To D

MW01283805

Romans 8:28

Into the Darkness

Memoirs of a Mission

In good times + bad, always trust the Lord.

Gina Doumaté

Gina Doumaté

This book is a very personal compilation of journal entries, letters to a dear friend, as well as personal insights. Hence the different typefaces. Unless otherwise noted, all letters were written to Alfreda, my pastor's wife and my dear friend.

The facts of this story are laid out as I understood them and as they were told to me. If any details are factually incorrect, please forgive me. Some names have been changed to protect the lives of people from retaliation. My goal is not to expose them to danger, but to expose the enemy's lies, tactics and deception.

I have provided a few maps for you to better understand where I lived, along with the village and places mentioned throughout this adventure. I have also included a list of people mentioned in this book.

To my beautiful, funny and amazing daughter, Hannah.
Darling, you were brought forth with much pain and sorrow, but have enriched my life and brought joy in more ways than I could imagine.

This is your story.

Forward

What can I say about Gina Doumaté? My friend, my sister in Christ, my trusted and reliable administrative assistant, a family member and definitely a prayer warrior for Christ.

Gina taught me so much about faith and trust while she was in Africa. Before she left I nearly suggested that she visit a doctor, a psychologist or a counselor to find out if she was still sane. I could not believe it when she told me she wanted to leave her job, family and friends to go to a place in Africa that was difficult to live even if you were an African...no running water, no electricity, no adequate medical facility and really not enough food. But her experiences in Africa showed to me that God was still on the throne.

Regardless of the difficulties, pain, trials and joys that Gina experienced in the Village of Aklampa and the country of Benin, they were all meant for her good and for the growth of her pastor--yours truly.

This is not a forward to a book but a testimonial on behalf of a friend, a sister, a truly dedicated supporter of her pastor. Gina is a true follower of Christ and a true armor bearer for her pastor.

Some great things happened in Africa under the ministry of Gina and all those who worked with her, and some are working still. I am forever proud of the decision made by Gina to give her life to Christ and to follow a directive that was not fully appreciated, nor subscribed to by others. With that obedience, several things happened to the Glory of God:

- Aklampa Village Baptist Church
- Mission Guest House
- MAFA / BAF Hospital
- (Beautiful) Hannah Doumaté
- Many who gave their lives to Christ!

Soli Deo Gloria!

Pastor Emmanuel O. Akognon
Village Baptist Church, Marin City, California 94965
November 2009

From the moment Gina stepped off of the bus from her first trip back from Africa, the trip referred to in this book as "An Eye Opener", I knew something had changed. She looked at me with tears in her eyes and said, "My heart is no longer here." What kind of shopping malls did she encounter in Africa? I wanted to go too. The reality was that God had begun in her the transitioning process which would lead her from sunny California to darkest Africa.

I was privileged to watch this process as God did some miraculous things in preparation for this journey. Even though there was much disbelief, unbelief and opposition, I am certain of two things: 1) If God sends you, He'll keep you; and 2) God DID commission and send Gina to Africa, in spite of, and maybe even because of, her weaknesses and failures.

Even though the letters contained in this book were mainly written to me, and I was aware of most of what she was going through in any given week, I was still riveted as I read these pages. It was as if I had never heard anything about these events before. I stand in awe of our Lord and Savior Jesus Christ, and the fact that He is Sovereign and does not need our approval to do as He pleases.

As you read, it is my prayer that you will recognize that God has a specific plan for your life. The question is, "Are you willing to obey?"

God bless,

Alfreda Akognon

Acknowledgements

This book is dedicated to the three most influential women in my life, my mother Bonnie, my dear friend Alfreda, and my daughter Hannah.

Mom, you have always supported me without passing judgment. You taught me how to be a mother who supports her children and then lets them go in order to do what God is calling them to do. Thank you for not getting in God's way.

Alfreda, you opened my eyes to an entirely new world of living for Christ. You pushed me to be all that God wanted me to be. You pushed me to never settle for a mediocre relationship with Christ. You encouraged me to go and build my ark, against all odds. When I began to believe the lies of the enemy, you shouted the truth. Thank you.

My daughter Hannah, looking at you made it all worth the trip. Besides my salvation, you are truly the greatest gift that God has ever given to me. May you also grow up to be all that God wants you to be.

Dad, thank you for teaching me the value of hard work, honesty, and commitment. It has not gone unnoticed.

Emmanuel, thank you for being my pastor, my mentor and my wonderful friend. I am truly blessed to have you in my life.

Aunt Lillian, thank you for your prayers, encouragement and friendship. I so enjoy our Saturday morning telephone calls.

Fred, you gave your quiet support and hugs on days you didn't even know I needed them. I'm honored to be your "daughter".

Village Baptist Church, thank you for your prayers and support while in Africa, and for holding me up when I was too weak to stand on my own. Thank you for being the most amazing church family ever.

To the village of Aklampa, thank you for welcoming me and treating me as a daughter. I was so proud to hear many of you proudly tell outsiders that I was an Aklampan. Thanks to those who fought to save my life, to the danger of your own. I know God will greatly reward you. To Village Baptist Church in Aklampa, I love you, pray for you and miss you. The foundation has been laid; now build on it.

A special thank you to Antuno, my Aklampa "mother". You welcomed me, taught me, and sat with me in good times and bad. You never gossiped about me, and saved my life on at least one occasion. You will forever be my "mother" in Aklampa. I love you and miss you so.

To the Adidemé family in Aklampa, thank you for letting me be one of your own. You brought adventure and laughter to my life. When I visit, sodas are on me.

Table of Contents

Significant People

Emmanuel – my good friend & pastor of Village Baptist Church, Marin City, California

Alfreda (Freda) – my pastor's wife and very close friend. The letters are written to her.

Adidemé Family – Emmanuel's mother's side of the family

Akognon Family – Emmanuel's father's side of the family

Ojo – Emmanuel's younger brother living in Lagos. One of my sponsors in Africa.

Godwin – Emmanuel's older brother living in Lagos. One of my sponsors in Africa.

Gab – Member of Medical Aid for Africa, native of Aklampa, living in Lagos and assisted with my visit.

Dossou Allagbé – Member of Adidemé family and first convert.

Sai Adidemé – Member of Adidemé family and second convert.

Fina – My house assistant and cook.

Bernard – My guard while staying at Henry's house.

Bayou – Woman hired to fetch water for me.

Henry – High ranking military official of Benin. Originally from Aklampa. I lived in his home for the first year of my stay in Aklampa.

Antuno – Wonderful woman who lived next door. She made me breakfast every morning and refused to take money.

Napoleon – My guard while staying in Emmanuel's mission house in Aklampa.

Map of West Africa

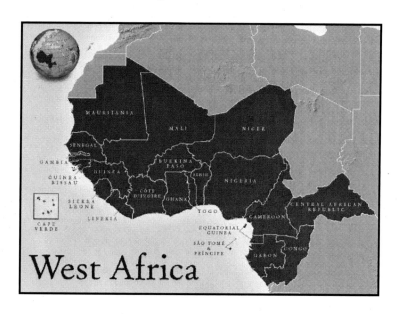

Map of Benin

Approximate location of Aklampa, the village where I lived.

Map of Aklampa

I drew the following map of the village in one of my journals during my stay in Aklampa. I lived in the Allawenonsa area of the village. The house I lived in for the first year of my stay is highlighted by the #1, and the house I stayed afterward is highlighted by #2.

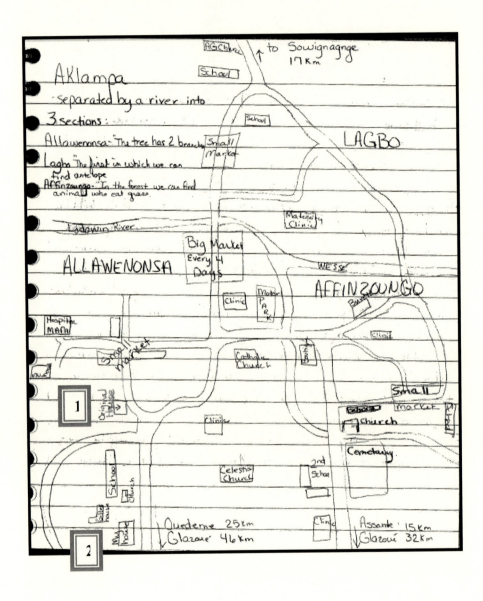

Preface

This is the story of a Christian woman whose greatest desire is to please God. It has cost her nearly everything, especially the friendships of those closest to her.

Was she perfect? Absolutely not. She made mistakes – some of them big ones. Yet, God in His infinite wisdom and mercy chose to use her and call her to go. So, go she did.

This is a story of the enemy's strategic plot to destroy a woman, and a story of God's divine protection, faithfulness, redemption, and ultimate victory.

How did she survive it all? Only by the grace, mercy and protection of God. If He had removed his hand for one moment, she'd be dead today. There was such a great attack that God often removed incidents from her memory shortly after their occurrence. The incidents were only recalled through the reading of letters to family and friends and her daily journals that captured every victory, defeat, joy, and pain.

This woman returned from her mission a different person. Part of her died in Africa while part of her became more alive than ever. She returned mentally, physically and spiritually exhausted. Except for one trusted friend, she kept most of her story hidden, knowing only God could heal such deep wounds. Only God's timing could bring her story to light.

After ten years, this is My Story…

Gina Doumaté

AN EYE OPENER

SHOPPING

Shopping! Yes, I was going shopping. That was the reason I was
going to Benin, West Africa. I was actually going on a short-term
mission trip with a group from my church. Never had I even
imagined traveling to Africa, so this seemed like a great opportunity to
see another country – and to shop!

I was single, had a well-paying corporate job, and also served as an
associate minister at my local church. Why not travel with the group?
I loved adventure. My only hesitation was the immunizations needed
to travel to Africa. I was more than a bit squeamish about needles –
heck, I was the type to faint when I saw a needle! Now, I was being
told I had to get seven or more shots to protect me from diseases I had
never heard of. Who was going to protect me from fainting and
hitting my head on the floor when I saw all those needles? I survived.
I'm here to tell the story, aren't I?

So off we were in October 1998 to the Republic of Benin, West Africa.
The purpose of the mission trip was to hold the ground-breaking
ceremony for a 20-bed hospital facility that our church was going to
build in a remote village in Benin, called Aklampa.

I remember flying over the country as we came in for a landing in the
early evening hours. From the air, I could see all these little lights in
the darkness. They were small fires by which people were cooking
dinner for their families.

As we landed and disembarked the plane, I was struck by the warm
and humid air. The heavy air literally took my breath away. I
quickly recovered and we were ushered into a metal barn-looking
building that served as our arrival gate. It felt like cattle being herded
into a corral. The atmosphere was loaded with tension. I understood
nothing of what was said since the national language is French and the
most common native language is Fongbe. My language of choice is
English. Well, actually, my ONLY language is English.

Amazingly, we made it through airport customs in record time and
were safely transported to our hotel in Cotonou.

We spent a few frustrating days in Cotonou because the Nigerian
government confiscated our passports. We had gone to their embassy
to apply for visas to travel to Nigeria. The embassy decided to
confiscate our passports in retribution for the US government not

granting visas to some of their nationals. After much negotiation, protest, and media and government involvement, we received our passports (with visas) and finally got on the road to travel to the village of Aklampa.

I was in a foreign land unlike anything I had ever imagined. Raised in the Midwest, I was exposed to very little "culture" and this was beyond anything I had ever seen on Discovery Channel. Yet, I was in awe and instantly fell in love with Africa.

A VERY LONG DAY

10/21/98 Journal Entry …
Well, here I am in Aklampa. I'm glad that I didn't write last night because my words would not have been holy. It was a very long day. I am now sitting on my porch in my compound and I have a crowd gathering to watch me. Everyone is getting ready for the new day and spirits are much higher.

Not far out of Cotonou, our truck which was loaded with food and luggage had a flat tire. That took about 30 minutes to change. We just stood by the side of the road and waited.

A funny thing happened along the way. We were going through a small town and I asked my pastor's brother to tell me the name. He said it, but I didn't understand a word of it. My response was, "Sure, got it." The whole van broke out in laughter. The real name of the town is Panwouan. Try to pronounce it. See, not so easy, huh?

We stopped in Dassa for dinner at Auberge de Dassa, a hotel and restaurant catering to tourists. Dinner was great. There were also weavers and wood carvers outside. A tourist trap. But clean bathrooms!

We then had to stop in Glazoué for an "African inquisition" with local officials. It was your typical political "dog & pony show" and personally a waste of daylight driving time.

To say the least, the road getting here was HELL! The drive from Glazoué to Aklampa, that we were told was supposed to take ten minutes, took four hours! Apparently, we had to take the "good" road which is a slightly longer route. The road from Glazoue to Aklampa is indescribable. We got stuck in the mud at least three times. We had to get out and walk while the men pushed the vehicles. To make matters worse, it was dark. No lights. I'm so glad that I had my little flashlights in my purse. It was very intimidating being in the middle of nowhere with stuck vehicles.

Along the road, we encountered an old truck hauling some type of goods. After men argued for 30 minutes about how to pass, we attempted to pass the truck. The problem was that there was a drop off into the water on both sides. As our van moved forward, you could feel it start to lean off the edge. I prayed like crazy!

4

It didn't help that a woman in the van was screaming that we were about to fall off a ravine and die. However, the two vehicles were able to pass without damage.

As we drove along the road, I was in awe of the sights and sounds. The crickets were singing and sounded like reeds hitting together. Even the crickets had a rhythm that was beautiful.

There were some humorous moments along this 35 kilometer, four hour trek. We decided that the only way this would have been a ten minute journey was in the bat mobile.

By the time we got to within a mile of the village, there were people waiting for us near the muddy spots along the road. At one spot, they had taken branches and laid them on the road for traction. All vehicles still got stuck. I was covered in mud.

We heard children screaming "Yovo" continually. This means "white person". We were definitely a sight. Most of the villagers have never seen outsiders so our arrival was a huge event.

When we were about a quarter of a mile from the village, we hit our final muddy spot. We walked ahead and the villagers set out benches for us while we waited for the vans to become unstuck. While sitting on a bench provided to us by some children, we even sang songs.

Now onto the festivities upon our arrival. We could hear the drums from about a quarter of a mile out. When we drove into the village, people were crowding everywhere. They sang and danced for us. We even joined in the festivities and danced for a bit. It was fun. They can really move.

I must foolishly admit that I was initially worried about the drumming. Here I was stuck in the middle of the bush in total darkness, walking through the mud into the unknown, being led by people I had never seen before. A thought that I was about to be a cannibal's sacrifice did run through my mind. Ignorant, I know. But remember, I was here to shop.

Upon arrival, we sat on the porch of the main house while villagers performed for us for a few hours. By the time the welcome celebration was over, we were exhausted and our nerves were raw. It took forever to organize people. We finally arrived at our compound (we are divided into two groups and my group is in a separate compound at the edge of the village with a gate and guards.)

Our house is more than a little rustic. It is basically a concrete structure with windows. There are screens and wood blinds on the windows. We have electricity via a generator. They built an outhouse for us to use. We have to take a pail of water with us for flushing. There are also no showers. I took my first cup bath. They bring an aluminum pail filled with cool water. We then take a cup and pour water on ourselves and lather up. We then take the cup and pour water over us to rinse. My room has an extra room to shower. It has a hole where the floor and wall meet to drain the water outside. After being as dirty as I was, the cup bath felt like heaven.

We also have beds. The villagers made sheets and pillow cases for us. It is more than a bit rustic, but I'll survive.

Well, everyone is pretty much ready to get going to the other house for breakfast, so I'll continue later.

2:40 pm

What a morning! I am sitting on the porch of the house where the other group sleeps. We came here this morning for breakfast. As the van drove us over, children chased behind the van. At the house, people gathered just to watch us. After breakfast, we were welcomed by some native drummers and dancers. The story goes that the ancestors have returned to greet us. Also, if one of the dancers touches you, you are to die. That's why there are men with sticks to guide them.

We also met Emmanuel's mother. All of us crowded into a small room in a clay house. She seemed very happy to see us.

We then marched over and met the king of Aklampa. I've never met a king before and shook his hand. We also met his "staff". His subjects stood by him and fanned him while his many wives sang songs and bowed behind him.

There were also voodoo dancers and two men on stilts to greet us and perform a ceremony. The people on stilts were amazing because they were able to flip back and bend over backwards at their knees and rise back up without falling over. To get on their stilts, they climb into a tree and rope themselves to logs.

After the festivities, we marched over to the hospital site for a dedication ceremony, prayer and song. It was very muddy, but fun.

Whenever I walk, I feel like the Pied Piper. Hundreds of children follow me. It is overwhelming. Most of them just want to touch my skin and hold my hand. It is really funny. They are commenting, "White woman, pretty, etc."

10/23/98 Journal Entry…
I had an interesting walk back to this house for dinner last night. I walked alone, except for 15 children, which grew to 100 by the time I got to the house. A group of men who sit under this hut and play games stopped me and asked me to take their photo. They were very friendly.

The children are overwhelming. They no longer stay behind the walls of the house. They come right into the front porch and sit and stare at me. You'd think they would get tired of looking at me. I am told by our hosts that this is a really big deal to them. Even some women stand around and watch me.

After dinner, we settled into a game of Pit. What fun! The children stood at the doorway in awe. They watched six Americans make total and complete fools of themselves. Even the Beninoise doctor travelling with us and the pastor's brother from Nigeria were shocked. The children were soon shouting "two, four, one, three…" It was very cute.

Suddenly, it started raining. It really rains here. It literally down poured. I've never seen rain like that. The roof of the house is tin and the noise was unbelievable. Reggie (one of our travelling companions) burst out in his own unique rendition of "Wade in the Water". He had verses with Emmanuel leading us out of here and another group member building us an ark to float us out. It was so funny.

We spent a total of five days in the village. We visited schools and attended numerous ceremonies. I had the most wonderful time, despite the hardship and heat.

Devotion 10/24/98
Exodus 23:1-9. What is God telling me? Don't follow the crowd. Stand up for what is right. Don't follow the crowd. Live in righteousness even if you have to stand alone. I must follow the Spirit's guidance and not the crowd.

10/24/98 Journal Entry…
Well, how can I describe how I'm feeling this morning? Since we leave tomorrow morning, it is my last day in Aklampa, maybe for forever. The people here are so beautiful and kind. We have not had anyone be less

7

than totally gracious. It is odd to walk down a trail and have people come out to greet you.

Even though life is very difficult for the people here, they are so close and support each other. It is true that tragedy (or poverty and famine in this case) brings people together. They are all working toward a common goal—survival.

It is going to be so difficult to leave this place, even though we have limited electricity, bathe out of an aluminum pail, do laundry out of a bucket, and use an outhouse. Somehow, it is all worth it. Even the drive.

10/25/98 Journal Entry, 11:00 am...
Here I am in Dassa at the same restaurant we ate on our way to Aklampa. Only one van made it out of Aklampa so we have been dropped off and are waiting for the others. I am not worried because things always work out, just not as quickly as we would always like.

So, since I have plenty of time, let me try to explain the past day.

After lunch yesterday, we relaxed until 4:30 when it was time for the closing ceremony in our honor. Once again, I had a great time with the people I have met. I even danced with my new friends as well. That ceremony was so significant to me. I am crying just thinking about it. These people live such simple lives and give it their all to dance for us. What a great honor.

After the ceremony, we returned to the house to await dinner. Dinner was exciting to say the least. Someone left a water bottle of kerosene on the table. A member of our group grabbed it, thinking it was water and took a drink. She instantly began vomiting and convulsing. The doctor had poison control tablets which she ate. She is fine today. Who would leave a water bottle with kerosene on a dinner table? I believe it was the enemy's attack. Yet, God's grace was more than sufficient.

After that, the festive mood was gone and we returned to our compound to pack and go to bed. I didn't sleep well at all. While everyone else couldn't wait to leave, I didn't want to go. It was so hard to leave such beautiful people. Each day, the children would gather at the fence or on the porch just to watch us. Sometimes, there were over 100 children sitting around just trying to get our attention. Just looking into so many poor yet innocent eyes was moving.

This morning was very tough. Packing was uneventful, except I should have known that we would have trouble getting out of the village when the truck got stuck for the first time between our compound and the other house.

We walked to the house which was emotional, but very appropriate. I was a bit surprised that at 6:30 am, everyone in the village would be awake. Also, as we walked to the house, people said goodbye vs. good morning so I knew they understood we were leaving.

I held it together until I saw one of the young boys to whom I had grown attached. Then, it was all over for me and the tears flowed freely. I told him that I would write and send him copies of the photos of him.

When our group prayed, a few members of our team broke down and cried as well. I was already sobbing. It was difficult leaving people you've grown to love, knowing you may never see them again.

After the prayer, I walked over to say a final goodbye to a new friend. I cried as I walked away and got in the van.

There were about 500 people out to greet us and tell us goodbye. God, it was hard leaving!

Now, what would be the most appropriate way to leave Aklampa, but to do it the same way we came in – on foot. We barely got to the edge of Aklampa when we hit the first big mud hole. We got out and walked through it and decided to keep on walking until we passed all the big mud holes – three miles out. Only a few of us walked that far. I cried most of the three miles.

We were informed that the other van had blown the radiator and the truck has a hole in the fuel line, making both unusable. Therefore, we waited at a farm along the road until the only drivable van arrived.

Well, the van finally took us to Dassa and I just ate the best meal I've had in a week. I ate rice, French fries, and an onion/tomato omelet. It was delicious. So is the cold water. We ran out of bottled water last night so we had been rationing water. That was tough since I've been drinking about three large bottles of water per day.

Since I have a few hours on my hands, let me try to explain living conditions of the people of Aklampa.

The road is nearly impassible and washed out in many areas. In order for people to get supplies, they must go to Glazoué which is 45 kilometers away. Not many people have transportation, maybe less than 1% of the population, and then it is mostly scooters.

Godwin told me that his father-in-law died last year because the road was so bad that they couldn't get him to a doctor in time. There are no doctors, only one nurse and medicine has to be brought from Glazoué.

The living conditions are deplorable. People live in clay houses/huts with two to three rooms. They have no electricity or running water so all their water is hauled in bowls on their heads. All the cooking is done outside on a fire. The homes have very little furniture, if any. The conditions are also very unsanitary because the pigs, goats and chickens are not caged and their feces is everywhere.

The children walk around with no shoes. In fact, not everyone has shoes. Some don't even have a shirt or pants and their underwear is torn. Some children wore nothing at all. It is hard to think that some children have absolutely no clothing. Yet, we have so much.

Stilt Walkers

THE BORDER FROM HELL

10/26/98 Journal Entry, 8:00 am...
The theme for yesterday afternoon – The Border From Hell

Shortly after my last entry, I took a short nap at a Dassa restaurant until the men arrived. After another argument (commonplace) about vehicles, we loaded up and headed for Cotonou. Dez's driver and another car met us half way. We unloaded the truck. The radiator problems made the truck virtually useless. Another woman in our group and I rode with Dez and his driver in the Peugeot. I had a nice nap while they drove.

When we arrived in Cotonou, Ojo and Emmanuel were waiting for us. We reorganized the vehicles and headed for Nigeria. We left the hotel, heading for Nigeria at 6:20 pm. Traffic was terrible. We hit the first checkpoint at 8:15 pm. It didn't look very official since the men weren't in formal uniform and the roadblock was a pole set across the road. The pole had spikes so if we had driven through, our tires would have blown. Also, since it was dark (this was our major mistake), only two candle flares lighted the checkpoint.

I believe one of our team members correctly labeled these checkpoints as "bootleg tollbooths". We had to pay the 'guards' to pass. Shortly thereafter, we hit our second, third, fourth and fifth checkpoints. This was where trouble began. This process took four hours.

We were delayed at the border until they closed at midnight. The only reason we were delayed was extortion. At times, we were held at gunpoint and tensions were very high. I remember walking onto one of the vans and asking people to pray. The only response was from one of our team members was a sarcastic, "It's a bit late for that!" Yes, this was a Christian woman. We were exhausted and had limited water and no food. Furthermore, at least two of our members were diabetic so being without food in such a tense situation can be dangerous as well as frustrating.

After four hours of waiting, fear, frustration, prayer, and politics, we were the final group to go through the border. The sad news is that they would not let Steve, a member of our group, cross the border because he only had a one-time visa which had been used to fly into Nigeria. He had a car take him back to Cotonou where he will deal with the embassy today so he can get into Nigeria to fly home. I feel really bad for him.

Tensions definitely rose yesterday among our group. By the time we finished the fifth checkpoint, people wanted to turn around and go back to Benin because there was grave danger in traveling in Nigeria at night. People from Nigeria do not even travel at night so some of the Nigerians escorting us were a bit on edge as well.

Two members of our team were campaigning to have us return, usurping Emmanuel's authority as well as that of our escorts. The problem with this is that our visas are good for only one entry to Nigeria. If we turned around, our visas would be void, because we had technically left Benin, but were not totally in Nigeria. (See, it is never a good thing to straddle the fence.) Also, it would take hours again to go through the Benin side of customs. They had closed anyway so we were stuck. What chaos.

I held up quite well. I trusted Emmanuel and Ojo's judgment and reasoning so I wasn't about to usurp their authority. There were enough people trying to overthrow leadership decisions and I didn't need to add to the chaos and rebellion.

I really wanted to go to Lagos and felt as if God was protecting us even in the midst of chaos.

Once we were finally allowed passage past the fifth checkpoint, we hit the sixth about a mile down the road. This was one of the most dangerous points of our journey. It was well past midnight and our escorts knew that any checkpoint on the Nigerian side of the border could be deadly. A decision was made to pay off the first checkpoint to get us to safety. While stopped, we had gunmen shine flashlights in our faces. Their sole purpose was to make money and they were willing to get paid at any expense.

Fortunately, God protected us. After arguing with the men for another 30 minutes, they agreed to a sum of money in exchange for passage to a guarded hotel a few miles up the road where we could lodge for the night. I am sure that this "escort" paid off the other two "checkpoints" on his way back.

The hotel where we stayed is quite nice and I slept in a great bed with a great pillow. I also had real baths – last night and this morning. Since this hotel is behind a guarded gate, I'm sure it costs a pretty penny.

Right now I'm sitting under a grass roofed gazebo near an outdoor bar writing this entry. I think it's going to be a good day.

10/27/98 Devotion

Exodus 23:20ff. What is God telling me? Listen to God. Listen to all that God tells you. Follow Him and he will lead your future. He will reward you and heal you. Don't bow to other gods as many do, but be faithful to Him alone. God has already prepared your future. Walk in it.

We spent three days in Nigeria before returning to Benin. While in Nigeria, we met with the local staff and some patients of Medical Aid For Africa, a ministry that our church started. MAFA provides high blood pressure medicine on a regular basis for patients in six clinics in Nigeria. We were also able to do some shopping for souvenirs. Once in Nigeria, we had a wonderful time.

10/28/98 Journal Entry…

We made it back to Cotonou safely. We arrived at our first checkpoint around noon. We went through four checkpoints before even hitting the border checkpoints. Godwin had to pay officers at most, if not all, the checkpoints. At two of the stops, after being paid, the officers then approached our van to joyfully wish us a safe journey.

Oh yeah, we even picked up three border control people and gave them a ride to work, thinking this would help. They were definitely on our side, but Nigeria is corrupt.

After the first four checkpoints, we arrived at the "real" border. There were three more stops on the Nigerian side of the border. We arrived there at 12:50 pm, to be met with so much corruption in the daylight that I was shocked. Right away, a man walked up, asked for our papers and led Godwin away, expecting he would pay the man. This cost 2000 naira, or about thirteen dollars. As we went through these three checkpoints, I took a look around me. Let me try to describe it.

Most of the officers were in uniform and some had guns. Some had whips. If people weren't walking in the right place (as if they would know in such chaos), the guards would whip them. I saw a young man whipped until he dropped his goods and his goods were taken away. It was crazy. Two guards even "playfully" wrestled over money they were pocketing. I also saw some of the guards grab the goods of people to search their bags. They didn't ask, they just pushed and shoved.

It took over two hours to get through these three checkpoints, which were within 20 feet of each other!

Once we drove across the border and had the gate come down behind us, everything changed. Even the Beninese man who lowered the gate was a drastic contrast to Nigeria, only inches behind us. No uniforms, friendly and talkative. He even offered me some of his sugar cane which he was gnawing on. No thanks!

There were four main checkpoints on the Benin side of the border. They took less than 20 minutes. There were two more checkpoints past the border. We were told to stop at one, but were only detained a minute or so. On the other, we were ushered right through. The Benin side asked for no bribes.

All total, there were thirteen checkpoints to pass to get home. Oh my gosh, I just called Cotonou "home". What's up with that?!

LEAVING AFRICA

10/30/98 Journal Entry…
8:05 pm. I'm now at the airport in Cotonou, preparing to return to America. What a strange experience. We were so rushed through the departure system that I didn't get a chance to say goodbye to anyone.

So, I'm on the plane awaiting takeoff from Cotonou. How do I feel? I have no idea but I'll try to describe them.

First of all, this has been a life-changing experience. If I could do it all over again, there's very little I would change. Right now, I dread going back to work. I feel as if my job has no real meaning compared to what is happening in Africa. There are so many people in need of so much. Just think, $6 would send one child to school in Aklampa for an entire year.

I feel as if I see things so differently now. I wonder how I will feel after a few weeks at home.

I'm so very sad to leave the wonderful people I've grown to love in Benin. I will especially miss Emmanuel's brothers, Godwin and Ojo. They were invaluable and worked so hard to make our stay enjoyable. I will forever be grateful. Godwin has become like my very own big brother. He really took me under his wing like a family member.

I'm going to stop writing now, because I'm sad and wasn't ready to go.

… Well after a brief nap, I'm awaiting take off from Abidgan. I have no idea what country I am in.

Everyone in our group is so anxious to get home. Why am I not excited? I feel as if I left part of me in Africa, and more than just the weight I lost. I don't know why; I can't explain it. I wouldn't want to live there permanently because of the living conditions. Yet, I miss it already.

10/31/98 Journal Entry, 6:44 am Brussels time…
Well, it's approximately 20 minutes before landing in Brussels. I slept most of the way. I kept dreaming that we were landing at small strange airports.

A few days ago someone in the group asked if any of us could become missionaries after a trip like this. I was the only one who said yes, and I did it without a second thought. That comment just came back to my remembrance. I wonder why.

All I know right now is that I am NOT anxious to go home. I really miss Africa already. I'm going to begin saving money immediately to return next year, even if the hospital is not complete.

10/31/98 Journal Entry, 3:00 pm California time…
Well, I'm on the final leg of my flight home – Cincinnati to San Francisco. I'm still not overly excited to get home. I feel as if I've left so much behind and am returning to nothing special. I know that's not true, but its how I feel.

I am still wondering what the whole purpose of this trip was, from God's perspective. I guess it may take some time for me to fully digest all that has happened and its meaning. My main question is, "Now what?" In light of all the experiences of the last three weeks, what is God's plan for my life? My biggest desire right now is to make a difference to the people of Aklampa.

Another question I have is, "How does this experience affect my ministry, my job, school, etc.?" For example, my job seems so unimportant right now. The business I am in, does it really help people or is our company more worried about making money? If it takes only $6 to send a kid to school, how many people at my job will pitch in?

Yes, I know I'm tripping right now. I also know that God has a plan for me and this trip was part of my journey with God. I'll just have to trust in Him to give me peace because right now, I have no peace. I miss Africa already and can't wait to return.

I guess it's all in the hands of the Lord and I truly thank Him for this opportunity!

A CHANGE OF PLANS

THAT UNSETTLED FEELING

After returning from Africa, I returned to my secular job, school and volunteer work as a minister. I felt so unsettled. My prior desires and goals suddenly seemed so insignificant. Following are some of the journal entries noting my discontentment and how God began leading me down a completely different path.

11/15/98 Journal Entry ...
I haven't recorded any feelings or thoughts since the trip, but I'll try now.

It was very hard leaving Africa. I felt as if part of me was left there – my heart. Sometime during the trip, someone asked our group if anyone could become a missionary after going through what we were experiencing. Without thinking, I said I could and then later thought, "How did that come out of my mouth!?"

Since returning two weeks ago, I have had a burden that I can't describe. Actually, I didn't even label it a burden until a few days ago. I just felt this drawing to go back to Africa. Every time I tell people about Aklampa, I get choked up.

In talking with Freda, she has been encouraging me to seek God's will. On Friday evening, Pastor Small had Pastor Debra at his church to preach. At that time, I was really struggling to break some type of stronghold. There was something standing in the way and my prayer was for God to show me His face. Pastor Debra approached me to pray for me. She told me to seek His face. My exact prayer! She also prophesied that God was preparing me for something that I wasn't prepared to hear. I was frustrated because I wanted to know what it was. However, I now know that I wouldn't have been ready at that time.

This morning I woke up with the same burden. I felt as if God was preparing me for something that my logic can't comprehend. During prayer with the praise team, I began to feel something break as I read Psalm 34.

During worship, I had a vision. Christ was leading me through a doorway. I don't know what was through the doorway, but I knew that I was leaving something. However, Jesus was holding my hand so I felt ok. I remember stepping over a threshold and not looking back.

After worship service and a number of meetings, I went up to Pastor Small's house for our weekly Sunday family dinner. Debra, a friend with prophetic gifting, was there. She had preached this morning in his church. We had a nice visit. Right before they left, Freda asked Debra and a few others to pray for me. Seven people surrounded me. They prayed only the things that God gave them to say. One man noted that he saw a curtain that I was afraid to step through because I don't know what's on the other side. (Very similar to my vision of the doorway!!!) He also mentioned that God has already prepared the way. I just have to step through.

Debra saw a vision of a baby eagle who takes flight. They are forced out of the nest and fall. They never fall too far before the mother swoops under them and catches them. The mother teaches them to fly. She saw me as that eagle that needs to get the courage to fly. I have to step out in faith, even though this is all foreign to me and totally out of my comfort zone.

Robin had a vision that I had wings under my feet.

Other things were said confirming that God already has the plan and I can't worry about what I'm leaving behind at Village. He has a "ram in the bush" who will take my place.

I was also told that I am not alone. There are people who will support me through the journey. I knew this related to the Small and Akognon families. It was very comforting to realize that my relationship with them will not cease.

I'm going to write about this, even though it may seem foolish.

I know that I feel a longing to return to Africa and I believe God is leading me to the mission field. Of course, my logic kicks in and says that's impossible. Why? Well, because I'm not done with school, I may have an opportunity to leave my current job and start my own company, and I just began my youth liaison position. Going on mission would mean leaving everything, and my logic can't figure out how to do that!

Well, I guess if that's God's plan, He will work it out. I'm still processing how to deal with this. I have questions like, How? When? Who will financially support me? So many questions. No answers.

I guess I need to stay in prayer, keep journaling and let God direct my future. I just have to give up my will and step over the threshold!

CONFIRMATION, CONFIMRATION, CONFIRMATION

Even before traveling to Africa for the first time, I remember visiting a friend's church one evening. As I stood in line for prayer, I heard the Holy Spirit tell me, "You can't handle right now what God has in store for you." I had no idea what He was talking about at the time.

I also remember kneeling by my bed one evening in prayer. I heard God ask me, "What are you willing to give up to follow Me?"

A bit of advice. If God asks you this question, Stop! Do not answer immediately! He just might take your answer seriously. Consider the implications. Are you truly willing to give up everything? Your great home, new car, wonderful job, ministry, friends, family, etc. In my eagerness to please the Father, I quickly answered, "Everything" without considering that He might take me literally. He did, and I had to live up to my word.

It is easy to say with our lips that we would give up everything to follow our Lord and Savior and the plan He has for us. However, how many would be willing to walk away from everything that is comfortable? It is not an easy calling. It is very rewarding, but very costly.

So, I said "everything", and God led the way. He began confirming his call for me to go to Africa. He confirmed my call through the Word of God, prayer, other Christians, non-Christians, friends and family, radio, the internet, and even a Christmas gift. He was quite clear.

11/16/98 Journal Entry…
I wanted to write a few things that happened today. First of all, on the way home from class, I was listening to Charles Stanley preaching on faith and how Abraham's faith was tested by God. He had to give up his home and family to move to a strange land to follow God. Another point in the message was that the more time we spend with Him, the more clearly we hear His voice. Another point: Reason is not always the answer. God makes a way when we can't find a way!

In class tonight, someone reminded me that my first sermon dealt with living by faith.

I called a friend today and was sharing that I'm reevaluating what God wants me to be doing. Her response was, "As long as he doesn't take you to Africa." We weren't even talking about Africa!

In speaking to Freda today, she let me know that I need to speak to Emmanuel and let him know my thoughts. She understands that part of my anguish is in leaving him and my church family.

I have such a difficult time talking to my pastor regarding this issue. I'm afraid that he will analyze me from a theological viewpoint and not feel where I'm coming from. I need to tell him because, not only is he my pastor, he is one of my best friends, and I want his help and input. I think that's going to be an emotional and difficult discussion.

11/17/98 Journal Entry...
This morning on the way to work, I was listening to Chuck Swindoll on the radio. He was preaching about how Aaron was a spiritual friend/encourager to Moses. It made me think of Freda. Then, out of the blue, his message switched to: "Are you dealing with a very important decision? It may be the most important decision of your life..." I literally screamed at the radio. I also became emotional. He went on to mention how important it is to let God have control and guide you. You have to put total faith in Him.

I have a strange peace about things today. I'm not sure why, but I know it's God.

11/18/98 Journal Entry...
Just a few things happened today. Yeah, right! Today blew my mind.

This morning on the way to work, I was listening to Chuck Swindoll. I had to take notes while driving! He was talking about how God parted the Jordan & the Red Sea. It was more than just a crossing on dry ground. They crossed from one lifestyle to another! He also said it's not enough to have faith and see the miracle; you also have to have the courage to pass through the miracle. I wonder what the Israelites were thinking as they walked through with a wall of water on either side.

While at work, I went into the InTouch website for the first time and clicked today's devotion. It blew me away. If I hadn't been at work, I'd have shouted. It was about Abraham's faith and all he gave up to follow God. It was similar to Charles Stanley's message a few days ago. It was totally amazing.

On the way home, I was listening to Charles Stanley again. He defined three levels of faith:

1. Little Faith: I know God can do it, but don't know if He will.
2. Great Faith: I know God can do it and I know He will.
3. Perfect Faith: It's Done!

I need to have more than just great faith.

God has been confirming in such a powerful way. I love him so much!

11/19/98 Journal Entry...
Just when I thought today would be an uneventful day, God drops another confirmation. Tonight, Freda told me to listen to KFAX at 9:00 pm. She told me that she didn't know the topic, but that I may want to listen since Marcus told her to listen. I ignored her until she phoned back and told me to quickly turn on the radio.

The program was about a man who lived deep in the South American jungle and was part of voodoo. A missionary, who actually interpreted the man's story, had gone to South America, had given up his comfortable lifestyle to serve God as a missionary. This man's story was amazing but the part that hit home was that the missionary left everything to spread the Word of God.

11/20/98 Journal Entry...
A date stood out in my devotion and that has never happened. The day that Noah's ark came to rest on the mountain was the seventeenth day of the seventh month. I don't know its significance, but felt led to journal it.

Much of Noah's calling seemed significant to me. God told Noah to build an ark in the middle of the desert. People laughed at him, yet he obeyed God.

That Christmas, Freda gave me a Noah's Ark throw quilt along with a card which read, "Go build your ark." That note and blanket would accompany me to Africa and serve as a reminder of my calling to follow God, and not man.

Although God clearly confirmed to me that I was to go to Africa, some of the people closest to me, especially Christians, thought I was crazy. They questioned my calling to the preaching ministry. Also, I was in the middle of attaining a masters degree as well as a professional designation through my secular job. They questioned to my face, and

murmured behind my back, as to how could God call me to walk away from all that?

One of the greatest trials for me in leaving was the fear of disappointing those closest to me. Either they were not looking for the confirmation, or God withheld the confirmation in order to force me to choose between man and God. Either way, it was so painful watching the separation.

BREAKING THE NEWS

11/24/98 Journal Entry…
I met with Emmanuel today to let him know that God is leading me to Africa. I gave him a brief summary of what I've been going through these past few months. I also told him about all the confirmations that God has given.

He responded with caution. He wasn't exactly discouraging, but there was some restraint. His more cautionary comments were:

1. God won't call you into the preaching ministry which is a call to prepare and then switch gears and say, no; I want you to do this other thing. God also would not have me quit school. The encouraging side of this issue is that he sees that this could be a part of my ministry and I agree.

2. He mentioned that when God called him, he spent a few years in preparation. I think he sees this as a thing that will happen a few years down the road. He also told me that I needed to prepare before going. This included taking French, learning some of the local language, finishing grad school, etc. He also said that I need to make sure that God has laid out the entire plan before going because of the huge life-altering scope.

He did have lots of encouraging things to say as well:

1. He is glad that I'm willing to give up everything to follow God.

2. I've seen Aklampa and how it is. No one would willingly go there and live unless God called.

3. Aklampa definitely needs a mission.

Our game plan for now is:

1. He will be in prayer for God to confirm this call to him. He and I both agree that God wouldn't give us conflicting answers, especially since God has placed him as my overseer.

2. We need to be systematic and methodical and make sure every step is in God's will.

3. We will meet each week to discuss this issue and pray together.

4. I need to deal with my family. He read Luke 14:26-27; "If anyone comes to me and does not hate his father and mother, his wife and children, his brothers and sisters – yes, even his own life – he cannot be my disciple. Anyone who does not carry his cross and follow me cannot be my disciple."

I think he is a bit overwhelmed with this. SO AM I! One slight concern is that I don't want this process to become so "methodical" that we kill the miracles and movement of the Holy Spirit. I truly believe that part of the journey that God has for me includes recognizing and experiencing how God works in miraculous ways.

I believe God has a plan and will lead me through each step.

12/7/1998 Journal Entry…
What a tough day! I started out in a great mood, but things turned tough when I went to meet with Emmanuel. My first question to him was, "Have you been praying about my situation?" He said yes, but that he was still dealing with it from his mind's perspective. He is really having a tough time of it.

Some of his comments:
1) What is your call? Did God call you into an ecclesiastical and preaching ministry or into a missionary ministry? He sees them as two distinct, unique ministries. He wants me to pray for clarification on my calling? That comment hurt because I felt like he was saying I cannot be called to preach and do missions. I disagree.

   He also noted that he hasn't ever come across this type of situation where a minister was called to one thing, but then God calls them to another thing. I don't see them as two separate, but two parts of one ministry.

2) He doesn't believe that God would call me to prepare and go to school and then change His mind and have me quit school. I cannot comment on this since I don't know when and for how long He wants me to go. Actually, I think I know when (July 17th), but I don't know for how long.

3) When I told him the date, he said, "So you leave on July 17th. Then what?" I responded honestly. "I don't have those answers."

25

I told him I would pray for specifics. He requested that I pray with Freda on this issue.

It was a really tough meeting and he made me doubt God's call for a minute. However, God is still confirming this call.

Emmanuel's sermon yesterday was from Acts 1:8-9 "And you will receive power when the Holy Spirit comes upon you and you will be my witnesses in Jerusalem…even to the ends of the earth." God had a message for me.

In class tonight, someone preached on storms from Mark 4:35-41 and spoke of how, even when really tough storms come along, God is in the midst and it is a test of your faith.

When I spoke to Freda tonight, our prayer was for God to confirm my calling. She also quoted Luke 14:26-27 "… must hate mother, father, etc. to be my disciple." This is the same scripture Emmanuel gave me in our previous meeting. This scripture applies to everyone in my life. I must follow God, even if others refuse to accept my call. That's a tough one with which I have to come to terms.

"Lord, my prayer is that you would confirm to Emmanuel in such a way that he can't deny it. Also, show me the next step in preparing to go on your mission."

12/8/1998 Journal Entry…
Two confirming things today:

1) My devotion dealt with Jacob and Laban. Both had a dream. Jacob's was that it was time to move on; and to Laban to let Jacob go. I had even prayed for God to give those close to me a dream confirming the call.

2) On the radio on the way to work, someone read letters from Christians in Africa (Ghana and Ethiopia) who are faced with witches and demons. The funny thing is that the rest of the radio message had nothing to do with this.

12/15/1998 Journal Entry…
I know that I am called to preach. I also believe God has called me to the mission field. I think the two are definitely linked. I see me confronting spiritual warfare and preaching in Africa.

I think I will be in Benin, not Nigeria. I think I will be in Aklampa, although there is no house for me to stay in. I think I will be going next year, probably July 17th. Freda and I both think I will not be sent by the American Baptist convention. Now, I have no confirmation on any of the above. They are just feelings at this point and I need to await confirmation.

A HINT OF THINGS TO COME

Early Saturday morning, two days after our New Year's Eve celebration at the church, I was downstairs in the church library doing some studying. I had stopped and picked up a breakfast sandwich and was eating when I heard noises upstairs. Thinking our custodian had arrived to clean up from the service, I moved to the bottom of the stairs and called upstairs. Nobody answered me.

The sounds stopped briefly and then continued. It sounded as if someone were carelessly moving the drums. I looked outside and realized that the custodian's vehicle was not present. There were no other vehicles present. Something was amiss.

My body physically reacted. As my heart raced, I kept looking up the stairs to see if I could see any shadows. Suddenly a balloon fell down the stairs. I knew someone, or something, was upstairs. Boldly, I ran up the stairs, not thinking that I could be walking into danger.

Nobody was there. I knew it was demonic. I went downstairs and called Freda. She believed me. Emmanuel laughed at me. Freda wondered what I was still doing there. I said that some demon couldn't chase me out of my own church.

After hanging up, I returned to the library. All was quiet, but I could not shake this eerie feeling. I decided to leave until it was time to return for my meeting in a few hours. I had lost my appetite and decided to throw my breakfast in the trash. As I walked out of the library and toward the garbage can at the end of the room, a chair flew two feet into a wall beside me.

I would love to say that I boldly stood there and rebuked that demon. However, that would be a lie. I ran to the garbage, then ran out the building and drove to a friend's house. I returned after others had already arrived at the church building.

I believe God allowed this to happen to prepare me for the spiritual demonic manifestations I would encounter in Africa.

3/8/99 Journal Entry…
Last night I called Emmanuel to tell him what a wonderful job he did preaching. He then told me that he feels sad that I'm leaving and is not sure what he will do without me. (After all, he's my closest friend and

mentor.) We hung up right after that and I cried. I think I am beginning to go through a grieving process. It's going to be so hard leaving. However, I pray that I will be back in two years.

3/20/1999 Journal Entry…
I told my mom today about my call to Africa. I expected her to totally freak out. After all, she had a fit when I went for three weeks and with 17 people. Her response was, "I already knew." She was totally calm. She said that when she heard my voice upon returning last October, she thought, "I bet Gina goes back to stay awhile." She also said two years is not that long.

I had prayed for God to prepare her, but He's outdone himself. I couldn't believe what I was hearing. She was totally positive about it. God is unbelievable! God is so good! I feel totally privileged to serve him!

On Wednesday, Emmanuel and I were spending time together and he made some very encouraging comments about having a church in Benin. Then when I was talking to a wonderful woman in my church, she said that I may be going to start a church. I never really thought about starting a church in Aklampa. But, if it is God's will, I'll do it in His strength.

3/24/1999 Journal Entry…
On Sunday, I announced my call to Africa at the MAFA (Medical Aid For Africa) meeting. Most people were shocked. Everyone gathered to pray over me. After the prayer, Emmanuel mentioned Philippians 4:19 to me, the same verse he quoted when I first told him of my call, and the special scripture he gave me the day I was baptized.

It was strange telling a group of people. They reacted with praise and I want no praise for myself. I don't want the focus on me, but on God. I just want to go and do God's will.

We had a visiting minister preach today. One comment stood out, "Don't worry about building a church, just witness to the people about Jesus Christ and God will build the church."

On the way home on Sunday, Billy Graham was on the radio and said, "Let your light shine in Africa." He wasn't even talking about Africa!

4/11/1999 Journal Entry…
Emmanuel announced today at church that I would be going to Africa for two years. He quoted Acts 13: 1-3, how the church fasted before sending Paul and Barnabas out on mission. The youth that I teach for Sunday

School were shocked. DeShane was the most upset. He could hardly look at me. The boys (DeShane, Jerry, Josh and Naim) gave me a group hug.

I cried when I talked to DeShane. He's mad because he feels as if I'm abandoning him. It's going to be really hard leaving my students whom I love so much.

4/29/1999 Journal Entry...
Jack Hayford said something really profound on the radio on my way to work today. He was preaching on recognizing spiritual warfare and said, "The enemy will do everything he can to discourage, distract, depress and destroy you right before you begin doing a great thing for God."

That is so true. I've really felt as if the enemy is trying anything he can to break my faith. I'm up one day and down the next. That's strange for me since I'm usually upbeat.

5/31/1999 Journal Entry...
I called mom this morning to chat. She is such an encouragement to me. She is truly a blessing. She repeatedly told me about how she isn't worried about me because I'm doing God's will. She knows my faith and is excited to see what God will do.

She told me that a neighbor asked if she was worried about me. Mom's response was, "She's got more faith than you and me and this whole room put together. Why should I worry. God will protect her better than if she had the president and a whole army behind her." She also talked about how much she wants to come visit me, but can't. I think she will really be my encouragement through this.

"God, you sure gave me the best mom in the entire world!"

I've spent most of the day in prayer. I also spoke to Freda who has really pushed me to step out in faith. She knows some of the discouragement that has been thrown my way lately and has been praying for me. She called to encourage me. God is definitely using her to make me a possibility thinker.

As I sit here thinking about all that I am doing, I realize that God is totally in this. I also realize that the enemy is busy at work and is doing everything he can to discourage me and distract me. I can't let him win. I must come out punching!

6/3/1999 Journal Entry...

30

My devotions over the past few days have dealt with God's call on my life and how He will complete the call and work through faith. "He who began a good work in you will complete it." He will complete it, not me. I only need to be a willing vessel.

6/11/1999 Journal Entry…
I have been in a pretty good mood since last week. I realize that I can't think using my common sense. That gets me in trouble and I begin to worry. I really have to live by faith and not sight. However, some people are very logical thinkers and upset me when they chastise me for not raising more money by now. I responded that God knew my financial situation when he called me. I am not worried and I know that where God guides, God provides. God knows exactly how much money I need and will provide it. My job is to trust Him.

6/11/1999 Journal Entry…
Debra Westbrook ministered to me tonight. Following are the prophetic words that God gave to Debra for me:

1) Psalm 91
2) 'You have the Word in you. You will walk in the Word. The Word will have amazing effects.'
3) 'Angels will guard you. You will be protected by His angels.'
4) 'You will war in the heavenlies. You will do mighty battle. You will be involved in great warfare in the heavenlies.'
5) 'You are walking into Voodoo heaven.'
6) 'God will use you in mighty ways. You will have almighty power that you haven't even seen yet.'
7) 'The US doesn't pay attention to demons and angels, but Africa is well aware of them.'
8) 'You will be in a tight spot.'

Overall, she spoke much on the power of my ministry and the miraculous things God will do. I will experience things that I can't even imagine yet.

6/17/99 Journal Entry…
What a week! I've been so busy. I moved out of my apartment yesterday. I had people from both work and church show up. In less than two hours, I had everything out. It was a day of walking by faith! The person who was supposed to store my things suddenly went out of town. We prayed that if it was God's will for me to store my stuff there, He would have to tell that person to call. I figured that God is a better communicator than any phone. She never called.

I decided to walk by faith, get people together and begin packing. All my stuff fit into the vehicles that came so I didn't need to rent a U-Haul. After packing and loading, I sat down and decided to call storage places in Marin County. There were none! There was a storage unit available less than three miles away. By the time I completed the paperwork, my friends were nearly done unloading the vehicles. Imagine, all my worldly possessions, not including the things I gave away, fit into a five-by-ten foot storage space. Makes physical possessions seem insignificant. Everything flowed so smoothly. I know it was God's will.

I was also surprised and touched by how giving everyone was to help me move. I cried. It was also tough to see the move happen so quickly. It was out of my control so I had to just let go and let it happen.

I learned a good lesson through this process. My intentions may be pure and I think I'm in God's will, but when plans suddenly change, I still have to walk by faith. I can't just stop and wait until I have the whole answer. God won't always reveal the ending so I have to walk by faith.

This day of walking by faith served as a testimony to some of the people helping me move. They initially thought I was crazy to begin moving without any idea of where my things would go. God proved that when you take a step in faith, He is a faithful provider.

SAYING GOODBYE

The following was written while sitting in the Minneapolis airport awaiting my flight to San Francisco after visiting and saying my goodbye's with family and friends in the Midwest:

7/8/1999 Journal Entry…
Mom really cried when I said good-bye on Tuesday. She sobbed until I told her that I would think about coming to visit next year. She said "OK" and stopped crying so hard. Bernie (mom's very good friend) told me that she would take care of mom while I'm gone. I'm getting teary-eyed just writing this.

I started crying this morning when I said good-bye to David and Sheri, my brother and sister-in-law. I fell in love with Jordyn (my newborn neice). She is so precious and I cried just thinking of leaving her and not seeing her for two years.

7/10/1999 Journal Entry, 4:30 pm…
I'm sitting alone in Village Baptist Church. It felt strange and sad walking in here, knowing that it would be one of the last times I'll be here for a while. I absolutely love Village and its people and I'm going to miss them so much. This is the place where I accepted Christ, was baptized, accepted the call to the ministry, etc. The most important events of my life happened in this very building. I'm crying right now just thinking how sad it is to leave this place. Since I have no blood relatives here, these people have become my family.

God has shown me so much here and has blessed me so immensely. A large part of me doesn't want to leave, but the other part wants God's will so much that I'm willing to go wherever He sends me. I just want to be a willing vessel that He can use! However, I'm still human and will miss these people so much.

7/13/99 Journal Entry…
I must relay a vision that I had during worship on Sunday. Earlier in the year, I had a vision of me walking over a threshold and Jesus was holding my hand and guiding me. I had no idea what was ahead, but I knew I was not to look back. On Sunday, I had the same vision and felt as if I actually crossed the threshold. In the vision, I was walking toward a fire similar to the burning bush. I knew it was God and I felt like Moses – standing on holy ground.

(The following is being written after returning home from a powerful prayer meeting to pray for my journey.)

I just got home from the prayer meeting. It's late and I'm tired, yet my mind is racing from all that happened. I pray that the Holy Spirit will bring back all for me to write down.

Initially, one person from Robin's prayer team prayed for each member of my prayer team. They really spoke into their lives. Then, Robin's prayer team surrounded me and my prayer team stood behind them. The other team prayed over me and then traded places and my team prayed for me.

These are the words that I remember:
1. A fire surrounds you.
2. You are being filled with power to do His work.
3. You will walk more in the supernatural than the natural.
4. There is fire in your hands (my hands were burning and shaking at this point) and oil is dripping from your hands. God has empowered you to do miraculous healings, both physical and spiritual.
5. The fire surrounding you is God. He has commissioned angels to go before, beside and behind you. You will walk in the power of his fire.
6. You will be a great warrior. You will be an offensive player (this idea of offense has arisen a lot lately). I will fight battles and overcome the enemy.
7. You have a sword in your hand which you'll use to do battle. The sword is the Word.
8. Debra prayed and a fresh and fierce anointing filled me. There was much prayer regarding the power and anointing I would walk in.
9. Debra prayed the scripture, "Greater is He that is in you than he that is in the world." (Another woman had prayed that same scripture over me yesterday.)
10. You are about to begin a whole new life. All the old things that keep you in bondage are forgiven and forgotten. All is new and God has released you from all old things. None of your past is valid anymore. (I could feel God changing me. I could feel the faith and power of God filling me. I know I cannot walk in the natural realm any longer. God has a huge plan and I need to continually seek His face and walk in the anointing.)
11. The demons have already been put on notice (a prayer that was also prayed over me a day earlier) and they have no option but to flee at the authority of God. It will be a spiritual battle and the

34

demons already know you're coming. However, you are not to focus so much on the enemy that it takes away from your time with God. Your focus must remain on God. You can't give Satan too much credit.

At one point while Debra prayed over me, she laid her hands on mine and asked God to fill me more and more and more. I could actually feel the Holy Spirit's filling.

Then my team moved in to pray. One member prayed for me to have more faith. When another began praying, she broke down and began praying in tongues for the first time. Freda then prayed for me and we both cried.

Then Janice began making strange sounds and doing up and down motions behind me. At first, I couldn't figure out the meaning. At one point, she wrapped her arms around my ankles, then knees, then thighs, waist, chest, neck. She said she saw a wall of fire and many arrows. These motions meant she was girding me with a shield or armor of some type. She then fell at the back of my feet and began wailing and making sounds.

This continued for some time before she began hollering in tongues, also for the first time. Suddenly Debra shouted "Yes, Jesus!" and began laughing. She explained that Janice had approached the throne and was laying the path for me. She received the orders and was laying my path. That path led to the village and as she laid the orders, I noticed the tongue – it was Fongbe, the language of the village where I was going! I told Freda to listen and she agreed that it sounded exactly like the tapes we had heard. We began laughing, clapping and praising God. It was absolutely amazing!

After prayer, Robin said that God wants me to spend the last few days wisely. Spend much time in prayer and make sure I press into His presence. Gordon also gave me Isaiah 6:1 and read from his devotional where God saw how I gave up everything to follow Him and that as I gave up things, God would fill that space.

As we were visiting afterward, Debra also told me that "There are women who have made great mistakes. But great mistakes make great women." I didn't realize at the time just how prophetic this seemingly simple statement was.

7/16/1999 Journal Entry...
My devotion: Ephesians 1:15-23. God has great power for those who believe. This is the same power that raised Christ from the dead. You

don't need to be intimidated by any person or spirit, no matter how high their title. The ultimate King has anointed you and given you power.

7/17/99 Journal Entry…
I'm sitting at the airport waiting to board the plane. How do I feel? I'm not sure. I guess I'm numb. Am I happy? No. Am I sad? No. Am I scared? No. I just don't feel anything specific. A thought just came to me. Following God is not based on emotion. It is based on obedience.

I'm really tired right now and wish I could sleep. I think I'm emotionally and physically exhausted. I've done lots of running around lately. I hope I sleep well on the flight.

5:25 pm, U.S. time… Well, I'm in the air. I got a little emotional on takeoff, but I didn't cry.

Now some thoughts about my going to Africa:

I met with Rose and Yemi for prayer the other day. Yemi's prayer dealt with God shielding me on all sides and that God's armor would protect me. I guess Ephesians 6:10-20 will be my motto. I thank God for confirming so many things. I pray His voice will get louder and louder so I can always hear Him. The last thing I want to do is step out of the will of God.

As I sit here, I think of all that I've just given up for God: 1) a job that would have earned great money, 2) my parents and family, 3) Village Baptist Church and all its members, 4) my home and car, 5) all my friends, 6) my relationship with a wonderful pastor who emptied himself to teach me and guide me, and 6) Freda, my great friend and wonderful mentor.

I know God has a plan and I want to be part of it. Therefore, it was all worth it.

I also wonder what God has in store for my future. At this point, I only have vague ideas and dreams. I do believe I will experience miracles and healings and salvation. I think my first goal is to just get settled and learn the custom and language.

HELLO AFRICA

HERE I GO

7/18/99 Journal Entry, 11:20 pm …
Well, I made it here safely. I'm in my room and just showered with cold water. Welcome to Nigeria! However, I have air conditioning and lights for the time being so I can't complain.

On the flight from Amsterdam to Lagos, I sat next to a man who is originally from Nigeria but now lives in Nashville. The man, Emmanuel, used to live near me in California. He asked about my travels and I told him very briefly of my call and my salvation. He was flying to Lagos from Jerusalem. He had just visited the sites of Jesus' ministry.

He says that he's a Christian, yet believes that Jesus, Mohammed and Buddha are only prophets. Our first conversation ended because I didn't want to argue with him. I sat beside him silently praying that Jesus would convict his heart. The topic arose again and we both realized that God had a plan for us to sit together. I shared more with him and witnessed to him and he acknowledged his need for Jesus. My prayer is that the blood of Jesus Christ would soak him and change his heart to know the fullness of God.

I was met at the airport by Caroline (who recently married a fellow church member and is working on her immigration papers) and her family member who escorted me through all the checkpoints. Therefore, I didn't have to put up with any of the typical political hassles. Everyone was very nice.

I didn't meet Ojo, Godwin, or Gab (my sponsors in Africa) until we walked outside the airport. They brought me to the hotel and fed me a home-cooked dinner. After praying, they left. The plan for tomorrow is to take me to the American Embassy to register.

Later that night in my journal…
I was just praying and something came out of my mouth that shocked me. I thanked God for bringing me home. I said "Home", not Nigeria or Africa. What's up with that? Only God knows.

My stay in Nigeria was interesting. The original plan was to spend 2-3 weeks there getting acclimated and buying supplies. Due to the condition of the house for me in Aklampa, as well as some other politics, this "brief" stay lasted over 5 weeks. There were times when I was frustrated because my movement in Nigeria was limited due to

political unrest in the country. The hotel had a guarded gate and was located in a guarded estate. I was not allowed to go beyond the estate walls without an escort because it wasn't safe. At night, you could hear the gunshots.

Corruption was rampant in Nigeria, especially within the police force. They would stop your car for no reason and demand money. One day they were even posted outside the estate gate. I was never allowed to be outside after dark – 7:00 PM!

7/18/99 Journal Entry…
I spoke to Freda today. It turns out that she was praying for me at the same exact time that I was ministering to Emmanuel on the airplane.

Mom also called me. I could tell by her voice that she was emotional but happy to hear that I was fine.

8/2/99 Journal Entry…
Ojo took me shopping in Lagos today. From the moment we arrived, I could tell Ojo was tense. Now I know why. I also know why he wanted me wearing African attire. The answer -- 419. That's the Nigerian police code for fraud. He was really worried that we would encounter trouble and that it would cost him lots of money to pay off thieves.

Only one person approached him. The thief boldly said he had a weapon and tried to show Ojo. However, Ojo thought quickly and replied that he was also armed. The guy let Ojo know that he wasn't alone. Ojo countered that we weren't alone either, hinting that we had security secretly watching us. This wasn't true (in the physical sense), but it worked. Ojo gave him 100 Naira. He thought he'd be approached much more. I recognized what was happening so I just kept walking nonchalantly and following Ojo. I was not in the least afraid.

These thieves are also involved in fetish worship to the extent that they actually see smoke over the heads of people carrying money. However, we serve a God that is greater than the devil and He was protecting us. Ojo agreed because he was sure we'd run into trouble. Also, my wearing African attire helped because it made people think I somehow live or belong here. Once we got in the car to return to the hotel, we relaxed and had a good laugh.

8/2/99 Journal Entry, 9:45pm …
I'm watching a television show called "Miracle Hour". Actually, lots of the "Christianity" in Africa focuses on miracles. Pondering this, a few

thoughts come to mind. This culture is loaded with the supernatural workings of the enemy. Is this simply another ploy of the enemy, or is the atmosphere so supernatural because the people believe and have faith in the supernatural ways of God? Something in my spirit is troubled by this movement. It's too much like some American "miracle workers" who aren't really healing, but looking for fame and fortune.

I'm beginning to understand what Debra said when she said I'd live more by the supernatural than natural. My "supernatural" is their "natural". Africans are used to spiritual manifestations. I'm overwhelmed that God would choose me to deal with such issues. My mind can't begin to conceive God's plan.

8/5/99 Journal Entry…
A friend took me to the National Museum today. It was an interesting experience. One area of the museum contained three separate sections – religious power, political power, and warfare power. There was also another area that detailed the political history of Nigeria.

It is difficult to describe my feelings as we walked through the first area. These three sections are tied to religion. Even the political and warfare areas have religious ties. This was one of the first times I've physically felt the presence of evil. My eyes began to sting, my breathing was a bit labored, and my body began to ache, especially my upper arms. At one point I was looking at some of the masquerade costumes and almost began crying. It was overwhelming to realize how extensively religion is tied to everything. It permeates the entire culture.

I also felt compassion. These people work so hard to appease their gods. It's really sad because salvation is free.

THE PRESSURE'S ON

8:00 pm…A day that started out great, but ended awfully. We went to await a call from America. The call was less than encouraging. I was informed that information is still being gathered regarding who will financially support me. Then, I was admonished for not going to the Baptist Mission House to meet the missionary there. (The Baptist Mission House is located across the street outside of the compounded area where I am staying at the Bible Guest House.) I was asked, "You say you're a missionary, don't you?" "Well, do missionary work. You don't have to wait until Aklampa." I tried to explain that there are security issues. He said, "Don't worry. God will protect you."

I feel as if people are sitting back and thinking, "I told you so." They think I shouldn't have come and that I'm proving it by failing to fulfill their ideas of missionary work. I don't take failure well so I'm very upset. I held it together until we returned to the Bible Guest House and Godwin left. I just sat down and cried. My friend tried to explain that he's sure this person didn't mean it in the manner I received it.

I feel like a burden on everyone and I don't like that either. A very tough day.

Most of the pressure revolved around money. I was repeatedly told that I absolutely had to purchase a car to drive to and from the village. The estimated cost was $6,000 -- money I did not have. Daily, the pressure increased to find a way to buy a vehicle as well as other purchases that later proved unnecessary. God kept closing doors and frustrating our plans. The plans were just that – our plans, not His plans. Still, it was so difficult to have people pressuring me and hinting that the lack of money was proof that God did not call me.

Just think. Right now, I could be working at my old job and making good money, driving my new car, living in a great apartment and doing ministry at my church. There's one problem with this scene: I'd be out of the will of God! So, here I am, alone in a hotel in Lagos, Nigeria, with money problems and frustration. Yet, I somehow know God wants me here. I guess this is really a night for prayer.

Godwin finally told Emmanuel that it is not safe for me to stay at Henry's home in Cotonou and that Henry should not be allowed to select house help for me because they can't be trusted. People are finally realizing that this man is not what he originally portrayed. The plan for now is to go to

Cotonou late next week and stay in a hotel for a while. However, I'm learning that everything is subject to change at any time.

8/6/99 Journal Entry...
God is so unbelievably faithful, especially in my weakness. My devotion this morning was 1 Peter 4 and spoke of suffering as a Christian. Then, while reading the New Estate Baptist Church newsletter (I had attended this church in Lagos a few times), there was an article about the sufficiency of Christ. I need to rely on Him and He will provide for all my needs, especially as I serve Him. It spoke of not looking to men, but to God, to provide my needs. I really needed to hear these messages from God today. Also, scriptures kept coming to mind about Him being my strength, shield, fortress, and provider.

So, I feel a bit better today.

8/11/99 Journal Entry...
I began my devotion in Joshua this morning. I can already tell that its going to be powerful. The book opens with passages about being strong and courageous in all circumstances and that God will be with me and will never leave me or forsake me. Also, God wants me to keep my eyes forward and not look to the left or right. If I meditate on the Word and follow God, I will prosper and be successful. I can tell I'm going to love Joshua!

8/13/99 Journal Entry...
I've found out more about Henry and the "house help" (maid) situation. I'm quickly learning that I need to stay away from him at all costs. The person he's <u>ordered</u> to be my help is very sick and can hardly take care of herself, much less someone else. The motives are purely wicked. Also, its come to my attention that Henry has designs on me. He's trying to find a way to control me. He even made a comment to one of the MAFA members about wanting me sexually. The thought makes me sick! I have been warned that he believes all women want him, due to his high ranking political and military power, but it's their "duty" to say no. So he will force himself on them. Sounds like rape to me.

The way things are going, I may not even live in his house in Aklampa. After all, he's not done any work to it that he had promised to complete. I am wondering if Kinti's house is available. It is much more private, has a ceiling, better ventilation, and the back room could be used as a kitchen.

I believe I will reside wherever God wants me so I'm not worried. I'm not even worried about a car. I really believe God will provide exactly what I need and at the time I need it.

I fasted until noon today. My only prayer was that I wanted to grow closer to Him and know His will. Worship and fellowship this morning at the Strong Tower Mission orphanage were part of His perfect blessings.

My devotion today was in Joshua 3. The Holy Spirit said to consecrate and prepare for God to use me in mighty ways and that He would use me to show people the miraculous power of God.

8/14/99 Journal Entry…
I can hardly believe that I've been in Africa for nearly one month. Time moves so quickly. Today is another beautiful day. There's a light breeze so it is not so hot. If only it would stay this cool. However, I've learned that November to April will be very hot and dry. A good time to sweat off some weight!

I'm sitting on my deck and must mention that I spend a lot of time watching the lizards that hang out on the wall. I'm fascinated by them.

During my long stay in Lagos, I spent most of my time alone at the hotel. Some days I was nearly insane with boredom since I could not leave the estate. No visitors, no electricity, nothing. I did volunteer at an orphanage located within the estate walls, and worshipped with them three times each week.

ROAD BLOCKS BUT OPEN HEAVENS

How quickly plans change! We won't be going to Cotonou until at least next Wednesday. There are more issues with the house in Aklampa. Therefore, three planned weeks in Lagos has turned into nearly five. I know the enemy is doing all he can to keep me out of the village. Too bad! I know God already ordained that I go there and He's already won the battle.

Also, I hear that the villagers are already awaiting my arrival. We're not sure how they found out. I hope they're not kept waiting too long. I originally thought I would get to the village before my birthday on the 22nd. Now, I'll be happy to be in Cotonou by then. I really hope I'm in Cotonou no longer than one week. (Yes, I can dream, can't I?)

8/15/99 Journal Entry...
I attended New Estate Baptist Church today for Sunday service. The message was confirming in so many ways: 1) The lead scripture was Psalm 91 and the message was about God's protection. Psalm 91 is the scripture Debra prophesied over me. 2) The preacher also spoke about being the apple of God's eye, which Gordon prayed over me before I left. 3) The preacher spoke that people shouldn't be afraid to go to villages because of the witches. We are much more powerful in Christ. 4) He mentioned Elijah, which I have been studying. 5) He quoted Exodus 14, which I just read this week. He noted how God put a cloud between the Israelites and Egyptians so that the Egyptians could not see the Israelites. God can literally hide me from the enemy. Also, their choir sang two songs that my home church regularly sings.

I'm confined to the Bible Guest House today. As we left for church this morning, there was a white Mercedes with two men parked outside the gate next door. The hotel security guards called the police and were very cautious about letting my friend onto the grounds to pick me up for service until they recognized him. As we left, the car was still parked around the corner. Security determined they are either armed robbers or hired assassins. That's good enough reason for me to stay inside! This is one of those events you never tell your mother.

8/18/99 Journal Entry...
Last night before going to bed, God urged me to go in my room and pray. I got on my knees and my Lord met me. He is so faithful and sweet. I prayed and sang unto the Lord. I could literally smell the presence of the

Holy Spirit. The room had the fragrance of men's cologne, but nothing like I've ever smelled. It was wonderful.

This morning I went to Strong Tower Mission to meet with Reverend George. They were having staff prayer time. **The Strong Tower Mission, an orphanage, was begun by a wonderful Christian woman, Reverend George. The main office and orphanage for the babies and toddlers is located inside Palmgrove Estate and is just down the street from my hotel. Three times a week, this orphanage requires staff to meet for one hour of worship and a short message. No wonder this ministry is successful and has continued to grow. Christ is at the center of everything they do.**

Towards the end of service, Rev. George called me up to give a short testimony of my call to Africa. She then prayed over me. She prayed Psalm 91! She also said she sees fire in my mouth and on my hands and that she sees the power of God. By that time, my hands were shaking. She also rebuked anything the devil may try to do to me. She also prayed that God would bless me financially. She also spoke of mountains and prayed that mountains would become graves. It was a powerful prayer.

Afterward, she took me to another orphanage location where I met the older children. One had malaria and another seemed to have a skin rash. One little girl latched onto me so I picked her up. Her name was Patience, something of which I said I needed more. We then went to the hospital to visit a sick baby that I had previously held at the orphanage. After seeing him on Monday, he had become sicker. Turns out that the feces and urine that he had been laying in when discovered had soaked through his skin and into the bloodstream. He was awake and restless when I saw him. I knelt down and prayed for him before leaving.

Later that day…
A letter was sent to Henry informing him that my visit is NOT MAFA association business, but a family issue. The Akognon family is responsible for my well-being. Henry was given money weeks ago to prepare his house in Aklampa for my arrival. To date, there is only a ceiling in one bedroom and no other renovations have been made, or are going to be made. He has declared that Fina, my house help that we selected, cannot sleep in the house. There will be further meetings with him when we get to Cotonou.

We were due to leave for Cotonou today, but the money in the Lagos bank is still not available. The money has been at the bank over a week, but still not available. Our departure date is now moved to Monday or Tuesday of next week. However, my goods departed for the border today. They also took two of my suitcases so my border crossing would be easier. I hope it's easy. However, judging by past experience, I doubt it.

I really need to be in prayer. I refuse to let the enemy win and I believe that he's attacking in all directions to keep me out of Aklampa.

8/19/99 Journal Entry, 8:00 am …
I woke up angry at the enemy this morning. So, I'm in a fighting mood. My plan for today is to stay inside, pray, fast, and read the Word all day. I know that the enemy will lose this battle. I know this based on the Word of God. Until 1:00 this morning, scriptures kept coming to my mind as I slept. I kept hearing: "Greater is He that is in you than he that is in the world", "No weapon formed against you shall prosper", "You're more than a conqueror through Christ Jesus who gives you strength", "God shall provide all your needs according to his riches in glory in Christ Jesus", "For this war is not against flesh and blood, but against powers and principalities."

I also know that the offensive weapon of the armor is the Word. Therefore, my battle and fight will be with the Word of God!

8/21/99 Journal Entry…
Yesterday, Ojo and I went to the bank at 1:30. We didn't get the money until 6:20 pm. Still, we finally got the money. God is faithful!

8/22/99 Journal Entry…
Ojo and I went to the market to exchange some money yesterday afternoon at Yaba. We walked down a dark alley and entered a small hot cement office. As we were sitting in the room, there was a commotion outside. Our hosts closed and locked the office door and everyone became very quiet. Armed robbers had arrived and were outside causing mayhem. After the gun shots stopped and things calmed down, we left, with Ojo leading the way to the car which was parked on the opposite end of where he usually has the driver park. If we had parked on the other side, we would have been in the same exact area where the robbers were located.

As we were leaving and drove by the corner at the edge of the market, there was a commotion in front of our car. A group of about ten young men, all under the age of twenty, pushed over a man on a scooter and then jumped on the back of a bus. Ojo told our driver to go straight, but there was traffic so the driver turned right, in the same direction as the bus of young men. Turns out these were the armed robbers. When they saw me in the car (a white woman in a sea of Africans), they ordered the bus to stop and they jumped off to come after us. Our driver took off past them and we got away. If they had seen me at Yaba or had spotted me earlier in the car, it would have been horrible. We'd have been robbed and possibly shot. As we later discussed the incident, we clearly saw the hand of God protecting us.

I lived to see my 31st birthday today.

8/23/99 Journal Entry…
I just had a meeting with an associate pastor of a local church. He had seen me sitting on the deck a few days ago and asked the woman who manages the kitchen about me. He is her pastor.

We visited for over two hours. It was an interesting meeting. He has a deliverance ministry. He also works with local pastors and leads revivals. His intent was to travel with me to Benin and assist me. He's looking for a way out of Nigeria. Many people approached me, seeing me as an opportunity to advance their purposes. Therefore, I had to be very wise and cautious in my dealings with strangers.

I thanked him, but told him kindly that I believe I'm to go alone. He led the closing prayer, which in spite of his motives, was quite powerful. Here are some of the visions he said he saw as well as his prayer:

1. Saw fire from my mouth.
2. Saw the finger of God.
3. I'd walk in the spiritual more than physical realm.
4. Saw so many angels around me and saw a forest of young trees. The angels were clearing a forest.
5. Saw a strongwoman, not strongman, who's overpowering the village in evil.
6. Saw an immense light of God around me.
7. Saw an open door for me that God opened.
8. Said that God will fulfill and bring to pass that which He promised.
9. Saw great power and miracles.
10. Demons would be exposed and have to bow to God.
11. Saw the chiefs approve, receive and welcome me. It would be a positive welcome.
12. Kept calling me God's chosen daughter.
13. Prayed that God knows my sacrifice to go to the village and that He will reward the sacrifice.
14. Spoke of my spiritual eyes.

It was a powerful prayer and the presence of God was awesome. However, I still kept my guard up because of his motivation for meeting me. I believe he has a heart for God, but also really wants out of Nigeria.

9:15 pm…
I was beginning to think I'd never leave Nigeria. We are leaving tomorrow at 11:00 am. I feel funny about leaving. Not scared, but maybe a little sad. This has been home for over five weeks. Tomorrow begins another adventure!

OFF TO BENIN

8/25/99 Journal Entry…
Yesterday was a wonderful day. God was totally with us!

We didn't leave Lagos until 1:45 pm. We made one stop on the way and arrived at the border at 4:30 pm. Before the border, we hit three checkpoints. We were stopped less than two minutes at each stop. At one checkpoint, the guards made us pull over (a sign of trouble) and then immediately let us go without explanation.

At the border, I walked across the border versus riding in the car. We were met by a family friend who works there. He escorted me through all checkpoints. It all took less than 30 minutes. Everyone was so friendly. We passed through three more checkpoints on the Benin side with no problems. We arrived in Cotonou at 6:30 pm. Everyone was shocked at how little time the border crossing took. They recognized that God was really with us.

I remember that as we were driving into Cotonou, I felt as if I had finally arrived home. I became quite emotional and began silently crying. I turned to my friend and said, "I'm home." I loved Benin instantly, even though I didn't understand the languages. It was peaceful, clean, friendly and easy-going. The downside is that Benin is not technologically advanced and every task took lots of time. However, I didn't mind too much. It was such a simpler way of life.

We initially drove to Dez' office and then left to find the Baptist Mission House. Only a guard was at the mission house; no one else. He directed us to the manager's house. I met him; he's a missionary. He was quite rude. He flat out told me that I could not stay at the mission house. He said they were full, which we knew was a lie. Anyway, we had an uneasy feeling about the place because I'd have been completely alone. I decided that this was not where God wanted me.

We checked one hotel which was full and another that didn't feel safe. Gab then suggested Hotel de France. That's where I'm staying. The best thing is that the staff and many guests speak English.

I had dinner in the hotel restaurant after my escorts left. The hotel manager came and we visited for over two hours about Christ. His name is Claude and he's Catholic. He knows the bible but has so many questions. We very openly spoke about our beliefs and what the bible says. At one point, I went to my room to get my bible and we researched passages together. He now wants to meet each day and discuss the bible.

I returned to my room and praised God for the opportunity to minister to someone. It was so wonderful.

HOUSES AND CARS AND MONEY, OH MY!

Journal Entry, 8/25/99, 4:55pm…
The guys arrived at noon. They again approached me regarding the car situation. They really want me to press Emmanuel into buying me a car. I refuse to speak to him about it. Ojo spoke up for me and commented that buying a car is not possible right now due to finances. He told them about the garage in the village where I could hire a car and driver. They didn't like that idea at all.

8/26/99 Journal Entry, 9:20 pm …
Oh, boy, is the enemy busy. We met with Henry. The meeting began with me in attendance, and in English. It then moved to Fongbe, the local language, and then the men left the room to meet without me. They were gone for over two hours. I spent that time in prayer, reading the Word and praising God in song. When they finally rejoined me, the following decisions had been reached:

1. It would shame Henry to have me stay at Kinti's house (Of course that was not said in his presence.) Henry initially said Kinti's house was not available. Therefore, I must stay at his house in the village. However, only the one room (his own bedroom) is completed. I said that my understanding is that two rooms and the kitchen would be completed. He agreed that he and Emmanuel had discussed the other room, but hadn't discussed anything about finishing it.
2. The kitchen still needs to be completed.
3. The wiring wasn't done because he thought we had scratched the idea of a generator. How foolish is that?! We still need to complete the wiring.
4. The toilet/outhouse needs to be redone. As it currently stands, it will only last for about a month before being full. He agreed this needs to be done but didn't commit to anything.
5. It was decided that I would leave the hotel Monday and stay at Henry's house in Cotonou. This one left me speechless so I didn't respond in front of him because I didn't know how on earth they came to that conclusion based on all the issues we had discussed earlier.
6. It was agreed to buy a car versus a 4x4 because when the road is impassable, it's impossible, regardless of the vehicle. However, Godwin and Ojo said this issue is on hold due to finances.

I also noticed that Henry called me his landlord a few times. Sorry, I only have one Lord. He also directed that I was to be his personal guest! No way!

After he left, I was briefed on the meeting. Henry wants us to ask Emmanuel for help in finishing the house. I really object to this! Also, I asked how in the world they decided to have me move to Henry's house. They had expected me to speak up, but how could I since I was so shocked. I told the men that I believe God wants me at this hotel, no matter the cost. Money was not the issue. The real issue is that it is not safe for me to stay at his house. If the enemy wants to play, he can only play on God's field. He must walk into my territory! I told them that I will inform Henry of my decision to remain at this hotel to do ministry. This is spiritual, not political.

Also he had trouble looking me in the eye and almost seemed to cower. I could see the demonic oppression. Still, all the signs of control are there, and he thought he had backed me into a corner. He doesn't realize that he's messing with God, not me. I relinquished control to God so it's not my battle. My job is to walk beside God and He will do the warring. I just held up my shield of faith and stood firm.

Another observation. Henry saw my bible lying open on the desk and joked to one of the men about it. Basically, he was ridiculing the man for reading it. It is amazing how easily the enemy exposed himself!

I'm sitting in the hotel lobby thinking about all the attacks, including an impassible road to the village. I would normally fall apart in tears. However, its humorous. It's obvious the enemy is doing all he can to discourage me or make me worry. I refuse to back down. I knew I was going to encounter spiritual warfare so what should I expect? I'm just excited to see how God wins! I just called and left a message for Freda to call me ASAP. She's going to love this!

10:25 pm...
Can God get any better!!!!!! I feel like screaming!!!!!!!

I just called the guy at the front desk to ask for toilet paper. He said he'd bring it right up. He has been telling me that he loves my smile because I am always happy. He's never met anyone who is always happy before. Last night, he said he had some questions for me, but we never had a chance to talk.

When he arrived with the toilet paper just now, I said thank you. He asked me what makes me so happy. I said "Jesus". He said, can you give me Jesus. I said that Jesus can give him Jesus. He said, "Yes, I want that." We are planning to meet tomorrow to talk. As he left, I asked his name – Lazarus. I said that was Jesus' friend's name.

10:35 pm…
Lazarus just returned with a towel and more questions about Jesus. His main question related to John 14:6. He wanted to know what this scripture meant to Muslims and voodoo. I told him that Jesus is the only way to God. They can see God only if they go through Jesus. We were then interrupted from the front desk calling him back to work.

The flood gates seem to be opening. God wants me right here, right now.

8/27/99 Journal Entry…
I just woke up and a question came to me. Why am I playing by Henry's rules? What would he do if I backed him in a corner by laying my ground rules? In thinking about this, I realize that I'm the one with the control, not him. I need to take back what is mine.

Here are my decisions: I'm not concerned with Henry's reputation or honor. That's his problem, not mine. If we keep his reputation as a consideration, it may be months before I get to the village.

I will not stay at Hotel de France for an extended time. If the house isn't done, I'll still go and they'll have to complete it after I arrive. I'll make do with tough conditions if necessary. If the house isn't renovated as promised, or if other conditions and "rules" arise, I will take it upon myself to find other lodging until Emmanuel's mission house is completed.

I don't care about the road. Once we go, God will find a way to get us into the village. That's not our battle.

I received a phone call from Freda today. She also thinks it is not imperative that I get a car right now. I believe this was confirmation.

By this point, I had been hearing so much negativity, from both sides of the ocean, which discouraged me and tried to make me doubt my calling. Freda encouraged me so much. God consistently used her to keep me focused on my mission versus what man was thinking and saying about me.

9/1/99 Journal Entry…

We've decided to leave for the village on Tuesday, regardless of the house status. Henry was given money today to complete the toilet and wiring. I've been told that I have surprised Henry. He thought I was some sort of "enemy" based on the fact that we never included him in our preparations. Then, when we visited his wife and children, they reported to him how nice I had been. He didn't know what to think. He said he felt bad, but he really just wanted to control me by having me stay at his house. I really threw him by refusing to stay there, even if it was free housing.

Now, he's been informed that we are leaving on Tuesday and are going with or without him. I praise God and give Him all the credit for working things out and taking control. I serve an awesome Savior!

I am beginning to pick up pieces of conversation in Yoruba and Fongbe. I don't know any words, but I seem to be able to understand things and find myself responding in conversations. I'm not sure how I know, I just do. **I believe God was giving me divine discernment to understand portions of conversations.**

A MOMENT OF REFLECTION

9/2/99 Journal Entry…

I've done some thinking about my life today. So much has changed. So much of the old is gone. I used to have goals about making lots of money. Now, my goal is to get close to God and be wealthy in Spirit. I used to spend sleepless nights worrying about money. I was so consumed with it that I became a slave to it. Even upon my arrival, I worried about money. However, I remembered words of prophecy that the old me would be gone. I claimed victory and turned the worry over to God. He replaced the worry with peace of mind.

Speaking of worrying, I worried about so many things before. I used to worry about appearances and what people thought of me. I worried about my relationships and friendships. Now, I can't afford to exert energy into worrying. To worry is to not believe and I believe God can do anything. I used to doubt His promises and now I'm starting to grab hold of his promises and claim them. Doubt is unbelief.

Romans 14:23b "…and everything that does not come from faith is sin."

Overall, my faith has probably been the biggest change in me. I now know that all things are possible through Christ. This change has been facilitated by spending so much more time in the Word and in prayer.

(Following is a prayer that I wrote to God in my journal on 9/3/99.)

Dear Lord,

All glory and praise truly belong to you. You are all mighty, all powerful, and all glorious. You are beautiful, sweet, loving, kind, patient and so much more than words can express. You are my sustainer, my joy, my peace, my strength, my foundation, my Savior. You have blessed me so much. You've brought me to the other side of the world to live in a totally foreign culture (race, socio-economic, and language) and I couldn't be more at peace.

People here cannot understand how I can be happy to be here, leaving America. However, I think I'm in a beautiful land with beautiful people. Also, I know that I'm exactly where you want me to be so I'm content.

I was just thinking back to the night in my apartment when you asked me what I'd be willing to give up for you and I said everything except my bible. Now, here I sit at a hotel in Africa, having left my entire life behind me; but my Bible is sitting at my side. I no longer have to deal with the politics of my secular job, paying rent, a car loan, etc. My entire old life is gone. Everything I've worked for in the first thirty years of my life, I've let it go to follow you. The only important things I have to show for my first thirty years are my salvation and education. I thank you for both of them.

Lord, thank you for all the changes in my spiritual walk with you. I pray that you would continue to increase my understanding of your Word, your will and your ways. I love you so much and truly consider it a privilege to serve you.

I pray that you'll continue to break me and clean me so your Spirit can reside and flow more freely. I pray that I will never take any credit for your marvelous work. I want your Name alone to be glorified. I just want to serve you and allow you to use me.

Lord, once again, thank you for your many, many blessings and encouragements. I love you so much, Gina.

9/12/99 Letter to Prayer Team in America...
I've learned a lot about African Traditional Religion:

1) *The village of Aklampa is known throughout Benin and is famous for their "spiritual power". People travel to Aklampa from other parts of the country to get fetishes and idols because their power is so strong.*
2) *The witches in Aklampa meet on certain nights between 11:00 pm and 2:00 am. I've been told this is a good time to be in prayer. (We're 8 hours ahead of you so that's 3:00 pm to 6:00 pm your time.)*
3) *The witches and "priests" are known for asking for a personal item, such as a shirt. They then take it and cast spells on the owner.*
4) *I've been told not to step in or over strange puddles of liquid, especially if they are in my own yard. They are curses.*
5) *There are people who sold their soul, and in exchange, Satan puts smoke over the head of people carrying money. They then rob the people.*

At our prayer meeting on the Thursday before I left, I remember Debra said that I would be completely new and that none of my old worries and ways would remain. However, once I arrived in Africa and realized I would be spending much more time in hotels before going to the village, I began to worry about money – my biggest vice. I spent a lot of time worrying about my finances.

One day I was in my hotel room in Cotonou and began praying. I was almost angry as I asked God, "You told me I'd be new but I still have the same worries as before I left. Why am I not new?" His response shook me, "I promised it, and I've provided it. But, you've not claimed it. It's waiting for you to take."

All I could do was cry. My devotions at that time were in the Old Testament and I was reminded how God promised it, and provided it. They just had to claim it.

I stopped worrying temporarily, but this proved to be a short-term victory. Money would continue to be a point of attack throughout my stay in Africa. This is a stronghold that I had such difficulty releasing. As you read on, you will see how such a stronghold affects relationships, self-esteem, etc.

I want to give you a list of my specific prayer requests, so we can be on one accord:

The house I will initially occupy in Aklampa is owned by Henry. He needs Jesus. I won't go into any specific details. He is a very powerful military man but is afraid of me. Actually, he's actually afraid of the presence of God. However, the enemy is using him as my main obstacle in getting to the village. It's taken lots of prayer (and a talk from the pastor) to keep me from telling this man what he can do with his house and "control" over me.

Please also pray for the spiritual atmosphere in the village. I've already been informed that there are traditional celebrations and ceremonies which must take place upon my arrival. I'll have to grin and bear it because I can't afford to offend the king and chiefs before I'm even settled. I need wisdom on how to deal with this without compromising my beliefs.

THE TREK INTO AKLAMPA

9/30/99 Letter…
Well, I finally made it "home" to Aklampa. How do I feel? Relieved.
However, it was quite the journey. There's no way I'd ever expect you to
do this trip! You'll see why as you read on….

I'm learning patience. Nothing happens on schedule in Africa. **I've**
always been neurotic about being on time, often arriving an hour
early everywhere I went. You'll see that God must have enjoyed
messing with me in this area.

Godwin & Gab were to be at my hotel by 9:00 am to depart for the village.
They didn't arrive until 10:30 am. The plan was to load my truck and
leave. Wrong! We loaded the truck and then Godwin and Gab ran around
for building supplies until after 4:00 pm. Godwin finally dropped off Gab
and picked up Ojo and I, and we were off – 4:50 pm – my blood pressure
rising as the day progressed.

The old man we hired to drive my stuff took his sweet time. A 3.5 hour
journey to Glazoué, a village about 30km from Aklampa, took 5 hours! It
was past nightfall when we arrived in Glazoué. There was no way we
could get to Aklampa that day. Our plan was to unload my goods at the
pharmacist's house and then drive back to Dassa (20 miles) to stay in a
hotel. Wrong again! We unloaded my goods and Ojo told me to pack an
overnight bag. I thought we were going to Dassa so I packed clothes,
shampoo, makeup, etc. (PS – You're about to find humor in the items I
packed.)

At 11:30 pm, after getting somewhat organized, a man grabbed my bag
and led three of us down the main road. I then realized we weren't going
to Dassa. After one block, we turned left onto a dirt road with garbage,
mud and weeds. Only the moonlight lit our path as we had no lantern or
flashlights. After about a quarter of a mile, we turned left again onto a
"path". I use that term loosely. There were trees on one side and a drop-
off ravine with water on the other! At times I had to grab onto trees to get
along the path.

By this time Ojo was about to have a panic attack. I think he was more
scared than I. After about another quarter of a mile, we came to the place
where we were to sleep. Freda, it's hardly describable. It's a simple
cement structure with two rooms – a sitting room and a bedroom. It was
the home of the guy carrying my bag. He put a sheet on the bed and left us

a lantern. There was no water, and the 'toilet' was out the back door of the bedroom. Just pick a spot of grass, squat, and watch out for snakes!

You think I'm exaggerating, don't you? I wish I were! Anyway, after changing into pajamas, we settled in for a night of swatting mosquitoes. Not much sleep.

At daybreak, we woke and got ready to return to the pharmacy. Since there was no water or a place to bathe, I took a bit of my bottled water and poured it on my washcloth to at least wash my face. Ojo teased me and called me a "bush woman", but he soon realized what a good idea I had had.

Well, news of a white woman sleeping in the bush travels fast. When I stepped out of the back door to brush my teeth and go to the bathroom, there were at least fifteen people (men, women & children) waiting to catch a glimpse. Well, I decided to only brush my teeth. Some things are too personal to share with perfect strangers, especially my white buttocks.

Our host returned for us (having given up his home for the night) and we hiked back to the pharmacist's house. He has the post office box I am using in Glazoué. After breakfast, we visited the post office, the local government, and the doctor who checked my legs which had begun tingling. His verdict – my blood pressure is sky high. It's never been high. It's usually low. He figures my body is trying to adapt to an entirely new environment, culture, food, etc. (Plus some spiritual stuff.) He put me on some medicine with Vitamin B. I've been on it for a week and feel no difference. Actually, my index finger on my right hand is almost completely numb. I think its 100% spiritual.

We finally loaded my goods on two smaller trucks and left for Aklampa. This drive was supposed to take one hour. It took over 4 hours! Fifteen minutes into the journey, our truck (carrying Ojo, the driver and me) got hung up in a mud hole. While we worked to get us out (45 minutes) the other truck carrying Godwin, Gab and the driver tried a different route around a mud hole and broke the front axle. This meant waiting for someone to come by, pick up the driver, take him back to Glazoué, find a mechanic, and come back to the truck and fix it (2 or more hours). It was during this time that I began to realize the warfare I was entering.

I suggest you sit down for this one because it is almost unbelievable.

While waiting for the mechanic, our driver worked on jacking up the truck. To do this, we needed logs so he grabbed one by the side of the road. An older woman came out and began screaming at us for stealing her property. We tried to reason with her. No way! She called for her son. He was clearly demon-possessed. He was screaming and then began chanting and shaking and foaming at the mouth. All I could do was pray.

Turns out that there are two warring villages in that area and tensions are high. The son left to go get men and weapons and said he'd be back to kill us. Gab hopped into action and finally calmed the mother down. She called off the battle. The son came back anyway and stood by, watching us until we left. WARFARE or what?!

Then I received my blessing for the day. As we were still working on jacking up the truck, a frail little old lady walked by. She had been walking barefoot from Glazoué and was on her way to a funeral near Aklampa. She had no money for transportation. She saw our situation and felt sorry for us. She walked into the mud on the road, pulled out a small log and brought it over to us. It was so touching. I can't even describe it. So simple, yet so meaningful. Now, this woman is probably in her 70's but looks 90. She visited for a minute and then was on her way. After Ojo interpreted what she said, I decided that we would pick her up and carry her to her destination.

Once we got both trucks free and fixed, we prayed as a group and were on our way. We met up with the old woman about a half mile up the road. She was thrilled, even though she had to ride in back of the truck. When we dropped her off, I also gave her some money for transportation back to Glazoué. It was the least I could do, given her kindness.

Now, the road. As our driver described, there are seven "gates" to Aklampa, meaning seven bad spots on the road. I noted the biblical significance of the number seven and the term gates. However, in my mind, there were at least 15 bad spots. By bad, I mean that the drivers get out; survey the best route through the mud (or drop off). The men walk ahead and the drivers get back in and go for it – full speed ahead! If one vehicle makes it through, the other takes the same route.

More than once we were airborne. It was harder for Ojo to watch from the roadside than for me to be in the truck. I thought he'd have a stroke at one point. Remember, I'm a country kid and we used to drive through mud for fun.

The Road to Aklampa

We finally arrived in Aklampa. People had seen me in Glazoué so they knew I was due that day. Remember the boy who danced for me during my first trip to the village? Well, he walked up to the truck, said welcome and started unloading my truck. Others pitched in and soon I was unloaded.

The next day one of the men and I visited a family compound. The caretaker escorted us inside and sat us down. The other two men were outside at that time. The woman caretaker came in and offered us a drink of water. I asked my escort if I should drink, thinking of health issues. He said to take just a bit so I did. He then took a drink. She then asked one of the other men to come in the house. She then started chanting something and then had the two men pour water on a grave. We then left. My escort kept looking to see my reaction, but I said nothing. I knew it was some sort of "traditional" ceremony.

At dinner, Godwin told us that he was upset that we drank the water because the woman is a witch. She is known for poisoning and cursing water and food. Also, since the water was also used in the ceremony, we can be sure she "prayed" over it. My escort and I both thanked God that we were fine. His attitude is similar to mine. As long as we are firmly grounded in Christ, God will protect us. I won't take food or water from villagers again, but there will still be situations of which I am unaware. However, I praise God for his protection.

On Friday morning, Ojo, Godwin & Gab took me to present me to the king and chiefs. Gab did all the talking until they said they wanted to hear from me, which surprised all of us since I wasn't sure a woman could talk in such settings. Some of the chiefs speak some English. I explained my call to spread the gospel of Jesus Christ, thereby putting them on notice since they are the voodoo leaders of the village.

Ojo, Godwin & Gab were surprised that I was so open about letting them know my call. They had been using the MAFA project (the hospital we were building) as my official reason for being here. They were sure that the king and chiefs wouldn't accept me, but once again, Christ won. They joyously welcomed me to Aklampa.

Someone had "informed" the king and chiefs that I had no intention of informing them of our arrival. Therefore, they were initially wary. However, once I explained my calling and requested that they take me under their wing and teach me their language, they openly welcomed me. They were impressed that I would leave the comforts of America to live with them in suffering and poverty. I explained that I believe God created us equally so I feel as if they are now my family.

During my entire stay in Aklampa, the chiefs and king were always very nice and courteous to me. When I attended any ceremonies, the king made a point of having me join him and sit beside him, which was a very high honor.

For the first year of my stay in the village, I lived in Henry's house. I was given two bedrooms, as well as the main salon for my use. Henry routinely visited the village and stayed in his rooms across the hall from me. He acted cordial to me most of the time. However, God usually revealed when he was plotting something against me.

I was finally able to negotiate with Henry to allow Fina, my house help to work for me and sleep in the house. However, my guard was assigned to me by Henry. It was a firm condition of my staying in his house in the village. However, this guard was more trouble than help. Essentially, I paid him to spy on me, torment me, not do his job, cheat me out of money, and attempt to kill me on a number of occasions.

Hard to believe? Read on...

HISTORY OF AKLAMPA

Aklampa is named after a child named Akla. A mother, father and the child named Akla were traveling. The mother carried the child on her back. As they were trekking, they arrived in this area. It was the dry season. At one place, there was a hole dug for fetching water to drink. The mother, baby and father reached the hole. The mother drew water for her husband and then took some for herself before giving the baby a drink. This was against their traditional custom.

The devil saw her error and dried up the hole. When she drew water the third time for her baby, the hole was dry. She turned to the baby, Akla, and told the baby that there was no more water. The baby cried and cried. The mother shook the baby and it cried even more. Finally the baby died. During the time she was shaking the baby, she was speaking Yoruba (their language) and said, "Akla, Omi o ton." This means, "Akla, the water's finished." In Fon (the current language), it's "Aklamita". When the Europeans came and asked the name of the village, they couldn't pronounce Aklamita so they changed it to Aklampa.

The village of Aklampa is separated into three sections, Allawenonsa, Affinzungo and Lagbo. The sections are separated by two rivers which intersect in the village. The rivers and their meanings are:

Lodowin: "The area where they went to capture the tortoise." This river is in Lagbo.

Wessé: "The river for fetching bath water". This river is in Affinzungo.

WE'RE NOT IN KANSAS – A PORTRAIT OF LIFE IN AKLAMPA

The following are excerpts from my hometown weekly paper, the Napoleon Homestead. They requested I send information describing my living conditions.

1/26/00 Napoleon Homestead Article...
... Let me try to explain the lifestyle here. I shower or bathe out of a pail of water. There's a room off my bedroom for it so I have privacy. I have a toilet/outhouse outside. My kitchen is a simple, small cement room built beside my toilet. I have a kerosene stove that's the size of a hotplate (no oven). I bought a toaster oven but can only use it at night when the generator is on. I have electricity from about 7:00 pm to 7:00 am, so I have a fan at night to keep me cool. I have a refrigerator which keeps things relatively cool, considering it's off all day. I pay a woman to bring water each day. The cost is 40 francs per three gallon basin. She fills a barrel each day.

I ran out of fuel for the generator yesterday so I paid a man to take my keg to Glazoué to fill. The cost: 5,000 francs to pay for the fuel and 5,000 francs for transport. For reference, 620 francs equals $1.00. The keg is 50 liters.

I have a maid, who is great and a guard who I don't like at all. I'm not sure what to do about him but I know I can't do anything until the men return.

It's near the end of the rainy season. You can tell when it's going to rain. The sky turns dark and the wind suddenly begins to severely blow. When the wind hits, people run for cover, because they know the rain will hit in less than one minute. There is no such thing as a light rain. It pours! I'm guessing they get at least five inches in less than a half hour. You can hardly see my front gate which is about 25 feet away! Hey, send me a rain gauge that I can stick in the ground. However, it doesn't rain long. It started raining when I began writing this letter and it finished a while ago so I'm back out on my deck. I have fifteen children watching me.

I'm learning Fon faster than French because it's all I hear. I've just started greeting people in Fon which really surprises them and makes them laugh. The other day, Ojo's uncle sat down to teach me some simple phrases and made me write them down. However, everyone laughed when I said, "this is my pregnant belly". I had meant to say, "This is my house." It was very funny.

Tomorrow is market day in the village so I'll try to get some fresh fruit and veggies. They aren't easy to find here. I can't wait to receive your garden seeds so I can plant a garden in my new yard. Make sure to send carrots, cucumbers, peas, bell peppers and tomatoes. Their tomatoes are the size of a quarter and bell peppers are almost impossible to find!

So, I'm settling into bush life quite well. The men responsible for me worry that they'll return and find me covered in mud with dirty hair. I'm tempted, just to scare them, but if I did, they said they'd kidnap me and not let me return.

Well, I had better go.

3/13/00 Napoleon Homestead Article, Part I...
The purpose of this letter is to describe life in Africa and how the average villager lives.

The Average Day: The first activity of each day is to visit the family voodoo shrine. After feeding the shrine, villagers go to the toilet, brush their teeth and begin their day. The toilets are concrete huts with holes in the ground. I guess they're similar to our outhouses, but without seats. However, I've not been close enough to inspect them and I have no need to know.

(Note: most villagers do not own outhouses, so they go into the bush to go toilet. There are areas of the village with high brush where villagers go to relieve themselves. Many do not own toilet paper so they use leaves to wipe.)

Most villagers don't have a toothbrush or paste, although they are available. They use sticks of which they chew and grind on their teeth and then spit out. Amazingly, I've not smelled anyone with bad breath, but have seen some horrible teeth.

Most men own a farm. The main money-making crops are cotton and cashews. They harvest these crops in December and January. For the other part of the year, they plant crops which they use for food and local trade. They raise corn, rice, cassava, peanuts, melons, tomatoes, hot peppers, bananas, oranges, papaya, yams, beans (two types), okra and greens. There are no machines. Everything is done by hand. The only two instruments are a long knife (two feet long) to clear brush and a shovel to dig. Their shovels are different from ours. Whereas American shovels are straight, these are v-shaped.

The men farm until late afternoon unless it is too hot. In that case, they'll farm until noon and then return in late afternoon once it begins to cool off. To get to their farms, they walk up to ten kilometers each way. A few have bicycles.

Some of the women also farm especially if their husband has died. However, many women engage in trade. For example, each morning my next door neighbor makes a corn porridge (which is delicious) to sell and in the afternoon she makes and sells a creamy corn flour mixture that gelatinizes and is wrapped in leaves. One bowl of the morning porridge costs 25 cfa, or about four cents. I add sugar to sweeten it.

Many of the women sell their goods at the small market in the village. The market is a set of lean-to's under which they sit throughout the day. If we need meat, tomatoes, or other necessities, we go to this market. However, I've learned not to personally go for the meat because I lose my appetite. The raw meat sits outside in the sun and is covered with flies! I've learned to send my house help early in the morning to avoid as much contamination as possible.

Before opening for business, the women sweep their area, even though it is dirt. They also sweep their front yard. For example, I have an employee who comes each morning at 7:00 and sweeps my entire yard. This employee is also responsible for fetching water. For most families, this is the responsibility of the teenage girls.

There's no running water, but there are wells to find water. They carry the water in large basins on their heads. I pay 100 cfa per day for an oil barrel full of "clean" water. There is clean and rough water available. The rough water is brown. The clean water is not too bad, but definitely not drinkable for me. It makes me very sick.

Laundry is done outdoors by hand in a basin. Homemade soap as well as commercial soap are available. The clothes are hung on a clothesline to dry. They use charcoal irons to iron. Charcoal is placed in the iron and lit in order to make the iron hot.

All cooking is done outdoors. Each house or compound has a set of three mounds that form a triangle. The mounds are built so wood can fit under the pots. They burn wood for fire to cook. Some people have various size mounds to accommodate various size pots. To grind tomatoes, pepper, onions, etc., they use a flat concrete board about the size of a large cutting board. They lay the food on the stone and then have another stone that's a half circle and about six inches long. They grind the food with this stone.

I'm eating much of the village food and it's all foreign to me. They eat many starches, such as pounded yam and amala. Pounded yam is made by peeling and cooking yams like you would potatoes. When tender, they put the yams in a wood cauldron. They take a long clublike stick and mash the yams until they glutenize. Pounded yam feels doughy. They eat this with a stew with their hands. Actually, most foods are eaten without utensils. They eat with their right hand only. Even I've mastered this skill.

The common meats are chicken, beef, goat, some pork, tiny dried fish (disgusting) and bush meat. Bushmeat is the term for those ugly beaver-like animals that don't really have a name. I refused to eat it for a long time, but I've grown to like it because it's so tender. (Bushmeat looks very similar to American muskrats.) I hear they also eat turkey, pigeons and snake, but I've not indulged.

There are virtually no vegetables available in Aklampa. If I want potatoes or carrots, I have to go to the port city of Cotonou (3 or more hours' journey). Onions, tomatoes, peppers, rice and peanuts are readily available. They also use corn, beans and cassava for many different foods. If I want coconut, oranges, or bananas, I let someone know and they bring them from Glazoué which is about 30 kilometers away.

Every fourth day is Market Day in Aklampa. It's the center of activity. There are lots of stands where you can buy goods such as fabric, recycled clothes, food items, hygiene items such as soap, fetishes and traditional medicine items for voodoo worship, etc. The cost of items is cheap compared to the U.S., but it is still costly for villagers.

Of course, the cost goes up for me because I'm white. Therefore, I quickly learned the real price of things and negotiate/argue with them. The locals treat me fairly well. It's the traveling marketers who travel from village to village on market days to sell their goods that give me a headache. A good example: I bought a watch today for a friend. The original quoted price to me was 15,000 cfa. The final price we paid was 2,000 cfa.

Besides market day, other social activities include voodoo ceremonies, traditional dancing and singing, stilt walking ceremonies (also voodoo) and funerals. Yes, funerals are huge social activities that last for seven days.

Wednesday is market day in Glazoué. Many people go to trade and buy supplies. On Tuesday evening, a big truck loads the goods and goes to Glazoué. The traders follow the next morning and begin trading at sun-up.

Transportation: No one in Aklampa has a private car. If they own a car, they use it to chauffer people and make money. The village has about ten cars with chauffeurs. They pack as many people as possible into a car, such as twelve or more. They load the goods in the trunk and on the roof. Each chauffer also has a "motor boy" who acts as his assistant and does most of the labor. When I go anywhere, I hire the entire car, so I can ride in comfort. I refuse to sit with twelve people in one car. My chauffer, Jonas, runs errands for me such as bringing my mail, and buying water and fuel.

There are also motorcycle taxis available. Due to the bad road, I initially wouldn't use them in the village. When I travel to Cotonou, they are my main source of transportation to get around the city. They're quick and cheap. And fun!

Housing: Most houses have one or two rooms which are formed from clay. The roofs are tin or grass. Usually there is a set of houses that are close together and form a compound with a central common area outside for cooking, bathing, etc. All cooking is done outdoors. There are some

concrete homes as well.

Families all live together; therefore, you can't escape your in-laws! At marriage, the wife literally moves to the husband's family compound. By the time of marriage, the husband will usually have built a hut for his wife. Since many men have multiple wives, they build separate houses for each wife and will keep a separate house or room for himself. Essentially, the village is sub-sectioned by families. The eldest male will be the chief of the family. All his brothers and their families will live together.

The children are taught to highly respect their elders. They never call them by their first name. They also bow to all elders. Even I bow to anyone older than I.

Since there is no hospital, the women give birth at home or in the bush. It is not uncommon for them to begin having children in their mid-teens. The women breastfeed as well as feed them regular food from birth, including food with peppers!

The boys aren't circumcised until 2-5 years old and it's not done by a doctor. The electrician performed the circumcision that I witnessed!

The babies are carried on the women's backs and they wrap material around to hold them against the mother. This leaves the mother's hands free to work. If the baby gets hungry, they pull the baby to the side, hook them up to the breast and keep working.

3/20/00 Napoleon Homestead Article, Part II...

Babies have a naming ceremony seven days after birth. The baby is given a number of names based on African tradition. The parents then pick two or three names to retain throughout life. However, there are some automatic names given in certain circumstances. For example, the first child born after a set of twins is Dossou. The next child after Dossou is Dossa. If a twin is a girl, her name will be Hoho. I'd tell you the boy's name, but it's too long.

69

<u>Marriage</u>: I haven't witnessed a marriage so I can only give brief details. The men are required to pay a dowry to the bride's family. This will usually include money, a goat, chicken and other food products. There are also other items which are used as part of the ceremony. As mentioned earlier, many men have multiple wives. The first wife holds the most power, unless she doesn't bear children. The more children they have, the higher the honor. For example, my friend's father has many wives, and has fathered over 40 children!

It is also no big deal for a man to cheat on his wife. I was visiting with a man who is married with one child and his friend who has two wives. I explained how marriage, infidelity and divorce happen in America. For example, if men cheat on their wives, the wife often divorces the husband and gets the house, the car, and the kids. They were shocked and asked what the men did after wives give birth and cannot have intercourse with them for some weeks. I told them that husbands have to wait, just like the wives have to wait. They thought I was crazy and said there's no way they would wait that long. They're also allowed to beat their wives, but I've not seen it publicly.

<u>Medical</u>: My church is in the process of building a hospital in the village. The nearest hospital is about 80 kilometers away, which would be tolerable if the road was good. However, during the rainy season, the road is virtually impassable. Therefore, many people die because there's not a real doctor or equipment. There are pharmacies where we can "self-medicate". They have basic drugs such as aspirin, penicillin, etc. There are no prescriptions needed.

<u>Politics</u>: Aklampa is made up of three main sections which are separated by a stream. The village is led by one king and six chiefs (two per section). All matters go through them and then on to the regional government in Glazoué. There are no police in the village.

3/27/00 Napoleon Homestead Article, Part III...

<u>Technology</u>: There is no electricity, no phone, no running water, etc. There are a few generators. An electrician who fixes mostly radios has a speaker hooked up to a pole to make announcements and sometimes play music. Remember the TV show M.A.S.H. and their announcements? Same thing. Many people have small radios run with batteries. Many people have never used a phone. For example, my friend Dossou spoke on the phone for the first time last week and he's 25. He said hello to my mom.

School: School runs from early October to July. Uniforms are required. There is a small fee to pay, but many people can't afford it so they don't send their children. The fee is approximately $6.00 for the entire year. There are six years of primary (elementary) school. If they pass an exam, they can move onto secondary school which is another six years. The fees for secondary school are higher; therefore, few students are able to go.

Also, very few girls attend school because many don't see the need for a woman to be educated. As I think about it, I've not met one girl or woman who's pursued an education and gone on to the university in Cotonou. Maybe that's why they can't imagine how I chose an education over family first. The women in the village think I'm crazy not to want to have a baby yet. The entire village of 20,000 people has six primary schools and one secondary school.

Pets: Many people have dogs as pets. There are a few cats, but I was told that witches own cats. That's the easiest way I know who the witches are. However, I'm not intimidated by most of them because they are very nice women. They truly believe they are worshipping God. They are blind to the truth. However, there are some very bad witches. I know of only one for sure and I keep clear of her.

There are also chickens, goats and a few pigs running around, but they're eaten.

I later learned that anyone may own a cat and I was given a cat as a pet. I named it "Grace" and taught it to play with a ball. This was quite the spectacle for the village, and I soon gained a nickname translated, 'the cat plays ball'.

Clothing: The men wear shorts or pants with a t-shirt or button top. The women wear a top with a wrap skirt. I've seen very few women in shorts or pants. Many women also use a wrap top (similar to how we wear a towel after a bath). I've mastered the skirt so it doesn't fall off while I walk. They are actually very comfortable and cool. Babies usually run around naked or wear a t-shirt. There are no diapers. A few women use cloth and make make-shift diapers. Needless to say, I've had more than one baby pee on me. Not a pleasant experience.

From birth, the girls have their ears pierced. Men and women wear necklaces made of gold, silver or beads. The beaded ones usually contain a voodoo fetish. Both men and women also wear rings which seem to be made out of bent copper or metal. Many people have beaded chains on their waist. Some specific ones are used to keep away evil spirits – voodoo.

Furniture: Most people sit on benches, not chairs. The villagers usually sleep on straw mats which are rolled up in the morning. There are a few beds. I've seen only three and most of these had no mattresses. Other than that, there is very little furniture.

Weather: Hot! It rains from April – October. November and December are hot and humid. January and February are cool in the morning and hot and dry in the afternoon. March is just plain hot! I can't wait. Only joking!

Religion: The main religion is voodoo. There are other "Christian" churches here, but most of them combine Christianity with voodoo. For example, they still allow sacrifices to pray for healings. Jesus was the last Sacrifice. I flat out tell everyone that voodoo is against Jesus. You can't do both. No church in Aklampa boldly took a stand against voodoo. Therefore, they posed no real threat.

Some parents put white powder on their children's faces at night. They also put a black mark on their forehead. This is to keep evil spirits away. Many of the children also have beads around their neck, arm, ankle, or waist with fetishes attached for protection.

The village has "dirt devils" – those tiny whirlwinds that pick up dust for a few moments before dying. However, they are viewed very differently in Aklampa. These whirlwinds are believed to be evil voodoo spirits. I have seen them. They don't just show up any place. When these "dirt devils" manifest, they always follow voodoo members as they walk.

Openness to Outsiders: This has drastically changed in recent years. Aklampa is known for doing anything possible to keep away outsiders, including killing missionaries! That was only three years ago! I found this information out after arriving here!

However, they are realizing that they need help to modernize them and they don't have the money to do it themselves. They're fine now, as long as you respect their culture. Needless to say, I'm the first missionary that's been allowed to stay (and survive). Many people, including villagers, thought I wouldn't last a month. My willingness to stay really opened their hearts to me. Praise God.

Well, that's life in an African village. May God bless you all, Gina.

MY DAILY ROUTINE

I spend my early mornings next door with a woman who cooks hiavi, a porridge that is similar to cream of wheat, but made with fermented ground corn. I visit with her and greet my neighbors. Greetings are a big deal and quite lengthy. After returning home, I eat breakfast, bathe, and then settle in for my daily prayer, worship and devotion time.

Dossou sometimes joins me for a bit of prayer afterward. He's walked in a few times in the middle of my prayer, but he can tell he's intruding so he quietly leaves and goes into the next room to read his bible. He only reads a verse or small passage because he reads very little and doesn't comprehend French well. I have a Fongbe bible, but very few people can read Fongbe.

By this time, it's nearly lunch. I may visit a few people or do some writing. After lunch, I'll rest for about an hour. Everyone sleeps in the early afternoon. Around 2 pm, I go to visit people. I try to visit at least three people each day. I also play ayo with some adults who get a kick out of beating me. What do they expect?! They've been playing for years.

I also ask different women to teach me certain cooking skills. For example, I've helped make "gee" which is ground corn flour cooked until thick. It is then wrapped in large leaves to gelatinize. I've also helped grind and sift cassava, which is eaten both cold like a cereal and heated in water as a starch with dinner. I'll never need these skills in America, but its good bonding.

Around 5pm I return home to relax and play with some children, if I don't go out with some church members. Dinner is at 7pm. After dinner I relax and write, or play cards, or go out for a bit. By 10:00 pm I'm in bed after prayer.

In the afternoon, many women peel local seeds to prepare their sauce for dinner. I would often grab some seeds out of their bucket and join them under the shade of a mango tree or market stall roof. Although they spoke only Fongbe, I began to understand at least half of their conversations and often joined in the conversation.

During this first year in Aklampa, life was wonderful. Looking back, it was probably one of the most joyful times of my life. I was accepted by the villagers as one of their own. I sat with them, prepared food and cooked with them, danced with them, mourned with them, prayed for them, etc.

73

The outside world became much more foreign to me than my life in the village. I even caught myself carrying things on my head just like the villagers. My English, both spoken and written, changed. Even when speaking to friends from America, my English was broken at times. I unknowingly incorporated many local phrases in my conversation. There are a few phrases that still slip into my speech even today.

MINISTRY BEGINNINGS

"Every morning in Africa a gazelle wakes up. It knows that it must run faster than the fastest lion or it will be killed. Every morning a lion wakes up. It knows it must outrun the slowest gazelle or it will starve to death. It doesn't matter whether you are a lion or a gazelle. When the sun comes up, you better be running." Author Unknown

9/27/99 Journal Entry…
I was settling in for a nap when I heard a commotion in the front yard. I opened the window to see a man in voodoo masquerade costume. I quickly got on my knees and prayed. I then went out for him to greet me. He asked for something, which is common in the village. I went back to my room for 100 cfa. However, I knew the potential of its use in voodoo. I felt led to anoint the coin with oil and pray that the Holy Spirit's presence would affect the man, and protect me. I set the coin down for him to take. We are not allowed to touch these masqueraders. He then left. Somehow I feel I've just won a victory.

The voodoo that visited this day was Kpadjé, which means witch killer. The inhabitant of this voodoo costume was Dossou Allagbé who became the first convert in my ministry.

The masquerade voodoo routinely walk throughout the village greeting people before their public ceremonies in the late afternoons. Young men are the main members. These members go into some trance-like state and allow the demons that represent the costumes to take over their bodies. The person "dies" and the demon inhabits the costume.

9/28/99 Devotion…
Romans 15:20-21. "It has always been my ambition to preach the gospel where Christ was not known, so that I would not be building on someone else's foundation. Rather, as it is written: 'Those who were not told about him will see, and those who have not heard will understand'." This passage was encouraging in that I believe people here will accept Christ. I know there are other churches in this village, but are not scripturally based, and some are cults.

10/1/99Letter…
I thought I would be here for months before starting any ministry. Wrong again.

The other day a young girl came with her two month old baby. The baby weighed no more than five pounds. She wanted prayer so I anointed them with oil and prayed. Two days later as I sat on the deck reading the bible, another woman came with her baby whose hand had been caught under a log. The hand was bruised and badly swollen. The baby was clearly in intense pain. She too wanted prayer.

By the time I finished, two other adults, one man and one woman, arrived with their babies who had fevers. All they wanted was prayer. So I prayed. When I opened my eyes, guess who was standing beside me? The king. He'd come to greet me. Oh boy, what timing! I bowed and greeted him. He then left. I'd love to know what he thought. I'm sure God had a reason for this timing. I know one thing, if he was displeased, knowing he is in voodoo, I'd better be prayed up.

It is customary in West Africa to bow when greeting an elder, especially royalty. However, because my eyes were closed in prayer, I did not see the king enter the house and did not bow to him until I was finished. However, I believe he recognized that I was praying and could not stop what I was doing to greet him properly.

Then an older woman came with some skin disease and wanted prayer. She took off her shirt (no bra) and I prayed for her. I have no idea how people know. All I know is that it made me check myself and make sure my life is in order so God can use me. It was totally humbling. Some of them have returned for prayer.

Before I step out the door in the morning, I had better be prayed up!

I'm sick as a dog. I have stomach cramps and diarrhea. I'd like to think it's something I ate, but I think it's also spiritual. Let me explain how I think this and you can tell me if I'm off base.

Yesterday, I had an intense day of prayer. I'm reading "The Mind of Christ" and realize I have a lot of issues in my life. They may be subtle, but they affect my ministry. Here's a prime example. I believe I've given up a lot to move here and want to please God. However, I realized yesterday that I also worry about pleasing Emmanuel (my pastor) and proving my calling to Village (my home church).

My focus was wrong. It needed to be focused totally on pleasing God – not on proving a point. I also have some fears about the future. I've always been goal oriented and it's throwing me off to not have any worldly goals. However, I realize that fear equals lack of faith. Therefore, I asked God to reveal everything in me that doesn't imitate the mind and life of Christ and asked Him to clean me out so He can use me.

Now let me explain my stomach cramps. A little while ago I was praying and I think God told me that this process is not only a physical cleaning to get rid of a foreign substance, but spiritual as well. Oh, I forgot to mention that the Lord also led me to fast today. It's interesting that all this should happen on the same day.

4:35 pm...
I had to quit writing for a while and rest. I just took my temp – it's 101.9 and rising. OK, maybe this isn't of God, but it's definitely spiritual. I'm breaking my fast at 5:00 pm. We'll see what happens then. PS – Your Christmas gift- the blanket- came in handy. I'm freezing!

7:30 pm...
At exactly 5:00 pm the fever broke for a while. I sweat so much that my clothes were soaking wet. Sweat just poured out of me. It was amazing. I'm still not well, but I can function. My fever is 100.7 right now.

Now onto other spiritual matters. The other night, Henry's brother brought me a case of bottled water as a gift. I thought, "How nice". Wrong again! My guard and Henry's sister, who is the caretaker of this house, sat me down and begged me not to drink the water. The man who gave the water is from the "other" association and they fear that the water may be poisoned, even though it's never been opened. I agreed to wait until Ojo, Godwin & Gab come before using the water.

The other association was a rival to whom we were working with to build the hospital in the village. They come from separate political positions and had competed for our assistance in building the hospital. This man is a well known witchdoctor and lives in Savalou, a town about 40 kilometers west of Aklampa.

Another water issue. The other morning, a neighbor poured some "bad" water outside my gate. The caretaker of this house had a fit. The water is bad because it's used in some ceremony and then thrown out the next morning. However, the "water" doesn't dry like regular water.

10/2/99 Letter...
The fever returned. At 1:00 am, it was 103.1. I thought I wanted to die. I was so cold that I couldn't think straight. Then I began sweating. I

changed my pajamas twice because they were soaked. I'm feeling a bit better this morning although I still have a slight fever of 100.

I remained sick until Ojo, Godwin & Gab returned to the village. The source of my sickness was the water that had been given to me as a "gift" from the witchdoctor from Savalou. I hadn't opened the case, but realized that I became sick the same day the case of water was placed in my room.

Ojo, Godwin and Gab were immediately informed of the "gift" upon their arrival. Sure enough, even though the case was never opened, nor the seals on the bottles broken, it was poisoned. The water was tested on a chicken which died instantly. The water was removed from my room and destroyed. Within one hour of the water being removed from my room, I was completely well.

Now, you may wonder, how can a Christian be influenced by voodoo curses? I firmly believe that a Christian cannot be possessed by demons. However, I also know there are biblical references to the fact that Satan can afflict Christians. If you don't believe it, read the book of Job.

I also believe God used this, and many other situations, to teach me that spiritual warfare is real and I was a target. The enemy did not want me in the village and would try many different tactics to get me to leave. However, through it all – and this instance was just the tip of the iceberg – God protected me in miraculous ways. Did He keep me from all danger? Not always. But, He divinely brought me through it, which made me stronger and bolder.

"For our struggle is not against flesh and blood, but against the rulers, against the authorities, against the powers of this dark world and against the spiritual forces of evil in the heavenly realms." Ephesians 6:12

10/10/99 Journal Entry...
Today was the final ceremony for a man who recently died. There were voodoo masqueraders which came to visit me. They danced for me and sang a song to me about love being more important than money and wished me well in Africa.

Of course, I realize it is voodoo. I also know that I'd have been wrong to insult them – the humans under the costume, not the demons. I need to gain these people's trust. One of my tactics is to say nothing yet about their customs until they ask and even then I will let them know that I still love them and so does God. I have to separate the person from the demons that inhabit them.

LORD, MY PROVIDER

My pastor once preached that a church's success isn't based on its seating capacity, but its sending capacity. However, our church has always had limited financial resources so my financial support was never set in stone. Therefore, there were times that there was not enough money to cover my expenses. However, God always provided what I needed in surprising ways.

One day as I was praying about the shortage of funds, I felt the Holy Spirit leading me to go through my paperwork. I found 10,000 cfa in the paperwork!

On another occasion, I was in Cotonou awaiting the arrival of the Americans who were traveling to Africa. However, their flight was delayed an extra two days and I did not have the funds to cover my hotel expenses and food until their arrival. God put it on my aunt's heart to wire me money, all the way from North Dakota!

Again, there were times that I would be out of money and my mom would send a box of goodies to me with $100 bills hidden in them. She would have sent the box months prior, but they always arrived at just the needed moment.

Finally, there was even a time that a few of the villagers provided for my needs. This was the most humbling of times. I was out of food and fuel. They provided food for me, loaned me money, and filled my fuel kegs.

Through all these difficult times, I learned some valuable lessons:

You don't necessarily need what you think you need. Everyone told me initially that I was required to purchase a vehicle. The stress related to this was immense. However, I never was short of transportation and I made many close acquaintances as a result of traveling with others.

Also, I was initially told that I had to run the generator all night, using lots of fuel, to ensure my safety. I later only ran the generator for a few hours in the evening and was fully protected and safe. God was my protector, not man-made light.

If God guides you to a place, He will surely provide. Yes, there were very lean times when I was eating dry blueberry muffin mix that mom had sent, thinking I had access to an oven. The mix proved useful when other food was gone. I initially laughed at the mix when it arrived, but God had a plan in everything.

Pride is a terrible thing. You cannot imagine how humbling it was to have villagers provide for your needs. I was there to minister to them and help them, yet, here they were, taking care of me. I think it was one of the most humbling moments of my life. I felt so low and embarrassed. Yet, God had a plan.

10/11/99 Journal Entry…
I had a phone call from America. Very few people have pledged to support me on a monthly basis (although I had over $500 in support pledged before leaving and I had originally believed that they would support me with $500/month). I have been told to pray about my call to determine if this is God's mission and if He is actually sending me. I was told that VBC has agreed to support me partially, but it's ultimately my responsibility to find the funds and supporters. This is so discouraging because those close to me are not sold on my mission.

However, I was also told by the same people that if I did return, it would be saying that God had failed. Catch 22! I disagreed and said it would be saying that we failed God. God sometime chooses to work through people, and we can choose to disobey His will.

I also registered my concern that leadership may not be convinced of my calling. If not, it's a serious problem because God has placed me under the leadership of VBC.

After this difficult and discouraging conversation, I had a telephone call from Freda. I asked her if she had doubts of my call. She said she had no doubts and noted that God has confirmed each step of the way. She told me I wasn't going home because God wants me to shake up Aklampa. She committed to getting Village on track to do their part in supporting me. She agreed that if I have to go home, it means that VBC failed, not God and Gina.

She also noted how immense the warfare is. She is going to speak to the prayer team. Only three of seven are committed to financially supporting me.

Is the enemy busy? Very. Even last Saturday evening as Ojo, Godwin and Gab were returning to Lagos from visiting me, their car broke down on the most dangerous stretch of road. It's an area known for armed robbers, and people who kill, cut up and sell body parts for sacrifices. They were sure they were about to die. They pushed the car back to the police checkpoint (the lesser of two evils) and convinced them to take Godwin to get a mechanic. They know that God literally hid them from danger because nothing happened.

I've really got to put on the armor and fight. I can't let the enemy win. Aklampa needs Jesus. They deserve to have me stay.

10/16/99 Journal Entry…
I'm back in Aklampa after a brief trip to Cotonou. It was quite the adventure. We left the hotel at 6:45 am. The hotel driver drove us to Tokpa market to catch a cab to Glazoué. We stopped a few times along the road to purchase fruit, vegetables, bread, frozen popsicle-like treats, etc. We arrived in Glazoué around 11:00 am.

We were told that no cars were going to Aklampa because the road was closed due to the rains. However, money talks. We had lunch in Glazoué (goat), bought coconut, water and soccer balls, visited with the pharmacist and were off to Aklampa via Dassa/Savalou route. This was a three hour journey. I had to push the car twice and get out and walk many more times. I didn't mind because I wanted to get home. We arrived home at 4:30 pm. The guard was not present, although he was supposed to be on duty. We finally found him to unlock the house. I was in bed by 7:30 pm, exhausted, but happy to be home.

10/17/99 Journal Entry…
Every Saturday night the traditionalists have their "service". My guard explained that there are many different traditional religions and each Saturday service has a different meaning. Last night's ceremony was to remember a recent event when a Beninoise man living near Togo came to Aklampa. The Aklampa man was very sick. The foreigner forced himself sexually on the man's wife. He then threatened to bring a tornado on the wife if she ever revealed the event. She felt guilty and told someone. All the fetishes came alive and formed a tornado which killed her.

There is also a sect which serves as community protection. They move about the village at night and "pray" over the community. At that same time, other members of this secret society are moving about other areas of the village looking for thieves. They even hide in trees. This is more common during the dry season when people return from the farm.

ICE BREAKERS

My strategy to begin ministering to the villagers was to have "open house" every afternoon at 4pm. I had a supply of board games, card games, soccer balls, etc. People would come over to play games. This served as an opportunity to meet people, interact with them in a non-threatening manner, and begin learning the language. This games ministry was the launching pad for witnessing and founding a church.

11/1/99 Letter...
I've been keeping myself busy with three ministries. I told you about my games ministry which is really a success. I've had over 60 people here at one time. The average is 40 people. Many of them are children, but the dominos and cards have brought in an average of 8 young adult men per day. They come by every day to play games. One day I took my stereo outside and was playing Christian music. The only word they recognized was "Jesus". Praise God!

I've been trying to think of a way to bring Christ into this ministry and thought it would be good to close each night with prayer before people leave. I asked God on Saturday to confirm if he wanted me to include prayer. My confirmation came yesterday. One of the young men came over to the house and brought his bible. He belongs to the Celestial Church (a cult) and I asked him if he'd be interested in attending a bible study at my house. He said Yes. Oh, I love Jesus!!!!!

This leads me to my second ministry – Bible study. I had the first formal session last Sunday and it went well, although only 3 people were present. One disturbing thing about this village is no one has a bible, even the people who belong to one of the local churches. I keep thinking, how can they live by the Word if they have no access to it. I've been praying that God will open a door to finance bibles for people here.

My third ministry is a prayer ministry. I'm now also going to another section of the village to pray for a few specific people, and God is definitely at work. It started when a woman came asking for prayer for her child with mental problems. I asked for her to bring him to my house. She said she couldn't because he is chained up so he cannot hurt anyone. I agreed to go to him. He's a 20-year-old man who was totally fine until a year and a half ago when another man put a curse on him. He's now demon-possessed. It's even affected him physically. He looks like a wild monster. He doesn't talk much at all. He's kept in a room with no furniture, he's naked, and he has chains on his feet. His name is Thomas.

The first time I prayed, he shut the door on me. I stood outside the door and prayed with my eyes open. I knew it was the demon responding and was encouraged. The second time I prayed, the door stayed open, but he smiled at me. Based on the look in his eyes, I knew it was the demon smiling, as if mocking me. Did I mind the smile? No, because the demon is revealing himself and this encourages me to pray all the more. Now when I go to pray, he usually sits on the floor and just looks at me. Thomas knows some English so I hope he understands me.

His mother comes here to give me progress reports. A local gentleman and I had a lengthy discussion about her son's situation and what other things she's tried to heal her son. She's tried herbs and traditional religion, witches, and voodoo priests. She's also paid for visions and sacrifices in the Celestial Church.

I delicately explained that all of these methods contradict Jesus and haven't worked. I asked her to not do anything other than pray in Jesus' name. She agreed because she's seen a slight improvement in her son. One day after I left their home, Thomas allowed his brother to give him food to eat. He took the food from his brother for the first time without becoming violent. Praise God!

The first time I prayed for Thomas, three men approached me and asked me to pray for their sick wives. The first two wives recently had babies but had little or no breast milk. The third had a terrible case of rheumatism. I prayed for them and then returned two days later to pray again, but was met with some great news. The first woman had had no breast milk at all, but after I prayed the first time, she took out her breast and by faith tried to feed her 10-day-old baby. When I returned two days later, her breasts were full of milk. The second woman had milk in only one breast and remains the same. The woman with rheumatism is completely pain free! God healed her too! He is so great!

AFRICAN TRADITIONAL RELIGION

*I've been trying to understand the traditional religion of the village.
Doors are finally opening and people are beginning to explain things to
me. I witnessed a public stilt-walking ceremony on Saturday. I went with
Fina and Bernard. I received an education. I was seated with the elders.
They offered me some of their alcohol to drink, which I kindly declined.
One man walked around in front of us carrying a wooden statue of some
god. It had a bunch of skulls on it. The elders touched and kissed it, and
even poured some of their alcohol on it. The man with the statue would
put the alcohol in his mouth and then spit it on the statue and rub the
statue while praying. I was also praying – for them and to Jesus!*

I wonder what was happening in the spiritual realm at that moment.

*There were also drummers, dancing and singing. I could tell when a spirit
overcame them. I could see it in their eyes. I was told that they do this
competition in Lagos and it's even more spiritual. In Nigeria, they often
chop off part of the stilts and they grow back in front of the audience's
eyes.*

*There are lots of shrines around the village. There's one right outside my
gate for the family next door. They look like mounds of clay dirt, usually
two or three side-by-side. They are about 12-18 inches high. Some are
shaped like gods but some are plain mounds. The strangest thing is that
many have a huge penis sticking out of them. I'm trying to figure out what
they are used for, but I know that some type of burnt offering is made
because there are ashes present.*

**These shrines are called "the first devil". They are the head devil for
a family. Every morning people literally feed food to the shrine. Each
family has a shrine. Before they do any curses or ceremonies, they
must first consult the shrine. They even build it a house – a tin roof
and back like a lean-to.**

**There are also many small huts which they build for the devil. These
huts store all secret voodoo things in them. The tell tale sign of these
small huts is that the doors are only about three feet high and are not
solid doors. They are bars of wood. There is one right behind my
house. I walk by it at least twice per day.**

**There is a compound across the road from my house that is a voodoo
worship center. I initially had no idea because of the high wall. I had**

assumed it was a family compound. I've also learned that every Saturday night through Sunday evening is the voodoo sect's "worship" time. You can hear the drums, dancing, singing and screaming the entire night. I keep the generator on all night so I can sleep.

Voodoo hut along with a shrine shaped in a mound to the left.

...I'm glad that I didn't close the letter. It's only hours later...

I'm awaiting the arrival of Dossou and Koffi, two young men that attend my games ministry. They are taking me to another part of the village for some ceremony. I wouldn't go alone with Dossou because he's deeply into the masquerade voodoo and that's what we're going to see. I know he's deeply involved because the masqueraders came by my house when we were playing backgammon. Dossou stopped playing, took off his shoes, fell prostrate and bowed to each one that came by. It blew my mind, but I didn't let it show.

(The name of the masquerader that Dossou takes on is Kpadjé, which translates to "Witch Killer".)

These masqueraders all know my name so I probably know them. One in particular carried a large metal penis and kept wanting me to touch it. I know better than to touch anything near a masquerader. He then said it would allow me to have babies. I told him, "No, thanks".

OK, I'm back from the ceremony. What an eye-opener! I prayed and anointed my forehead, eyes, ears, nose and mouth before going. I knew I was walking into the enemy's territory and needed to be covered by the blood of Jesus. Only Koffi and I went. Dossou did not join us. I believe Koffi is involved in this voodoo as well, but not to the point of abandoning me.

Let me try to describe what I saw and felt. First of all, I soon realized that I was safe. Koffi told me that they cannot hurt me. I know it's because I'm a Christian, but am not sure of his reason for thinking this. There were about seven masqueraders. There was a section where drummers and singers played. Other people stood in a large circle about the size of a football field. The masqueraders would chase people who would run away. These people were smiling and enjoying themselves but they definitely took it serious. They quit smiling when they were chased. (It kind of reminds me of the bulls running through the streets of Spain.)

The masqueraders corner people and demand money and a bow. It's taken very seriously. The dancing and chasing went on for over an hour, then it got seriously spiritual. If the masqueraders touched anyone, that person instantly dropped unconscious (like falling under the power of the spirit, but the wrong spirit!) They were carried away to a secret place. I don't know what happens to them.

I also saw a group of men nearly dragging a very reluctant young man through some gate to a secret place. He was near tears. Somehow, I feel he was about to be initiated into this secret society.

Their target audience is young adult men. Very few women were present. I saw at least three of the young men who come to my house and play games. I was thinking that it was strange that most of the adults who visit my house are young adult men. Now I know why? God has a plan.

One of the masqueraders stopped to ask me some questions and bowed to me.

So, how did I feel during all this? My spirit was so heavy. It was as if someone were squeezing my heart. Oh, if only these people knew Jesus. Oh, if only Christians took worship so seriously. How many Christians take their shoes off and bow to Jesus Christ, no matter who is present? Christians don't want to stand out in the world, but Dossou stops everything to bow to a "god". He wasn't embarrassed. He was proud to be one of them! It nearly brought me to tears. He didn't do this just once, but at least four times for all the different masqueraders.

Another thing that upset me is that there were over a thousand people in attendance. Most Christian churches struggle to get a hundred people to a worship service on Sunday.

I was routinely asked to attend these ceremonies and take photos of the different masqueraders. While most people would decline, I saw this as an opportunity to gain the people's trust, learn more about the culture, and begin witnessing to them.

Although outsiders are not to know what person inhabits any given costume, I quickly found out because the members would come by the house to pick up the photos of them in their costumes. They would point out which photo was them so they could take that photo. Good strategy, huh?

It worked. Most of the initial converts came out of this voodoo sect.

11/2/99 Letter…
I learned more about yesterday's ceremony. One of the reasons the masqueraders didn't touch me was because Dossou ordered them not to harm me.

I also learned (very secretly) that one of the young men who comes by to play dominos is one of the masqueraders. Now, I've been praying about this and I think it's all God's plan. Even though he knows no English, I was able to explain that voodoo contradicts Jesus, and I follow Jesus. He said that both are good. I was encouraged because at least he's open to Jesus.

Today I realized that my target audience may be young adult men, the same target as those in the masquerade voodoo. I was playing cards today with three young men and four more were "hanging out" and watching, except Koffi. He was dancing to your CD.

During the card game (my partner is an active voodoo member, but not the one mentioned earlier), he asked if we could stop and pray to Jesus to help us win. He said "Jesus", not just "God". Oh, how I love my games ministry!

11/3/99 Letter…
A voodoo ceremony awoke me last night. They were marching around my house (and other houses as well). I usually hear ceremonies almost every night and I've learned to live with them. However, last night was much

different. The first time they marched around singing and playing drums, I woke up but didn't have any reaction.

Their second time around was an entirely different matter. As they passed by the house, I could physically feel a "presence" of evil. I believe it passed through my room. Then I heard howling and wailing that I've never heard before. I believe God opened my ears to hear the demonic forces. Reality hit me at that point – these people are totally controlled by Satan. I became so sad.

When I got up this morning, I was even more burdened. I've become attached to many of these people and do not want them to go to hell! I want them to know the peace, joy, and forgiveness of Jesus. Satan can't have them! Therefore, I spent time in prayer and fasting for some specific young man. These same men were at my house today to play cards and listen to Christian music. One young man even showed up with his bible. He belongs to the Celestial Church. **Most Christians in Benin consider this "denomination" a cult based on their foundation and beliefs.**

11/5/99 Letter to Freda:
Freda, I discovered the #1 reason why you wouldn't want to come to Aklampa. At 4:00 this morning I was awakened by something landing on my shoulder. I thought it was a cockroach since I kill one almost every night. I turned on the light and realized it was a bat! Actually, we found two of them. Needless to say, I screamed!

11/7/99 Letter...
Today was the best day!!

Remember the man I mentioned earlier who is deeply into voodoo – Dossou? He's been coming by the house almost every day to play cards. Yesterday I invited him to come here today for bible study. He agreed. He's really been on my mind and heart this week. I've even had nightmares about people using him as a voodoo sacrifice! I was in deep prayer for him today. He attended. There were six people today. The other new person was Koffi, the young dancer.

We opened with a game, followed by prayer and then the lesson. In the middle of the lesson, Koffi asked what the bible says about after our death. The subject changed and he and Dossou began asking simple questions about serving Jesus vs. voodoo. I told them that they can't serve the two. They conflict. They must choose one and follow only one. Dossou thought for a minute, turned to me and said, "Me. Jesus"! He chose Jesus. This is the same man who was bowing to masqueraders on Monday!

I brought him to a back room so he, my interpreter, and I could talk privately about his decision and make sure he understands it. We then prayed together. I asked if he had any questions. He asked, "Can we meet every week so you can pray and teach me?" I serve a wonderful God!

After bible study, Koffi asked for my stereo and "Jesus music" to dance to. We all danced for Jesus. It was so fulfilling. It was as if that moment, God said, "Yes, this is why I have you here." It makes all the tough times worth it.

Afterward, everyone but Dossou left. He wanted to play cards. At one point, he had to choose which card to lay and he asked Jesus for help. He won the game, looked up and said, "Jesus, Gangi (good)".

I heard drums a few minutes ago and found out that some family nearby was dancing to non-voodoo music. I went to see and determined that I want to learn to dance like that for Jesus. I had my first lesson and shocked the villagers to realize that a white person has rhythm. They shouted with glee. They claim that I'm no longer American, but Beninoise.

11/8/99 Letter…
Dossou came today and told me, "Voodoo finish. Jesus #1." I love the power of Jesus. While he was here, a blind boy came to greet me and for prayer. I had Dossou join me in prayer. He did. He also wants his best friend to come on Sunday so he can know Jesus too.

As you can probably guess, I've done a lot of praising God lately. He's so good. I can hardly handle it.

11/11/99 Devotion…
I felt led to read Ezekiel this morning. Ezekiel's call in Chapters 2 & 3 really touched me.
Ezekiel 2:2-5: "The people to whom I am sending you are obstinate and stubborn. Say to them, 'This is what the Sovereign Lord says.' And whether they listen or fail to listen – for they are a rebellious house – they will know that a prophet has been among them. And you, son of man, do not be afraid of them or their words. Do not be afraid, though briers and thorns are all around you and you live among scorpions. Do not be afraid of what they say or terrified of them, though they are a rebellious house."

11/14/99Letter…
At one time, some white European missionaries came to Aklampa to build a hospital. They were killed by villagers. I learned a new (and very

important) piece of information about this. It happened only three years ago! I thought it was 30-50 years ago. Wrong.

I realize that I'm sounding like the village hates me. 99% of them really like me. Therefore, I'm not worried. Do I think I'm safe because I have a guard and locked front and bedroom doors? NO! Voodoo have the ability to get in without going through doors. Therefore, Jesus is my only protection. However, he's the best protection. So, my adventure continues...

I observed the Catholic, Celestial and Apostolic churches in Aklampa. All three churches are highly syncretistic, mixing some biblical knowledge with much African Traditional Religion. Most of the voodoo leaders of the village have an alliance to the Catholic Church. Driven by fear, the other churches will not boldly denounce voodoo. They either embrace it and include some voodoo practices as part of their worship, or turn a blind eye to its effect on their churches.

Today, I had four new people in bible study – two Catholics, one celestial church member and one voodoo. We had a good time and God was truly blessing. My biggest surprise was that every single person who attended believed that Jesus was a small god. They don't know that Jesus is God. They know now.

11/14/99 Letter...
This afternoon, Dossou took me to watch the stilt-walkers. (Dossou is the man in voodoo who accepted Christ last week) I've been told by villagers that it's not voodoo, just tradition. I know it's voodoo. We had a nice time until a man walked up, greeted me by name and proceeded to grab Dossou and pull him a few meters away form me. This man did the same thing yesterday when we were together. In my spirit, I sense the man is threatening Dossou.

I secretly learned today that Dossou's conversion to Christianity has caused lots of problems. I learned that Dossou was one of the most powerful voodoo grand-masters. Even his family is upset because he was "dedicated" to be their voodoo representative. It's such an issue that it's been elevated to the chiefs. I act as if I don't know anything. "Wise as a serpent, innocent as a dove."

However, I've learned that both Dossou and I may be in danger. They are worried that Dossou may have leaked some secrets to me and they want to shut us up.

I've just learned that there is a special voodoo ceremony tonight, but I don't know what for. I may be paranoid, but I have a feeling it may have something to do with Dossou and/or me. Therefore, I made sure I prayed and claimed Psalm 91. At one point, in my prayer, I had a vision of God commissioning a number of warrior angels to surround Dossou. We'll see what the night brings.

I promised Dossou that I would escort him to any ceremonies that he's obligated to attend. Therefore, he asked me to go with him to a voodoo masquerade ceremony yesterday. I knew he was using me as an excuse to steer clear of the action. We sat a good distance away. I was safe until we prepared to leave. As Dossou returned the chair in the house, a masquerader appeared from nowhere and came within an inch of touching me. Startled, I flew back and screamed, "Oh, Jesus!" The masquerader came for me again, but didn't get as close – approximately one foot away. As soon as it was safe, Dossou grabbed me and we quickly left.

I could tell that the entire ordeal was very tough on him. Twice, he was even forced to bow to them and did it to protect me. I told him not to bow to them any more. Jesus will protect me.

Here's an interesting observation. Why did God choose to save one of the most powerful voodoo masters? He definitely has a plan, but Satan is definitely upset. Therefore, please make sure the prayer team is diligent.

11/17/99 Journal Entry...
There's a man in Aklampa who drinks heavily. I don't believe I've met him. When I moved here, he felt that it was a sign from God for him to quit drinking. He has been sober ever since. God works in mysterious ways.

Also, an old man from the farm came to see me. He had heard rumors that I spoke Fongbe and he wouldn't believe them. He came to see for himself.

Most people were shocked to see a white person speak their native language. Actually, most of them had never seen a white person, but had only heard of them. Watching people's reactions brought much laughter to our house.

One afternoon a young man living on a farm came to the village. As he passed the house, he saw me and became very frightened. He literally ducked down to hide from me as an animal would hide from a predator. He told my friend who was sitting with me that he was afraid I would kill him. He would run away and hide, then come a bit

closer to see. I couldn't help chuckling. I went inside to get some candy to hopefully show that I was harmless. He began to inch closer, but after getting within a few meters of me, decided a piece of candy was not worth possible death. He took off running, never to be seen near me again.

Many people were openly curious about this white woman. They often touched my skin and hair. Men questioned if my parents were also white, young children counted my fingers and toes, and young women wanted to know if my breasts were like theirs.

Another interesting observation: Aklampa normally has at least two cholera epidemics per year. However, during my stay in Aklampa, there were no cholera outbreaks. Even some of the villagers noted this and believed that my presence prevented the cholera epidemic from affecting them. I believe God staved off any cholera to send a message that the village was literally changed by my presence.

11/18/99 Letter...
My devotion yesterday was Romans 8:28 to the end of the chapter. Then, as I read from a book that Robyn gave me, the same passages were mentioned at least ten times. I knew God was preparing me, but for what? Well, around 7:30 pm, all hell broke loose.

Satan had a great time at my house. People in the village are very unhappy about Dossou being my friend and have started all kinds of rumors. It's so unbelievable, yet this village thrives on gossip. For example, I also heard that I have a 7-year-old child in the United States.

I had no children at that time.

The enemy repeatedly used gossip and lies throughout my stay in the village to cause confusion, and to try to discredit me. As you read, you will find numerous attacks through false information. Also, there was a power struggle to control me. There was infighting in the village over whom I "belonged" to and who had "authority" over my movement. The most controlling was my house help. She would prove to be a key player in the manipulation tactics of who could access me.

Anyway, my guard began screaming at a girl who took me to visit Dossou yesterday. She speaks English so she interprets for us. The girl got angry and went to get her big brother. Within minutes, everyone was upset and there were at least 30 people involved. I was confused and didn't know

93

who to believe. At one point I looked up and said, "Jesus, help me." It was so bizarre.

Dossou finally arrived, saw the commotion, and left. I hear he came back later to calm down my assistant. It was wild. People were physically trying to fight! Now, you know I'm not a fighter. I didn't know what to do so I just left and went for a walk down the street, drank a soda and prayed. Of course, people assumed that I had gone to see Dossou.

I finally returned home and went to bed, trying not to think about revenge. It was a sleepless night. All I could pray was "How in the world will God work this mess out for His good?" But He's God and His ways are perfect.

I woke up still upset until Fina and I sat down to discuss things. I'm now somewhat better, and things have been resolved.

11/20/99 Letter…
I've started doing some research on the religions here. I had gathered lots of internet material before coming here. It made much more sense after living here because I've seen many of the things about which I've read. For instance, I was wondering why many houses had an empty bottle (shaped like a soda bottle) hanging on the house near the front door. I learned that it's to ward off evil spirits.

I also learned that Dossou is the voodoo name for a twin. They believe that not two babies are born, but two bodies and one spirit as well. Therefore, twins are highly regarded.

11/21/99 Letter…
Praise God. I had six new people at bible study. They included my pastor's uncle, two people I had never met and three children. One child was Koffi's brother. My lesson was on being born-again. They've never heard this phrase so most of my teaching was on what it means to accept Christ. They all believe that Jesus is in their life because they know who he is. I had to explain that Jesus must be in their heart, not just their mind.

Brother Vincent asked, "What about voodoo?" It was "on" from there. Since voodoo is the accepted religion of the village, I'm realizing I need to fit this into my lessons. The topic slightly changed to comparing voodoo to Jesus.

Another young man, my guard's son, attended. He comes late because he goes to the Catholic Church and then rushes here. He's seventeen and *said he wants to follow Jesus. He said the bible says to honor your mother and father, but they want him to join voodoo like them. I gave him Luke 14:26 and asked him to pray for his parents' salvation.*

I've noticed a pattern in their prayer requests. Everyone's top two concerns are: 1) a long life, and 2) protection from evil. They are afraid to die and are very aware of the evil spirits in this village.

DREAMS OR REALITY

11/21/99 Letter...
I had a disturbing night last night. I was awakened by some young men chanting and passing back and forth in front of my house. Due to the darkness, I couldn't see their faces.

Then, I dreamed that a masquerader (in white with pastel colors) was coming at me in the front yard. I was inside my room and he was outside my window. I jumped and awoke.

Then, I dreamed that someone was loudly knocking on the door to my room, trying to get in the room. I knew it was very evil. It seemed so real that I woke up and listened for it again, but didn't hear anything. However, when I awoke, my room door was unlocked. I always double lock it. I shrugged it off yesterday, but now, I believe it may have been significant.

11/21/99 Journal Entry...
I've never had such dreams. Something is up. I can feel it in the atmosphere; I just can't place it. I somehow feel there's some dangerous plot against me. I pray that God will protect me through it all.

(There was another night where I woke up to knocking on my bedroom door and the knocking continued after I was awake and sitting up. I rebuked the demon in Jesus' name and the knocking stopped.)

11/21/99 Letter...
Freda, I really believe something is going on, but I can't quite figure it out. When I put on my armor in prayer this morning, I remembered Amani's comment in cell group that if we need to put on the armor, it's going to be a tough battle. I really believe someone's plotting something, but I'm not sure who – besides, Satan, of course.

I have a feeling that this has something to do with Dossou, but I can't really talk to him until Ojo comes to interpret. At this point, I don't trust anyone in this village to interpret such a conversation. This may sound far-fetched, but I wouldn't be surprised if he was being forced to choose between his life and mine.

Also, the man who gave me the poisoned water has been in Aklampa a lot lately. He lives with Henry when in Cotonou. He's a witchdoctor.

Prayer Request: My Protection!

11/21/99 Letter…
I learned some important information about voodoo & Dossou. His name keeps coming up because he was basically a "pastor" in the voodoo religion. This morning during bible study, I said voodoo and Jesus are opposites and the devil is the god of voodoo. Dossou loudly agreed. That seemed to shock a few men.

I knew Dossou was still involved in voodoo and he asked how I knew. I told him it was obvious by his actions and then confronted him on why he feels he has to leave voodoo slowly versus just walking away. His answer was honest. He fears the voodoo spirit will kill him. I explained that I know his life (and mine) are in danger. He agreed.

I also told him that God is more powerful than anything a spirit can do to him. He asked that I pray for him so God would enter his life very much and protect him. He's also afraid that his family will disown him. I told him that he's a grown man and must stand up for his beliefs. God will provide for him. It is also the church's responsibility to assist him. He has real concerns, but says he's leaving voodoo for good. He's just scared. Well, so am I.

11/22/99 Letter…
A masquerader came to my house yesterday. He called me by name so I went to greet him. It took me only a few seconds to realize that it was Dossou! I wasn't totally sure until late last night when I got in his face about it. He denied it, but it was obvious that he was lying. It is strange. I really believe he's accepted Christ and wants to get out of voodoo, yet he's still involved. He had to know that I would recognize his voice, even though they disguise their voice. I think he wanted me to know it was him. I told him we would talk when Ojo comes. He agreed.

Dossou and Justin (a Christian) took me to yesterday's voodoo ceremony. In prayer before going, God told me to "look for the little things." He wanted me to see the not-obvious. We sat right with the elders so I got a close-up look at things. The elders are all into voodoo based on their actions and orders given to the masqueraders. As the ceremony progressed, the intensity rose and you could feel the satanic power take over.

It was incredible. At one point, the elders left, and absolute chaos broke loose. The masqueraders became completely possessed and disregarded any "rules", such as staying within the log boundaries. They went wild. It happened very suddenly. By the way, it was a full moon and dusk had settled in.

Dossou and Justin quickly realized we needed to get out of there. However, we were seated in a place that required us to walk through part of the masquerader's territory and there were a number of them going crazy and chasing people.

At one point, Dossou stood up in front of me to shield me. I could see the worry on his face. He held onto me and we ran out of the area. We made it out with no problems. I can't begin to imagine what happened after we left.

Freda, I'm beginning to understand the prayer that Debra prayed when she said I would walk more in the supernatural than natural. It's not exactly what I thought, but it seems as if everything here is supernatural.

I think my relationship with God is also changing slightly. While in the US, I had time set aside for prayer. Here, I still set aside time for prayer and enter into worship. However, I now keep Jesus at the front of my mind and find myself talking to him all throughout the day. I realize that I need to pray over every meal, every handshake and every unusual encounter. I guess it's like spending the day with a great friend. You chat all day.

11/23/1999 Letter…
I found out more about my nightmares. The voodoo are "testing" me to see what I'm made of. They believe it is their duty to try to break me. My informant hasn't been told what they're doing, but when I told him of the nightmares, unlocked doors, and knocking, he said those are common practices.

He also warned me that they can take the face of someone else and come into my room. For example, if someone looking like Dossou appears in my room in the middle of the night, I must know it's not him and instantly pray and rebuke it. He also said it's common for them to touch me in my sleep, but when I awake, I won't see them.

11/24/99 Letter…
I had another nightmare last night that all the masqueraders came to my house and surrounded me. I was screaming and crying for them not to touch me.

This morning, Fina and my guard informed me that someone came into my yard in the middle of the night and killed a huge snake. It happened while my guard was away from his post. They left the snake and bloody mess for Fina and Bernard. We have asked around and no one claims to know who killed it. Here's the strange thing. It happened at the side of the house that no one would be able to see at night. What was someone doing in my back yard at night? Also, they used a long bamboo type pole to kill it. The pole is over six feet long and they left the stick (which was freshly cut). Why did they leave it here? Of course, I'm convinced it's spiritual.

11/29/99 Letter...
Dossou's really become a great friend. When I get upset or stubborn (usually at my guard), he calms me down. He's also someone I can trust to teach me what things should cost – the real cost, not the "Yovo" (white person's) cost.

For example, the other day my kids kicked the soccer ball into my neighbor's window and broke a wood panel. My guard called a carpenter. As the carpenter was finishing, I asked Dossou how much I should expect to pay. He said about 500 cfa. My guard then informed me that the carpenter wanted to charge 2,500 cfa. I said, "No way! I want to be charged the "Aklampa price", not the "white price". My guard totally defended the carpenter and wanted me to pay the amount. I informed him that I've asked about a fair price and wouldn't pay more than 1,000 cfa. He took the 1,000 cfa. My guard was supposed to have my best interest in mind. Yeah, right!

11/29/99 Letter...
Remember Thomas, the young man who is demon-possessed and in chains? I was going to his house for prayer. I haven't been there in a few weeks but have been in prayer for him. His mother came by yesterday to update me. He is much better. No more chains! I also had been hearing from other people that he was getting better. He's eating by himself and is more coherent. Oh, the power of Jesus!

NIGHTTIME FUNERALS

12/1/99 Letter ...
My maid's father died yesterday. Last night as I was getting ready to go to the funeral ceremony, I decided to use my blow dryer for the first time since arriving in Africa. Bad decision. I over-powered my generator and it died. I tried everything to start it again but it wouldn't even turn over. I sent my guard to get an electrician. Meanwhile, I felt led to pray. That sounds silly, but I laid hands on that generator and prayed aloud. I tried it again and it started with no problem!!! I shouted "Hallelujah!" Someone heard me and laughed. My guard returned and asked how I fixed it. I told him that I didn't. Jesus did.

The funeral began at 12:30 am – yes, the middle of the night. I returned home at 6:30 this morning and they were still going strong. It was totally different from anything in America. It was like a huge party, with lots of alcohol. The men drank gin like I drink water – by the glassful. Some of the men were not a pretty sight.

One of the drunk men kept trying to extort money out of me. Dossou told me not to give any more money. I had already presented the family with money as tradition dictates. Even my guard tried to convince me to give more money, but Dossou had already escorted me to the house where I dropped off my camera and money. Good thinking ahead!!

There were drumming and dancing throughout the night. The body was wrapped in white sheets and lying on a bed inside the door of a house. The women stand around the body and fanned it and sang throughout the night. I'm sure it has some spiritual meaning, but I don't know what.

Another odd tradition: a gunshot was fired behind us to let people know that someone had gone to the bush and killed bush meat (some ugly muskrat-looking animal the size of a large rabbit). They carried the dead animal to the house and hung it outside the door of the house where the body was located.

Before this man "died" on December 1ˢᵗ, I believe he had already been physically dead for some time. How do I believe this? Well, in the days prior, he was lying on his bed and was decaying with pieces of flesh flaking off his arms. Bodies do not decay prior to dying. I believe he was already dead, but that demons were using his body for a period of time. The demons released the body for burial on December 1ˢᵗ.

I also saw the body after the official death. The body was lying on a bed, wrapped in white linens. The entire body was covered, including white gloves, slippers, cap and mask. Only the closed eyes were visible.

12/6/99 Letter...
Oh, I love Jesus! The Holy Spirit has been speaking so much, I can hardly handle it. Saturday night I was praying and suddenly God told me to earnestly pray for Dossou, who had traveled to another village to see his uncle.

In prayer, God told me very clearly that Dossou went for some voodoo reason. That thought hadn't even entered into my head outside of prayer. I prayed for his protection and that he would not get involved in any ceremony.

He returned last night and I saw him this morning. I asked him to honestly tell me why he traveled. I told him what God had revealed in prayer. Yes, he traveled for voodoo reasons. He had to go pay final restitution (a goat) for something in his past for which he had been accused. However, he decided not to stay for the sacrifice which is today. Praise God.

He didn't tell me because he thought I'd get mad. He's right. I'd have been upset when he told me. However, God told me and I knew my duty was to pray for him.

I also gave him a French bible today and he was so excited. His first story he wanted to read about was Noah's Ark because he saw the blanket you gave me. He even had me take a photo of him sitting on the blanket reading his new bible. I love seeing people excited about the Word.

Dossou came to visit tonight and asked if he could bring his bible here tomorrow and we can read and discuss it together. He seems excited about Jesus. I love it! He's also totally not shy about praying, even in bible study. Yes!!!

12/12/99 Letter...
It's been a strange 24 hours. Last night and today were the final funeral ceremonies for my friend's father. I was required to attend since I'm her employer. Around 10:00 pm last night, we went for some drumming and dancing. Dossou escorted me. I refused to dance because my spirit didn't feel right. At 11:30 pm, people suddenly began to disperse, and I mean

suddenly! Dossou grabbed my hand and nearly yanked me away and quickly took me home.

He waited a bit for Fina to arrive. Since I thought she'd be here shortly, I sent him home. Bad decision because Fina didn't come until this morning and my guard is visiting another village. Therefore, I was alone all night and got very little sleep. When I did sleep, I had a horrible nightmare:

I dreamed that I woke up and went outside to find Fina crying in the front room. There were many people gathered. I walked outside to find my yard and house covered in white chicken feathers (Aklampa chickens aren't white) and blood everywhere. There was blood on the windows, house and even puddles in the yard. I then noticed some people were praying. I went back and asked Fina if this happened in all areas, or just my yard and my ministry. She replied, "Just your house and your ministry."

Before the dream, a voodoo ceremony passed by the house and I could physically feel the presence of evil. By the way, that's why Fina couldn't come home and why Dossou rushed me home. There was some deep voodoo ceremony that women cannot see, and we'd have been in danger had we remained outside.

Speaking of not seeing things, one of my neighbors asked me if I saw him last night at the ceremony. I had even looked for him, but didn't see him and told him so. He said, "Of course you didn't, but I was right there and saw you." He then made some comment hinting that he had spiritually hidden from my sight. (I had been told that some voodoo members have the ability to separate body from spirit.)

After a sleepless night, I woke early and got ready to visit Fina's family. I went with Dossou and two other cousins. I later returned again to Fina's family's compound as promised. I was greeted by quite the sight. Some men had come from the farm to greet the family and wish them well. They were dressed in costumes (peanut necklaces, woven straw hats, animal skins tied around their waist, etc.). They were so funny. They are from a different tribe and have their own language. Most did not understand or speak Fongbe. They sang and danced for me as well, and I even got up and danced to their music. I shocked them. These grown men have never seen a white person.

Afterward, the king and some men arrived at the family compound to play Ayo (a traditional board game). They did this to remember Fina's father who always used to play this game with them.

Lastly, the voodoo masqueraders arrived for the final ceremony. I thought I was seated a safe distance behind the barrier until one jumped over the barrier and ran toward me. He came very close and surrounded me on all three sides so I was told not to move. I obeyed because this same voodoo had just knocked out some people and it had taken a really long time (approximately 15 minutes) to revive them. The ceremony even stopped for some time until they were able to revive their victims, as they were worried they had really killed them. This was no joking matter.

I could feel their evil power, and even though the scripture "Greater is He that is in me than he who is in the world" came to mind, I knew better than to play with the enemy. When he finally left, I was shaking and couldn't stop until I got home. It was an indescribable feeling that I never want to repeat. I know I have Jesus in me, but the presence of evil was overwhelming.

To add to this confusion, I've been emotional today and am thinking it's due to lack of sleep. However, the enemy's busy messing with my mind. I'm having the toughest time keeping my thoughts under control. This has been going on for over a week. I try to suppress the thoughts, but then I dream them. I'm at my whit's end and all I can do is persevere and pray and fast! Please pray for me to have the mind of Christ.

As you can tell, the enemy is busy. I feel as if something's about to happen and the enemy's torturing me.

On a good note, some friends and I encountered voodoo masqueraders while out on a walk today. All the men bowed to them except Dossou. Even when they called his name, he walked away. I believe Jesus smiled at that. I know I did. I gave the others grief. They say they love Jesus yet bow to demons. They said, "Tomorrow, voodoo finished". I don't believe they are sincere. Tomorrow never comes.

At the voodoo ceremony tonight, I noticed that these young men were in the thick of it! Dossou kept a good distance and didn't partake even though he wasn't escorting me.

12/14/99 Letter...
One of the young men mentioned above came to me yesterday morning and apologized for bowing to the voodoo masqueraders. I had noticed that as soon as he bowed, he got up and looked guiltily at me. However, I'm not the one to whom he needs to apologize. Jesus is the one who's been disrespected.

I'm really trying to witness to this man, even with the language barrier.

FALLING IN LOVE

12/8/99 Letter…
I have a problem. How in the world am I going to be able to leave this place? Before coming, I never thought about the fact that I would develop deep bonds with these people. I can't imagine how hard it's going to be to leave people like Antuno (my neighbor who teaches me the local language of Fongbe and feeds me breakfast every morning) and Dossou who has become such a good friend.

My neighbor Antuna making a breakfast corn porridge to sell. Her daughter and husband join her.

The worst thing is that I've only been here a few months. How will I feel after a year?! Even some people have shared that when I leave, it will be horrible for Aklampa. I've become part of their family. What a great honor.

As an outcome of my games ministry and bible study, I had grown close to a group of young adults. I spent lots of time with them and their families. We often took walks to visit people, or just went to the

local 'pub' for a soda. I really enjoyed these times because I felt part of a family and could relax for a few moments.

12/13/99 Journal Entry...
My devotions for the last two days have dealt with my association with people here. I've been concerned that my close association with people who are deeply into voodoo, and do not have a good reputation, will negatively affect my ministry.

In my devotion yesterday, God spoke to me about not worrying about eating food that may have been sacrificed, as long as it doesn't cause another brother confusion.

In today's devotion, Paul said that in his witnessing, he became like those he witnessed to. To the Jews, he became like a Jew; to the weak, he became weak, etc. There's a freedom in following Jesus and even Jesus was criticized for associating with a bad crowd. However, this was all part of Jesus' and Paul's strategy to witness.

Also, I am encouraged by some fruit from my associations. People have told me that they've seen a drastic change in Dossou. Another voodoo member has told me he wants to leave voodoo. All the men in this group are starting to come to church.

This biblical reminder would come in handy when I was later accused by some American Christians of being an anthropologist and not a missionary. I was criticized for learning about voodoo and associating with voodoo members. However, the fruit of my actions is that every one of my early converts came out of the very sect from which I had learned so much.

They did not understand God's strategy. I was able to be in the presence of voodoo members without partaking in their evil activities. Even Jesus was criticized by the religious rulers for his fraternization with sinners. If Jesus was persecuted, should I have expected anything less?

"Remember the words I spoke to you: 'No servant is greater than his master.' If they persecuted me, they will persecute you also." John 15:20

CHRISTMAS REFLECTIONS

12/25/99 Journal Entry…

A few thoughts this Christmas Day. I have given up much to follow Jesus. I thought it would be hard. Instead, it has turned out to be a wonderful blessing. So many pressures are gone – office competition, bills, money problems, technology, etc. Life is much simpler and more peaceful. I have more time alone with God. He has provided a safe living environment, income, health, and friends.

I feel so honored to be this blessed. I thought I'd be homesick, especially today, because I'm alone and it's Christmas Day. Yet, I'd rather be no place else. I'm happy to have this day to thank Jesus for His birth. I'd choose being here over anywhere else! Besides, I'm not really alone. I have Jesus with me!

I've read lots lately about how Jesus went totally against custom to reach out to people. He was ridiculed and even called a drunk for his association with sinners. Yet, he never defended himself. I want to be more like Jesus.

It makes me think of Wednesday evening when I went to the buvette (a restaurant/bar) in Affinzungo on the other side of the village. I know there are people who think it would be inappropriate for a woman missionary to go to a bar at night with four men and even have a drink with them.

(Alcohol consumption is viewed differently in Africa, as American taboos do not apply.)

I used this time at the buvette to talk about Jesus and Sai noted his desire to come to Jesus. He knelt before me in prayer, right there next to the table where we were sitting. What an opportunity for ministry! And this man is the son of the voodoo leader of an influential family in the village. He shared that his father makes him participate in the voodoo ceremonies.

A NEW YEAR

EIGHT DAYS OF NEW YEARS

1/4/00 Letter...
Well, as we knew, the world didn't end on New Year's. By the way, Happy New Year! How are things in the U.S.? What about all the technology problems that everyone predicted? Nothing is changed in Aklampa, probably because there's no technology.

New Year's in Aklampa is a huge deal! There have been plays, music, voodoo ceremonies, and other festivities every day. This will go on for eight days! I'm exhausted, but having fun each day. I go to the various events with Dossou and his cousins. On New Year's Day, I danced at one of the plays and shocked nearly 1,000 people. Then, the past two days, voodoo leaders have asked me to dance at their voodoo ceremonies. I'm so glad they ask, because I get to explain that I'd love to dance, but not as part of a voodoo ceremony. I explained that I follow Jesus and voodoo goes against Christianity. They understood why I couldn't partake in their ceremonies and were not offended.

I've also learned how deeply my neighbors are into voodoo. I actually think they may be the head of a voodoo sect. I've been watching how people respond to this family, even some older men bow to them. Also, the voodoo masqueraders totally respect and listen to them. It's amazing!

Yet, they try to convince me that they are not into voodoo, but love Jesus. I respond by noting how they bow to the voodoo, but I've never seen them bow to Jesus! Yesterday, I asked one of them why he wants Jesus and not voodoo. (PS – his father is a chief and head of voodoo for the entire family) He responded, "Because of Gina". Not a good answer.

I keep wondering why all my interaction seems to be with the masqueraders. There has to be a reason why these are the people whom I've befriended. I'm also realizing that I cannot be intimidated by them, which is tough because you see their power manifested so easily and visibly.

On another spiritual note, I feel as if the enemy has devised some very strategic attack against me that I don't yet see. I can't exactly put my finger on it, but I can feel it. I think he's being very subtle. All I'm hearing from God is "You're only seeing the surface of things". What "things"?

1/4/99 Devotion

2 Corinthians 10:7a: "You are only looking at the surface of things." This really stuck out. I'm not sure what God is saying, but I think it has to do with this village. I think I'm not really seeing the spiritual side of things in Aklampa. I think something deep is going on, but I'm not seeing it.

I think the enemy has developed a very extensive plan to destroy me and is doing everything possible to stop the gospel and salvation of Jesus Christ in Aklampa.

1/5/00 Letter...
Two of my friends were taken down by voodoo masqueraders during a ceremony. I was so grieved that I nearly cried. They thought nothing of it. They were declared "dead" and taken away where the voodoo perform incantations to revive them. Within five minutes, they joined us and joked about it. Dossou and Sai were the only ones to see how upset I was.

The other night I was standing on my deck. Fina and Bayou (the woman who fetches my water each day) were sitting on the steps. A voodoo ran into the yard and chased us into the house. Fina screamed. We ran all the way to my bedroom and shut the door. I was shocked that the voodoo came into the house. I've never seen them do that. Once he went back outside, we came out and Fina screamed at him. In retrospect, I wish I'd have stood my ground and not moved. I think the devil took authority on that one. I need not be intimidated at all. I was unprepared.

1/6/00 Letter...
The caretaker of this house is Henry's sister. She approached Sai to warn him that I belong to their family and am not an Adidemé, and they should stop trying to steal me from her family. She also warned him that if I die in Aklampa, her husband's family will murder the Adidemé boys. She also warned Dossou that if anything happens to me, the police will go after him first.

Now, I wouldn't put it past her to hurt me just to get Dossou in trouble. Her family is claiming ownership of me and using it as some sort of power play which I really dislike. They act like I'm some token prize which they brought to Aklampa. Therefore, others should honor them. When I go anywhere with that family, I'm on parade for them. It's disgusting.

The Adidemé family makes me feel like a regular human being. I'm not on display. They even go to lengths to make me feel as welcome as possible. For example, when I visit friends and family in other sections in Aklampa, there are tons of children who come to watch me. After a few minutes of greetings, we go in a house so I can have a somewhat normal visit. It gets

110

old having the same child repeatedly greet me many times within one minute.

1/6/00 Letter…
I wasn't going to go to the voodoo ceremony yesterday, but Sai came here and begged me to go with him. If I go with him, he can sit down with me and not participate. At first I thought I was a burden because he couldn't participate. Now I know both he and Dossou use me as an excuse to not participate. That's totally fine with me.

There was a new voodoo – a boy who's probably no older than ten, based on his height. A ten year old with spiritual power and he's taken very seriously. Pray for the youth of Aklampa. I often see young boys practicing the dances and movements of the masquerade voodoo. They dance to a very specific pattern which is symbolic. It is a serious obligation to learn them correctly.

Yesterday's ceremony was educational. I prayed before going and decided that I would not be intimidated by the voodoo. I hardly flinched as they came by. They didn't bother me. It was almost as if the enemy realized that I've taken back authority. Therefore, he didn't want to touch me nor come near me for fear of being exposed.

All the voodoo chiefs, drummers, dancers and participants (excluding the demon-possessed masqueraders) seem to really like me. They greet me, visit with me, ask if I'd like to dance (where I have a chance to witness and explain that I will not participate because voodoo is against Jesus). I keep thinking these people must realize that I disagree with their belief system. The enemy has to be telling them that I'm not a friend, but a foe.

MOUNTAINS

I just had a revelation! Remember when I said last year that the word "mountain" keeps coming up. It still pops up occasionally, but God never told me what the mountain was – until now. I recently read that sometimes we have to blast the mountains in front of us, even if I have to do it one stone at a time. Nothing is impossible with God.

What is the mountain established by the enemy in Aklampa? Voodoo! I think God's called me here to tear down this mountain and Dossou was the first stone. Now, my logical mind is screaming that I'm crazy and there are too many of them and they're too well-established. The Holy Spirit is saying, "If it weren't a big obstacle, it wouldn't be a mountain. It's not up to you to do this alone. I'm going to do it through you."

Freda, have I lost my mind. If your spirit does not bear witness, please tell me. This is one of those situations where I really need some specific direction from the Holy Spirit because I know so little about voodoo. I've only touched the surface of things. My mind is racing.

1/10/99 Journal Entry…
I'm seriously oppressed so I'm definitely going to fast and pray through tomorrow. Last night was a mess. I saw a voodoo ceremony in Lagbo. Sai and Janvier were with me and Dossou met us there. Sai kept me far away because he has learned that the voodoo want to harm me – badly. They want to touch me and do incantations over me. I was safe the entire time, but its time to cover myself.

1/10/00 Letter…
Convert #2! Sai accepted Christ yesterday morning. His father is the head of the Adidemé's as well as a voodoo chief. I was so happy for Sai. I can't begin to explain it.

We had a great bible study with six new people. I changed the format to more of an interactive teaching style. The questions weren't working. I also incorporated a visual example. It was reported to me today that one newcomer, an older man, was telling everyone in the village that the bible study made sense and he can ask any question. Praise God!

I've learned that I need to keep the lesson very basic and teach as visually as possible, which is new for me. God also revealed to me today that since many cannot read, they will learn through living examples. Therefore, I need to live the Word of God. Actions speak louder than words.

AN EYE-OPENING EDUCATION

A friend and I had a discussion. Fina joined us to interpret some things. I shared my call to Aklampa and how I believe God wants me to deal with the voodoo. The friend definitely tried to discourage this because I (and he) can easily be killed. He nearly begged me to only focus on the bible study.

He explained how dangerous voodoo is and shared some information about it. There were some questions that he was afraid to answer because revealing such information would cost him his life. At first I said that if he wouldn't tell me, I'd ask others. He got very serious then and said not to outwardly ask questions. He'd share and answer as much as possible, but in return, I have to act uneducated. Again, wise as a serpent, innocent as a dove.

He gave me lots of information. I'll share a few so you and the prayer team have some idea what I'm up against:

A white man once came to Aklampa and wanted to know what was so special about the masquerade costumes and what was under them. Somehow he gained access to one and as soon as he touched it, he died.

If the masquerade voodoo touch you, you're obligated to go down. If you don't go down for some reason, they kill you. On this point, let me digress. Dossou, Sai, Janvier, Dossa and I saw a ceremony today. I saw a voodoo touch his "assistant" who holds the stick. He went down instantly. It happened less than two feet from me. The boy was holding the voodoo back from me!!! The boy never knew what hit him. He didn't fall slowly. It's as if he was knocked dead and physically (actually spiritually) thrown down. I did notice that his heart was still beating as they carried him away. The voodoo also left me alone.

If you see any part of the physical body of the voodoo while in masquerade, you are either killed or you lose the body part that you saw on the voodoo.

After the death of a voodoo member, other members of that same sect take some of his hair, or whatever body part may be dedicated. Each member takes a hair, adds it to gin and drinks it. They believe that the dead person's spirit then enters the other voodoo members and they become more powerful, sometimes to the point of killing their own parents.

Some voodoo sects have the power to appear in front of you, without going through doors or windows, and then harm or kill you.

Freda, based on this and more that I learned today, I need to be fully covered in prayer. I know God is bigger than Satan, but I don't want to underestimate his power and ability. I'm literally dealing with life and death. I'm poking into the enemy's domain and he can't be happy.

As an endnote for today, Aklampa is known throughout Benin, and much of West Africa, as one of the most powerful voodoo villages. People from other villages are afraid to travel here. In Cotonou, the hotel staff keeps warning me to be careful and stay away from any voodoo.

Is it a coincidence that God chose Aklampa versus any other village in Africa? Probably not. Is it any coincidence that my first two converts, and good friends, were deep into voodoo and know so much information? Definitely not!

One final, final note. I asked Dossou if he misses the voodoo, especially the power and camaraderie. He answered honestly that he misses it very, very much, but doesn't want to go back because he doesn't want to serve the devil.

Please hold him up in prayer because I can see how much he misses it. It's hard for him to have been a "pastor/grandmaster" with all that power and now be an outsider. I try to encourage him to convert that faith to the power of Jesus and I believe God will work powerfully through Dossou.

His mind is already conditioned to work in the supernatural. What the devil meant for bad, God works for his own good. Amen! Goodnight.

The very next day…
Is it any surprise that my tonsils are swollen and I have a high fever today? Of course not. I think it's a spiritual attack to the fasting as well as from the information I learned yesterday.

Also, I had a strange dream/experience last night. I dreamed that one of the voodoo, named "Tailor" (his costume is made up of strips of fabric), was hovering over my face. He emitted a

114

horrible smell like dirt and sweat. I woke up and realized the smell had permeated real life and my pillows. However, I felt no fear, just annoyance.

I doubt it was a dream. Based on the odor, I believe I was visited by a voodoo spirit.

Dossou arrived this morning as I was praying. He sat down and joined right in. The Holy Spirit was definitely present. At one point, I prayed for Sai. He heard the name and began praying for Sai. Tomorrow morning, Dossou and I are going to pray for Sai's mom who is very mentally troubled. I really believe it's spiritual. Her sickness pains Sai. He wants his mom back. He worries that she will die soon.

Sai's mom did pass away a few years after my return to America. To my knowledge, she was not healed of her mental illnesses, which were apparently the results of a voodoo curse.

7:00 pm...
Dossou was excited to show me something today. He took off his shirt to show me the scars from his voodoo outfit. He's excited that they are nearly healed. The straps of his voodoo costume caused deep scars on his shoulders and down his back. There had been deep calluses but the skin is peeling and there's fresh, unscarred skin underneath! He's so happy that Jesus is even taking away the physical reminders of his past. This nearly makes me cry. This is a huge deal for Dossou. It's also a physical manifestation of the power of God over Satan.

HEALING WOUNDS

I love Jesus so much! I had the best worship I've had with Jesus in three months. After two blissful hours, I went to pray for Sai's mother who is sick mentally and physically due to a voodoo curse.

As I was sitting in the family compound while Sai gathered his parents for prayer, I took inventory of the fetish symbols. The place was filled with them. There were bottles on the outside walls of the house to ward off bad spirits. I know they house deceptive spirits. There were a few shrines, strange symbols painted on the walls, and wood posts in the ground for daily prayer sacrifices. There was a large clay mold that was stained red from animal sacrifices, as well as loads of other things that are voodoo, but I don't know their meaning. It was amazing to look at it all.

I explained to Sai and made him tell his parents what God has revealed regarding the mother's illness. Telling his parents was difficult for Sai because culture dictates that you do NOT give orders to an elder, especially a chief. Also, Sai's a very new Christian and this prayer meeting was completely foreign to him.

I had him inform his parents that her illness is spiritual and they should stop all fetish, voodoo and "traditional" medicine. The chief was absolutely open to this. I was shocked that they agreed, but as I said, they've spent four years trying fetish and voodoo and she's only gotten worse.

I took oil, anointed the family and prayed. Sai knelt beside me. Afterward, he took some of the oil for future use. He really wants his mom to recover and be his mom again.

I later told Sai that when he has some privacy at the compound, he should get me and we'll anoint the compound and claim the area for Jesus. He loved this idea.

A COVERT PRAYER OPERATION

1/14/00 Letter…
Today was quite the day. Please, please, please make sure the prayer team is covering me. Make any changes necessary to the team because my life depends on it. (She had shared that a member of my prayer team was inconsistent and not dedicated.)

Sai came to get me to pray for his father's compound. When we arrived, there were people present and I explained that I wanted only Sai present. He didn't understand why until later. We went back later.

I first anointed Sai and me, and prayed for our protection. I then had him point out all the fetishes and I anointed them with oil. I also anointed things that he said were not fetishes, but when he explained their purpose, I knew they needed anointing. For example, there are two structures hanging on a wall and one has feathers. I can't really describe them. Sai explained that they represent his dead grandparents and they feed these structures as a means of feeding their dead grandparents. Yes, they put real food on them. I anointed a shrine where daily sacrifices are made. At first I wouldn't touch it and poured a drop of oil on it. The Holy Spirit quickly reminded me not to be intimidated. I walked over and anointed it. I anointed skulls, bottles, etc. It felt strange to touch articles that are purely demonic. I also anointed the entry points to the compound, as well as the door and step to his mother's room.

There are numerous little things that they claim are non-fetish but still regarded as spiritual. For example, above many doorways, there is a sachet. This purpose has to be spiritual in some way, given that they believe nearly everything is spiritual.

Sai then sat down as I walked around the compound claiming the land for Jesus. I'd love to have seen into the spiritual atmosphere at that point. I felt completely safe, even though I knew I was engaging in a very serious battle.

All went well and we left. Sai told me he now understood why I needed privacy. He told Dossou what I had done. Dossou got worried for me and told me not to do it again. I told him that I understood what I was doing. He asked if I knew that my anointing them could make them powerless. I replied, "That's exactly my strategy!" I explained why I did it. Then he was fine with my actions. He's really worried about my safety. Realize that these are the voodoo fetishes for a chief in this village, as well as the head of a family. Dossou said that if this really works and Sai's mom is healed, the entire family would turn to Jesus.

As we returned home from Sai's compound, I suddenly felt physically nauseous. I knew it was an attack and prayed through it. However, I'm not about to underestimate the enemy. I'm sure he'll try again.

As I was just writing you, Sai came by my house to ask me to pray a big prayer for his mom tonight. I will.

A month later, Sai informed me that since I anointed the shrines for his dead grandparents, no one has fed them. The miraculous thing is that no one knows I anointed them! It's as if the demons lost the power to draw family to feed them. Amazing! I also learned that there is no one specifically in charge of feeding them. Any family member can feed them. They're usually fed regularly throughout the month.

A PERSONAL INTEREST IN ME

1/14/00 Letter…
I learned why Dossou doesn't like me wearing my hair down. The people in voodoo can take a piece of hair, use it in a ceremony, set it on fire, and that person would be killed.

However, I knew the enemy could do no more harm to me than what God would allow. They had no real power over me. They had to go to the King of Kings for permission to touch me. Furthermore, I know that what the King of Kings allows is for His glory and my benefit in the long run.

1/16/00 Letter…
I learned today that pregnant women are not allowed to play ayo, a local board game. They believe that if they play, spirits will come, tie up the baby and the baby will die. Also, pregnant women aren't allowed to have their photo taken. I've heard two reasons: 1) a photo steals the baby's spirit, and 2) its not good for ancestors to see a pregnant woman in a photo.

Speaking of pregnant, the latest gossip in Aklampa is that I'm pregnant. People saw me going to visit the doctor on Monday and Tuesday. I was visiting Dossou who was there with malaria. People began asking how I was feeling and if I was sick. I said I was not sick. Well, that left only one alternative in their mind – pregnancy. It's hysterical.

Since I'm tired of them asking if something's wrong with me that I cannot have kids, I'm letting them enjoy their latest revelation about my private life. They'll figure it out in a few months. Unfortunately, this culture just doesn't understand the concept of planning for a future and children. After all, they begin having children as teenagers.

Many of the elders of the village were very interested in marrying me off to someone from the village. One day I was summoned to one family's compound on the other side of the village to meet with approximately ten family members. One of the elders visiting Aklampa spoke fluent English. He inquired as to why I was not married, and why I didn't have children yet. After all, I was thirty years old. Something must be physically wrong with me. I calmly explained the cultural differences between Benin and America. They asked if I married someone from Africa, would I have a child in

Benin. I informed them that I would not have a child here. I would return to America.

PAYING ATTENTION

1/17/00 Letter…
I've seen two voodoo ceremonies in the past two days. I'm beginning to notice lots of little things about these ceremonies. I'm not questioning people in public. I play the role of "white woman with camera" and ask questions later.

I've learned that when I hand coins to the voodoo, it goes on the ground and they put dirt on it before the stick boy picks it up. It's to protect the stick boy from any problems. I think the dirt acts like a neutralizing agent. The funny thing about this is that I've been anointing and/or praying over the change I give them. The Holy Spirit is my neutralizing agent so they don't use the change to put a curse on me. I also pray that the Holy Spirit would touch them and turn them toward Jesus.

It's no coincidence that the majority of my bible study members and new converts have come out of this specific voodoo sect.

Yesterday, a voodoo came charging toward me as I threw him change. His cow's tail which he holds touched my hand slightly. I didn't react at all and, of course, felt nothing. I was informed that they use the tail to "bless people". Yeah right.

Today, I noticed that the voodoo touched some people who didn't "die". However, those people are very, very high ranking officers in that voodoo sect. They have ritualistic cuts/scars on their chest to provide their 'protection'.

At the end of today's ceremony, one of the chief voodoo came out from under his outer costume. He wore a simpler costume underneath the larger, more ornate outer costume. The voodoo sheds his outer costume if he gets annoyed.

I'm convinced the voodoo are trying to "recruit" me. The chiefs and young men who are leaders have approached me, asking me to participate. I inform them that I will not participate because it's against my beliefs in Jesus. Actually, I do secretly "participate" in the ceremonies. I sit there and intercede in prayer for them, especially the children. The enemy starts when they are so young.

I'm having a problem with Dossou and I know it's spiritual. I keep thinking he's still involved in voodoo, even though I have no evidence. He

121

openly tells me that he misses it, but would never serve the devil again. Also, he admits that the voodoo are really trying to convince him to go back. They're actually begging him.

Today a voodoo came to Dossou's compound and Dossou ran and hid so he wouldn't have to talk to them. Of course, they asked for Dossou.

All this, and yet I doubt. Today a thought came to me. I think it was God telling me, "It's not Dossou you don't trust, you don't trust the work I'm doing in him." It was as if the Holy Spirit asked me if I doubted the power of God to change lives. That was tough. I know the enemy's trying to destroy my friendship with Dossou and he's coming at us from all possible angles.

1/20/00 Letter…
I'm trying to do more "hidden" ministry. What I mean by this is that I try to privately help people. I don't like always having everyone know what I do. I want my reward in heaven, not here. For example, if I know someone is sick, I'll get them medicine and privately give it to them. Also, I give away food, especially to children. I've also given away some of my clothes.

Yet, I feel I should be doing more. I just don't know what. I'm so eager to learn more about this culture, but have to be very careful. Someone asked me today if I realize that I'm living in the devil's territory and inquired if I am afraid. I told him "Yes, I know I'm in the enemy's camp, but no, I'm not afraid." However, I respect the enemy and do not take him lightly.

FIGHTING ON MY KNEES

1/22/00 Letter…
I've started another letter which I'll mail later. This note is an urgent
prayer request!!!!! I just learned this information this morning and
haven't discussed it with anyone yet.

I have an urgent situation. A church attendee and interpreter informed me
that the secret sect of voodoo of which Dossou was a member is planning
something. They've been trying to get Dossou back and have begged him
but he's refusing. They've secretly met without Dossou and decided they
want Dossou – at any cost. Therefore, they are planning some sort of
secret "final" ceremony where they will "eternally" implant voodoo into
Dossou, making him one of the most powerful and deadly voodoo.

They are planning the ceremony to be completed within the next few
months. If Dossou refuses to go, they'll kidnap him. Even if he leaves
town, they can spiritually transport him to the ceremony and do something
to "implant" his brain.

They're also highly upset with me because I didn't ask their permission
before introducing Jesus to Dossou. Therefore, they commented that
they'll do whatever they need to rectify the situation.

Now, I know that God is more powerful than all their tactics, but I think
you understand my need to be covered in prayer. Specific requests:

1) For God to literally hide Dossou if they come after him.

2) Protect Dossou's belongings and hair – if they can even get a
hair, shirt, etc, that's enough to do the ceremony and 'curse' him.

3) For me to be ready for this battle.

Freda, I'm a bit emotional right now, but I mean what I'm about to say: If
the voodoo only pick one person to go after, let it be me. If this costs me
my life but somehow the power of God is revealed, that's fine with me.

The initial plan (after prayer) is that we will speak to Dossou and then
travel to meet with his father who is at the farm. His father is the chief of
a similar voodoo sect. Dossou's last name literally translates to the chief
of that voodoo sect. We'll explain the situation to the father and ask his
assistance in pleading with the voodoo to let him leave voodoo.

1/22/00 Journal Entry…

In prayer tonight, I prayed very differently. It was as if I prayed what God wanted me to pray; not what I wanted to pray. I waited for his leading on each subject.

God led me through each topic and I prayed things that my natural mind couldn't have thought. God gave me a powerful prayer to cover Dossou and to deliver him from anything demonic. I also prayed that any dedicated body parts be set free and curses broken. I also believed Dossou would arrive here and I was to pray over him.

Moments later, he arrived. I told him I was praying and asked him to join me. He never hesitated and sat on the bed, exactly where I had been praying. (He never sits on the bed – always in a chair – and he's always seen me praying in the chair. There was no way he could tell I'd been on my knees at that exact spot!)

I knelt before him, took his hands, and told him that Jesus had told me that Dossou was coming here and then prayed. The presence of God was definitely here. I prayed the blood of Jesus over his life. At one point, I put my hand on his head and dedicated him to Christ and informed Satan that Dossou no longer belonged to him. I broke any curses in the name of Jesus.

After Dossou left for Lagbo (a different section of the village), I was back on my knees. I then had a vision of Dossou walking to Lagbo and a light which seemed to be an angelic protective shield surrounded him. He was walking in peace and unaware that the enemy was trying to attack him. He was completely protected.

As I continued to pray and sing in the spirit, God brought certain people to mind for whom I prayed and God spoke. For example, a voodoo chief has started to come greet me almost every day. He's very friendly. I think he may be dropping something spiritual here, like cursed dirt. Yes, that sounds strange, but I felt led to rebuke whatever he's planting. God told me that "there's a reason he's coming to visit you so often."

There's a young man that's high in voodoo and looked especially strange a few ceremonies back. God spoke "That was the enemy looking at you at that ceremony." God also warned me that "he was dedicated to Satan from before birth."

God also spoke, "You were only seeing the surface, but I'm taking you beneath the surface."

The Lord also encouraged me with, "Your human authority is Emmanuel and I have prepared him for your ministry." This has been a worry for me. Emmanuel would think I'm nuts if I told him that I believe I'm here to stand up against voodoo. Furthermore, I don't have a specific plan to lay out for him. My only plan is to live as holy as possible, pray lots, and listen and follow the Holy Spirit. This is not a logical calling.

In closing my journal for tonight, let me say that I think the battle's just begun!

1/23/00 Journal Entry, 6:00 pm...
I realize Bernard (a villager who speaks English and visits often) is trying to scare me. I've noticed that he's made some strange comments lately that make me raise my guard. For example, I walked him home after church. He turned to me and said, "You're very clever. You think you can really change this village." It was not a compliment. I need to pray about him.

1/25/00 Journal Entry...
I received another strange comment from Bernard. He stopped by today and as he left, he said, "Gina, I fear you." I told him not to fear me, but to fear God. There was no response from him.

I shared with Dossou my vision that the Lord gave me last night during prayer. He then told me what happened to him. As he was going to Lagbo, he kept hearing strange cat-like sounds. Then a cat crossed his path, except the cat had a strange distorted face. He knew it was a demon. At Lagbo, he kept hearing the cat sounds, especially from his daughter's room. He also told me that some people are threatening to kill his daughter.

Is it any surprise that I have a terrible headache and neck ache, and so does Dossou? We believe it is spiritual and will go into prayer shortly.

INFILTRATION

1/23/00 Letter...
*Over the past few weeks, God has impressed upon me to pray for this
young man who's very high into voodoo. His name is Cyrille. He's so
high into voodoo that the voodoo masqueraders bow to him and if they
touch him, he doesn't fall. He's a high chief – at the top.*

*In prayer last night, God clearly said "he's been dedicated to Satan from
before birth". I even journeyed it. I prayed for God to break the curse
through the blood of Jesus.*

*This morning God directed me not to do prayer requests, but to lay hands
on each person in bible study. As I began, Cyrille arrived. Needless to
say, I was shocked. He's never come for bible study. As I came to pray
for him, I first told him that God had spoken to me about him last night.
Then I prayed very specifically for God to remove the blinders that Satan
has put over him, to break any demonic hold over his life, and to cover him
with the blood of Jesus.*

*During the lesson, which happened to be about what happens after death,
he asked lots of questions, especially as they relate to his voodoo history.
We spoke of the power of God over Satan. By the end of the lessen, he
turned to me and said that he now understands that voodoo is not really
God, even though they pray and sacrifice to their god. God seemingly
removed the blinders. Without me giving an invitation, he said he now
sees this is the right way to God and wants Jesus in his life. Afterward, I
explained the gospel message. He confessed and said he accepted Christ
as Lord and Savior.*

*Before our private discussion, when he said he wanted Jesus to come into
his life, I told him exactly what God told me about him last night. He was
shocked and revealed his past.*

*Both his mother and father were in voodoo. While his mother was
pregnant with Cryille, she became very ill a few days before giving birth.
They took the mother to the voodoo priest and the voodoo agreed to save
the mother's and baby's lives, as long as they dedicate the baby to voodoo.
The parents agreed, and the ceremony was performed. The mother lived
and gave birth a few days later. Yes, he was dedicated to Satan before he
was born.*

Cyrille kept telling me that he can really see God in me. He also said that he knows it's God because there is no way I'd have known about his history because we aren't friends and I've never even been to his home, and very few people knew this information.

As later revealed by his actions and plots, I do not believe that he really accepted Christ as Lord and Savior. I believe he was sent by Satan to infiltrate, cause division, and attempt to destroy the ministry. He tried to "act" like a Christian to get close to me. Although married, he even resorted to blatant flirting which was quite discomforting. His ultimate motive was to destroy my relationships with other church members. Through continual prayer, I quickly saw through the disguise.

I clearly heard the Holy Spirit tell me that Cyrille had been dedicated to Satan from before birth. However, instead of simply praying for his salvation, I now realize God was warning me of what I was about to encounter.

TEMPLES BUILT BY HUMAN HANDS & DEMONS

2/1/00 Letter ...
I traveled to Savalou (a village about fifty kilometers from Aklampa) for a few days rest and to call home. I was taken to visit the king of the village, who strongly encouraged me to visit his temple. Actually, he more or less gave me an order, so I did not have much of a choice whether I went or not. Although it is a tourist area, I clearly understood its spiritual significance.

The temple is guarded by two witches. The witches are caretakers of the temple, and responsible for offering sacrifices for the entire town. Before entering the outer courtyard where the two witches sat, we were directed to take off our shoes as a show of respect. This was tough for me because: 1) I'm tender-footed and the ground was very rocky and 2) I'm not into honoring the devil with this level of 'respect'.

I was escorted by a friend from the village, his brother-in-law and two taxi drivers who brought us on scooters. As we greeted the witches, we were directed to give an "offering" of 400 cfa (less than $1). As I reached into my bag for the coins, God nearly screamed at me. Yes, it was nearly audible. He told me NOT to touch the money because they were going to use it for a curse. I didn't know what to do because they were all waiting for me to give the money. Amazingly, a taxi driver reached into his pocket and pulled out the coins, knowing that I had the change. Now, have you ever heard of a taxi driver giving out money? And, he didn't know us at all!!! I never touched the money. God's ways are amazing.

The actual temple was very small. I had to step down to get in the door. Inside were hundreds of "stands" where sacrifices were placed. They were all covered with a tarry substance, blood and chicken feathers.

I didn't realize until later that this temple is very powerful and even most voodoo members are afraid to enter. However, I felt totally protected under the shelter of the Most High God. I believe my ability to enter the enemy's camp and be unharmed was a testimony to the power of God. What victory in the heavenly realm!

We then took the scooters twelve kilometers north to another touristy outdoor voodoo/fetish area. The area was about 30 feet long by 10 feet wide. It was a slightly raised area with stones placed in various spaces that were covered with this tarry substance. There were four main fetishes: 1) a "man", which was the largest and looked like a tree trunk;

2) a "woman", which was slightly smaller and placed near the man; 3) two "babies" which were a hole in the ground; and 4) a "garden" that had a stick, a penis shape and some other shapes. All of them were covered with fresh sacrifices of flesh, blood, feathers, this tarry substance, oil, corn, etc.

The area surrounding the 'man' and 'woman' had hundreds if not thousands of small wood or bamboo spikes in the ground. From the limited understanding of the explanation, they seemed to use these spikes when talking to the fetishes and making requests.

A man asked me in English if I wanted to talk to a fetish. I declined! When I later told my escort what the man asked, he told me that if I had spoken to it, I'd probably have been killed. It's that powerful. I know I would not have been killed because I belong to Christ, but I also had no reason to talk to demons.

There was one thing that was different from the other things I've seen. The sacrifices were so fresh and the sun shining so brightly that the fetishes glistened in the sun. They almost seemed alive. I know this seems like a strange thing, but I could feel their "life". I think my escort felt it too because he soon grabbed me and we quickly left. It was as if I was suffocating and needed to get out of there.

THAT UNEASY FEELING

2/4/00 Letter...
*I bought a mosquito net and Dossou and I hung it from my ceiling. I can
now sleep with the windows open and the cool air is heavenly. I laugh at
the mosquitoes as they fly at the net, but can't get me.*

*Please pray for Dossou. He told me that his "friends" are really
pressuring him to the point of threatening him. It's gotten so bad that
they've started trying to put fetish curses on him. They're even starting to
be unfriendly toward me. Dossou and I both know that it's only a matter
of time before they start putting curses on me, if they haven't already.
Now, I'm not really afraid for me, but I'm not ignorant. I need to be
covered in prayer!*

*Remember when I told you that Cyrille, a very high voodoo chief, accepted
Christ the Sunday before I traveled to Savalou? Well, he came back for
bible study and has been here at least once a day since then and seems on-
fire for Christ. The problem is that I cannot shake the feeling that there's
something not right. He's trying too hard to get close to me. What I'm
about to write is totally bizarre so if you think I've lost my mind, let me
know.*

*There are too many coincidences: 1) He's the son-in-law of a woman who
is angry with me and spreading rumors about me. Until recently, she
wasn't even speaking to me. Suddenly, she's totally nice to me. 2) I started
having huge problems with Dossou. I could not figure out why I was
constantly upset with him. It was totally out of character for me. Dossou
remained the calm one and told me that something spiritual is going on
and Satan's working on attacking me and I really need to pray. I was such
a mess that I sarcastically told him to pray for me since he's the one with
so much insight. Pretty bad, huh?*

2/4/00 Journal Entry...
I could be totally wrong, and I hope I am, but something about Cyrille
makes me so uneasy. Instead of trying to really learn about Jesus, he is
trying to get close to me and intimidate Dossou and others close to me.
Janvier, Sai and Dossou have all registered their concern.

My Prayer: May God give me wisdom and the discernment of spirits to
discover what's really going on. I know Satan's up to something.

2/4/00 Letter...

130

OK, I'll move on. I really believe Cyrille is trying to somehow destroy the friendship between Dossou and me. Dossou and he are not close, especially since Dossou left voodoo. Cyrille asked me yesterday if I would take him with me on my next trip out of the village instead of having Dossou escort me. Also, when Dossou arrives at my home, Cyrille leaves so Dossou sees that he's been to my house. It's very strange.

Here's what I feel may be really going on, but I hope I'm wrong. Satan has employed one of his chiefs to try to destroy my friendship with Dossou. If Dossou is not near me, Satan thinks Dossou will go back into voodoo. Even one of Dossou's "friends" who recently begged Dossou to go back to voodoo, made a comment to me that Dossou won't do voodoo because of me. I flatly retorted that Dossou won't do voodoo because of Jesus.

I don't think it's a coincidence that my problems with Dossou and my strange attitude (three days depressed and crying) began after Cyrille began coming by the house. Even Sai and Janvier sat me down and warned me that Cyrille has ulterior motives for coming here every day. They've never registered concern with any other person who comes here.

My main prayer is for discernment. If I'm right about this, I really need to pray for Cyrille.

In retrospect, I believe God revealed to me Cyrille was not truly converted. He stopped attending bible study and never really became involved in the church. However, he did continue to participate in voodoo ceremonies.

2/5/00 Journal Entry...
Dossou informed me that he probably won't attend any public ceremonies in Affinzungo in the near future. His "friends" are pressuring him – to the point of threatening him. Dossou believes they plan to curse him and me to either make us sick or kill us. He explained that if we go out and he refuses to participate, they will hurt us.

We both know that Jesus is our best protection. Part of me wonders if they've already tried some curses. It's not that I've felt anything, but I'd be curious to know what they tried that's failed because I'm abiding in the shelter of the Most High God.

2/7/00 Letter...
I learned that the voodoo masqueraders have been directed not to touch me because I'm a "sister". However, this only applies to the Affinzungo voodoo where Dossou and Sai formerly belonged. I'm trying to figure out

131

what that means – that I'm part of the family? Which family? I took it as
a compliment, meaning that I am considered part of the family in Aklampa
that heads this sect. However, I am confused as to why I'm so "safe"
when everyone else is running. Besides the voodoo chiefs, drummers and
singers, I'm the only other person they will not come near. It's odd, don't
you think?

I found their declaration as a sister especially odd, and likely deceitful, given that I stand against everything they believe. As a follower of Jesus, and only Jesus, there is no way I was really considered a 'sister'. Yes, I was considered part of their family, but certainly not part of their belief system.

THE BUSH WOMAN IN ME

Before you read on, I should share that I was raised on a farm in the Midwest. My parents also milked cows. I absolutely hated helping with chores. Usually, I was responsible for preparing dinner and cleaning the house while my parents and brothers were in the barn milking cows in the evening.

When my father was harvesting, or when my parents were away for a day, I was forced to help my brothers milk cows in the evening. I hated the smell of the barn. I was so disgusted that I would carry a can of air freshener and spray it in front of me as I walked so I didn't have to smell the barn smells. Of course, I would threaten my brothers into not telling my parents about my antics. They did. This has become a family joke. My father once called me the most "citified" country girl he had ever seen.

Needless to say, getting dirty on a farm was NOT my idea of fun. So keeping this in mind, read on.

2/8/00 Letter…
I'm a little worried about me. Dossou and Sai took me to visit two farms today and I had a blast. Since when did I begin liking farms? I grew up on a farm and my parents can attest that I disliked everything to do with farming – the dirt, the smells, the animals and the work.

I'm turning into a bush woman! At the Adidemé farm, I ate ata (bean cakes), cocoa (made from corn, not chocolate), roasted peanuts, pounded yam, peanut/tomato sauce and rabbit. It was all absolutely delicious. I love African cuisine. I took lots of photos and handed gum to the children.

This farm is along the main road from Aklampa and houses many people. There are approximately one hundred houses on this farm. It's nothing like America's farms. In addition to all the homes, I saw chicken coops and silos for peanuts.

I was surprised to see that the area was very clean – much neater than Aklampa. We mostly visited with Dossa, one of my friends who faithfully comes to Aklampa for church on Sunday. Today, he told me he'd like me to start a bible study/church at the farm. I need to pray about this. That's a big commitment especially once the rainy season begins.

133

After visiting, eating and playing ayo, a local board game, we traveled a bit further down the road to Dossou's father's farm. We stayed for a short visit. We ate again, which was also very good. I took more photos. This farm is more spread out into the bush so I only saw one section. This section had about fifteen houses.

We traveled via motorcycles. At first I was nervous with Dossou's driving, but he did well. I love motorcycles! At the Adidemé farm, Dossa gave me about thirty pounds of yams to make pounded yam. It was a thank you gift. I was very touched.

Have I mentioned lately that I love Africa!? I'm so happy here. I can't' even explain it. A small example: When we returned home, Pipi, a 12-year-old girl, ran up to me, hugged me and welcomed me. It was great. She's one of those girls who is very mature and lady-like. She's never asked me to give her anything. She's the granddaughter of Antuno, the woman next door who feeds me corn porridge each morning and refuses to let me pay. When I returned today, Antuno also ran here to welcome me. As long as I live, I'll never forget this woman.

After returning from the farm today, I visited Antuno and then played more ayo with Rosalyn before going back to the house. I taught the children how to play hopscotch. We drew it with chalk on the cement slab in my yard. It drew quite the crowd initially, especially when I hopped. They caught on very quickly.

A Farm

134

SHIELDED FOR THE ATTACK

2/11/00 Journal Entry, 10:20 am...
A word from the Lord during my prayer time: "My child, I have anointed you to do this work for Me. I have anointed your hands, your mouth to speak my words. You will be given a new vision to see the works of the enemy. Even through the tough times, I am holding you. Do not fear. I have stationed an army around you to shield you from the arrows of the enemy. You shall see them, but they will not harm you. You may have only been seeing the surface, but you will see in new depths.

Anoint your house with oil and proclaim My presence. You are in war and even your staff will be used by the enemy.

Remember, the enemy is a great strategist; but I will reveal his strategies to you. Even when you feel alone, I am with you. Don't battle in your own strength."

I also saw a vision of an invisible shield around me and under and over me. Arrows were flying and coming close, but they couldn't penetrate the shield.

This would all come to pass and God proved Himself true over the next few months and years.

2/29/00 Letter...
My guard is angry with me because I would not allow him and his brother to travel with me to Cotonou. He's more of a danger than help to me and even recently lied about the price of a spark plug for my generator. He told me double the price and kept half for himself.

Dossou and Sai were seriously worried that my guard had gone to voodoo to make me have a car accident on my way to Cotonou. I wasn't worried. We were scheduled to leave at 6:00 am, but due to car trouble, didn't leave until noon. We had more car trouble on the way so didn't really get moving until 3:00 pm. Do you think it's any coincidence that at the time I was traveling, you and the prayer team were beginning your fast for me? I was totally covered in prayer and fasting. Oh, how I love Jesus.

Thank the prayer team for all their diligence and support. I love them all.

2/12/00 Letter...

Aklampa has all kinds of gossip going on about how bad Dossou is. He wasn't the most reputable man prior to accepting Christ, and people don't quickly change their opinions. There's even a rumor that he stole money from me, which is false. It's chaotic.

The enemy is serious about his attack. This is no game! Dossou and I realize that the enemy's seriously mad and we also realize there are voodoo curses being said over us. It's gotten so bad that even Fina has been sucked into this mess. She's befriended Cyrille, who I'm convinced is involved in many of the curses. She's jealous of my friendship with Dossou.

This morning as Dossou and I were eating breakfast, Fina was in my bedroom chanting/singing a song about Dossou and me. I understood part, and Dossou interpreted the rest. She sang that "the problem between Dossou and Gina is over, but she's not happy about it. Dossou doesn't work hard and if his mother and father would die, he wouldn't eat because there'd be no money."

The chant was pure witchcraft! I later prayed and anointed my room with oil and broke off any curses in this house. Dossou also said that he won't eat here unless I eat with him because Fina could poison the food, but wouldn't dare poison me. Is this wild, or what!?

Now, about Cyrille. He came to my house twice yesterday and was too inquisitive about Dossou. He also said that Dossou's no good and claimed that he hasn't left voodoo. I don't believe this because Dossou has me attend all ceremonies with him that he is forced to attend.

Also, my spirit did not bear witness to what he was saying. I've really come to believe Cyrille's the problem behind my emotionalism of late. Problems with Dossou began only after Cyrille started coming to my house. And, suddenly he's good friends with Fina and now Fina has problems with Dossou whereas there were no problems a short time ago. It's all very strange.

Is it a coincidence that every time I have a conflict with Dossou, Cyrille comes by either during the discussion or just afterward?

I've really been seeking God regarding the Dossou/Cyrille situation. No one seems to like Dossou, yet everyone seems to like Cyrille. Yet, my spirit just doesn't bear witness. If Dossou really was so bad, he'd have tried something by now. He has full access to my house. Also, when we see voodoo ceremonies in progress, he's very protective. I just can't follow popular opinion. Still, I couldn't figure out why everyone seems to dislike him, but totally love Cyrille. I actually almost doubted my judgment and asked God to confirm if I was right.

My devotions have been in John. This morning's was John 15:18ff. Verse 18-19 read, "If the world hates you, keep in mind that it hated me first. If you belonged to the world, it would love you as its own. As it is, you do not belong to the world, but I have chosen you out of the world. That is why the world hates you."

No wonder everyone dislikes Dossou. He's no longer of this world. Yet they love Cyrille. This village loves who they can relate to. God made it so clear.

Now, I just need to know how to deal with this issue. Even tonight after dinner, Cyrille came to visit and acted like a jealous teenager. He asked if I still wanted him to come to bible study because I act as if I like Dossou more than him. I clearly explained to him that Dossou is like my brother/best friend and we're very close and Dossou has nothing to do with my wanting Cyrille at bible study. It was a very strange conversation.

OH, RATS!

2/12/00 Letter...
I just saw a most amazing/disgusting thing just now. If you're about to eat, don't read this yet.

My next door neighbor, Antuno, returned from farm today with two rats/mice. I called them farm rats. She brought them for dinner. They put them to the fire to burn off the fur. Then they cut them open and partially gutted them. They skewered them with a stick and roasted them on the fire. They then ate the roasted heart and lungs and added the rodent to their stew for dinner!

I truly thought they were kidding me when they said how tasty it was and that they eat them. I thought, "No way!" They weren't joking. I was nearly sick.

Here's the worst part. I just found out that it was baby bush meat. I'm eating bush meat nearly every day! No one told me that bushmeat was just a huge rat the size of a rabbit. Worse yet, it's 7:45 pm and I'm having bush meat with pounded yam for dinner at 8:00 pm. I've suddenly lost my appetite.

BUSH LIFE! I don't know whether to laugh or vomit.

9:00 pm...
I tried to eat the meat and was doing well until Dossou turned to me, smiled and said, "Ajaka" which is Fongbe for rat/mouse. That was the end of dinner for me.

To make things even worse, after dinner a neighbor boy brought over another bush rat, a huge one (about 8 inches long, 16 inches including the tail!). He wanted to know if I'd like to buy it! I clearly told him, "No way!"

I'm laughing writing this to you. I bet you thought we'd never have a conversation about eating rats. Heck, in the US, I wouldn't even eat pizza with my hands and now I eat nearly every meal with my hands – and don't even know some of the things I'm eating.

2/15/00 Letter...
I saw a circumcision yesterday. The boy was 2-3 years old. It was performed at his house by a family friend, not a doctor. They simply

pulled the foreskin forward and sliced it off with a razor blade. They then took the boy outside and sat him on a small stool/bench. The family friend held the boy still, (he was still screaming, of course) while Sai rinsed the wound with some red/brown herbal solution and then water until the bleeding stopped. He then applied some salve with a chicken feather (how's that for sterile?) and wrapped the penis with a piece of white cloth with penicillin ointment on it.

I gave the boy two pieces of gum and 50 cfa. He quit crying and shook my hand. I guess this is the circumcision season because I've seen loads of little bandaged penises running around. Of course, they were still attached to their owners, not running around on their own.

THEY'RE EVERYWHERE

The village of Aklampa had six masquerade voodoo sects -- two for each of the three sections of the village. Each had its own ceremony area. Of course, there were also many other non-masquerade voodoo sects as well.

2/16/00 Letter...
On Thursday night I attended a funeral ceremony for a friend's uncle. I returned home at 5:00 am. I danced a bit, but refused later when the type of music changed and became spiritual. The women were dancing in a circle. They kept telling me that it wasn't voodoo, but I knew it was religious. At one point, a woman sprinkled a white powdery substance on the back of the necks of the women as they danced. I found out that it is to keep the "bad" spirits away from them. No thanks. I'll pass.

They also had a voodoo masquerade ceremony yesterday afternoon for the man that died. It was one of the most powerful that I've seen and there were only four voodoo present. The Holy Spirit revealed that it is not about the number of voodoo, but about power.

Freda, I could literally feel their power. It was like a vacuum attempting to attract its victims. It was also chaotic. The atmosphere became so dangerous to the point that they wouldn't even follow their own "rules". We left. I believe the amount of power had something to do with the fact that the dead person had been a voodoo member.

I also saw a group of people walking/marching/dancing throughout the village and was told that they are very powerful voodoo. They were chanting and singing for another old man who had died. Four people have died in the last two days. I was told that it's not possible to take a photograph of these particular voodoo members. They are so powerful that the camera will break if anyone tries to take their photo. You'd never know from looking at them that they were voodoo of any sort because there were no costumes or fetishes visible.

Speaking of voodoo, a new sect of masquerade voodoo began this morning in my section of the village. They began marching at 6:00 am. I've heard their drums. I'm sure I'll see them later today marching around the house.

... Well, its half an hour later and one member has passed by my house and the rest are on their way. The one that came was known as Kpadjé

(witch killer) and he was a small boy – no more than ten years old. Remember, Dossou was Kpadjé for the Affinzungo voodoo sect.

...It's now 1:00pm. All the voodoo have been here and one spoke to me in English. I recognized some of the men who held the sticks and they all knew me by name. They came here to have their photos taken. Unfortunately, I'm out of film so I took a group photo with my Polaroid camera.

Dossou was in my house when the six voodoo arrived. However, he never came out of the back room until the masqueraders left. He secretly watched from the window. He didn't go to the morning ceremony and didn't come out of my house. Praise Jesus!!!

2/22/00 Letter…
The new voodoo are performing for seven days, not including today. They told me that they are tired. I told them that Jesus doesn't get tired so Jesus must be a much better choice.

I've realized that the new voodoo is led by the Adidemé family – the family I'm closest to. I personally know at least two of them. One is Dossou's 12-year-old brother. No one thinks I know he's involved. I knew this sect was led by the family just by observing who the chiefs are. Also, Dossou, Sai and I were sitting down and some voodoo came over to us and bowed to us! This could not have happened if they (and we) were not from this family.

A young man was disciplined by the voodoo last night because he opposed the voodoo. He was taken into a compound after the ceremony, stripped of his shirt, and forced to lie face down on the ground. They whipped and beat him for over four hours. He had pieces of flesh ripped off. He nearly died. He also had to pay 25,000 cfa, a goat, two chickens and some alcohol. That's severe discipline.

There was also an all-night voodoo ceremony across the road from my house the other night. They played instruments, danced and chanted/sang until 6:00 am. It made me wonder how many Christians would willingly give up a night's rest to praise God. Even I'm guilty of not doing this. Yet, Satan has his people worshipping all night long, and again the next day. They're more faithful than Christians. This really shows me how diligent I must be in my personal time with God.

2/26/00 Letter...
A church member sat me down to show me something today: a fetish he had used while still in voodoo. It's a medium sized padlock with a key. However, a fetish is attached to it. It looks like a lump of string wrapped around the lock, but it's so much more. Within the "ball" of string is a piece of cloth, hair, a tooth, chicken blood, a fingernail and a toenail. All ingredients except the chicken blood come from corpses. After a person dies, they dig them up and steal hair, teeth, nails and the cloth covering their mouth. This fetish's pieces came from five different people. It cost 25,000 cfa and was given to him by his great grandfather.

To cause great sickness, he would spit on the fetish three times and speak the person's name. Then he'd lock the padlock and remove the key. As long as the padlock stayed locked, the person was sick. To remove the curse, he'd simply unlock the lock. To kill someone, he'd lock it up and keep it locked until the person died.

Also, if the owner of the fetish was interested in a woman and wanted to have sex with her, he'd chant her name to the fetish and ask her to come. He'd lock the lock and within a few minutes, the woman would arrive for sex. She would not be aware of her actions as she would be in some type of trance. She wouldn't wake up and realize what she'd done until later. It's like hypnotism.

Also, if the owner asked to borrow money and someone refused, he'd do a chant to the fetish and within a short time the person would come with the money.

He claims that he hasn't used it since the day he accepted Christ. That's a lot of power to give up instantly, but I pray he's being truthful. I told him that there's much more power in Jesus. It's very difficult for him because he feels powerless in Christ because he knows so little, yet Satan is constantly tempting him to go back and utilize his old powers.

The other day Kpadjé (a voodoo that Dossou used to take on) ran after Sai and me as we were walking to my house. He came right after us. Sai

142

pushed me out of the way so I wouldn't be touched and calmed Kpadjé down. Sai admonished Kpadjé for coming after me and asked why. The inhabitant of Kpadjé was drunk and said he hadn't even seen me. He apologized. It's frightening to think that people with that much power are drunk and high.

The man who takes on Akpo, one of the other voodoo, knows me quite well and often engages in conversation with me. I do not know who he is. He tried to get me to escort him to a ceremony today. No thanks! When I was visiting Janvier's house the other day, Akpo arrived. They made everyone leave the compound except the young men and me. Akpo ordered me to stay. They shut the door and locked the compound door. I realized that something was about to happen. Sai grabbed me and said "We go." No way was he letting me stay. I think I may have been in danger. This was a bold move for him because he defied the very sect he'd left.

A GUARDED ATTACK

3/4/00 Letter…
I'm sure I wrote you about the timing of your fast and my travel to
Cotonou and my problems with Bernard, my guard. The problem is not
over. Bernard is convinced that Dossou initiated my decision to not allow
him to travel with us. Actually, Dossou and Sai begged me to let the guard
travel with me, but I was in a rather unwilling mood and refused to take
their advice.

In Cotonou, Dossou became sick. Ojo and I begged him to visit a doctor,
but he refused, even though I offered to pay the cost. We did go to a
pharmacy and get medicine. We returned to Aklampa on Thursday and by
Friday night, Dossou had a 103.8 degree fever, was shaking, breathing in
short gasps and somewhat incoherent. He rested on my sofa.

Around 6 pm, he finally admitted that he knew it was spiritual and was a
voodoo curse by Bernard. I felt terrible. My stubbornness had hurt
someone else. I went directly to my bedroom, dropped to my knees and
prayed. I then took oil and anointed Dossou and prayed. I spent the next
hour praying scripture over Dossou as well as continually repenting of my
poor judgment and stubbornness.

Even though I should have handled my emotions better, I don't
believe I sinned by not allowing an enemy to travel with me. As God
later revealed, my guard would attempt to kill me. My decision to not
allow him to travel with me was actually for my protection. I believe
God allowed this situation to show Bernard that his voodoo gods are
not more powerful than the Almighty God whom I serve.

Sai is also sick now. Dossou's better today, but is still very weak. His
mother begged Dossou to message his father requesting that he do a curse
to kill my guard. Dossou refused, but he was surely tempted. It's tough
for him because he feels so powerless. I told him that we need to set aside
time to teach him more about Jesus so he can build his faith.

It's difficult having your own employee as your most dangerous enemy. I
can't fire him because he's a condition to my staying in this house.
Therefore, I must wait for Emmanuel's house to be completed.

To let you know how sick Dossou was, his mother, stepmother, sisters,
brothers, etc. all came to see him. We were all quite sure he was dying. It

was a tough night for me. When Sai and I took him home that night to sleep, we nearly had to carry him.

3/4/00 Journal Entry...
A note about village "home remedies" for sickness:

1. Grind certain leaves and add them to water. Drain off the water and drink the green water.

2. Boil certain leaves in water. The boiling water is poured into a pail. The person sits on a stool with his head covered over the pail. The person is completely covered so the steam causes them to sweat. The sick person then bathes. Some of the hot water from the leaves is also drunk. I tasted it – yuck!

3. To clean out a sick person's digestive system, they swallow a small snake – live. Swallowing a small snake would definitely clean out my digestive system - I'd instantly vomit.

3/7/00 Journal Entry...
Last night in prayer, I began crying as I thought about the radical transformation of some people who've accepted Christ. Salvation truly is beautiful.

When I prayed and told God how hard it is going to be leaving here, I cried. I asked God how other missionaries do it. He quickly said, "You're not like other missionaries." I then said, "I can't just turn off my heart and not care." God replied, "I called you here because of your heart."

3/10/00 Letter...
Remember my mentioning Cyrille, the young man who said he'd accepted Christ but I had serious doubts? Well, he came to church yesterday, but in the afternoon, I heard him singing voodoo chants at the beginning of a voodoo ceremony. Then later, he was in masquerade and was dumb enough to stop by my house to visit. I recognized him instantly. I need to handle this delicately.

HELD HOSTAGE

3/12/00 Letter…
I'm a prisoner in Aklampa. However, so is everyone else. There's no safe
way to leave the village right now, because we stand a good chance of
being killed.

Let me explain why. On Thursday night, Dossou's brother Dominic shot
and killed a scooter taxi chauffer from Dassa. It happened along the
highway between Dassa and Savalou. He then stole the scooter, drove to
a nearby village, left the scooter with a relative (saying he had just
purchased the scooter), and left to supposedly go to Cotonou. That's the
last anyone's seen of him. The entire country is looking for him, but as of
yet, he has not been found.

Now if this had happened in America, things would be left to the law.
Well, this is Africa and people tend to take the law into their own hands.
There's already tension between Aklampa and Dassa over some
disagreement last year. Now, the village of Dassa is vowing revenge.

Dassa people have armed themselves and are setting up ambush sites
along all the exit routes from Aklampa. If we leave, we stand a good
chance of being harmed. If Dominic is found soon, it may minimize the
trouble. However, if he's not found, the Dassa people will go after
Dossou's family. Therefore, the entire family is in hiding. Not one person
is at the family compound and all the people have fled from the farm. They
are still in Aklampa, but at different parts of the village. For example,
Dossou is staying with a friend in Affinzungo and his mom is staying with
her mother in Affinzungo. They have literally packed up and moved out of
the family compound.

Dossou cannot visit as much as usual because we both know he's a prime
target. Dominic is his full brother and about one year older. Also,
everyone knows that he is at my house often so they will look here for him
first. He came here last night for a few minutes to let me know that he's
ok, but I can see that this is very hard on him. He even kept saying how
difficult this is for him.

People very seldom murder people in such a way in Benin. It just doesn't
happen. Therefore, this incident is national news. On a local level,
Dominic has shamed his entire family, which is very difficult for a well
respected family. Dossou's father was the first Aklampan to build a house

in another city (Glazoué), first to buy a vehicle, and first to build a big compound such as his. He is highly respected and liked.

When Papa Allagbé heard the news of what his son had done, he cried. Now he's the only person refusing to hide. He's all alone on his family farm. It's all very, very sad.

Fina said that if it gets too bad, I'll have to try to leave and go to Cotonou for a while. She figures that they won't kill me because I'm white. However, the trouble is finding someone willing to drive me out. I'm guessing I could get out with one of the cashew trucks. However, anyone who left Aklampa yesterday to go to Glazoué hasn't returned so we don't know the situation.

The Next Day...
They found Dominic in Cotonou. His uncle, the head of police for Savalou, found him. He's now in jail in Savé. Everyone is still afraid that Dassa will retaliate, but all is quiet so far. The cars that had gone to Glazoué have returned. They stayed in Glazoué due to the fear that they would be ambushed on the road back to Aklampa.

Dossou came by the house yesterday afternoon. It was so very sad. He sat down, then curled up on the couch and just cried and cried. All I could do was sit there and hold his hand. What was there to say? I knew he just needed to unload, so I let him cry (I also did my share) and talk. He cried off and on for three hours.

Dominic's actions have changed so many things. He will probably be in jail for 5-10 years before they judge the case. However, there's little chance he'll live that long. People are pushing to have him executed. That means he'd be soaked in fuel, set on fire and burned to death. Or, he'll be beaten to death.

Dominic was the oldest son of his mother. He was responsible for making sure his mother and brothers were well fed. Now, that responsibility is on Dossou's shoulders and it's a huge burden. Dossou was working on being trained as a chauffer. The plan was for him to save as much money as possible in one or two years and open a business of some sort. He was so excited about this new plan because there's decent money to be made. Farming isn't a money-maker here – it's a survival mechanism.

Well, he feels everything has now changed. Since he was due to begin his apprenticeship in a few weeks, he's not yet getting any income. He's spending money to pay for training. Now he can't use the money for training. He needs it to feed his family. Well, I thought I could solve that problem by loaning him some money. He turned me down because of another problem.

If he were to chauffer, the route to Cotonou goes through Dassa. Once anyone realized that he was Dominic's brother, they'd surely kill him. This is a small area and everyone knows everyone. There is no way they wouldn't find out who Dossou is.

All we can do is pray. When our minds can't find a way, God always has a way. It was so sad to see Dossou without hope. At one point, he just began crying out to Jesus and just talked to Jesus and cried and cried. Oh, it was so, so sad. It's times like this when I realize how attached I am to these people.

3/16/00 Letter…
There are a few things I never considered before coming to Africa. I knew I would see pain and suffering, but I never thought it would hit so close to home. We thought things had calmed down until today. Turns out that the Dassa people have demanded that Dominic be brought to them so they can kill him. The governor has denied their request. Therefore, Dassa decided to write an "open letter" to Dominic's family to inform them that they intend to kill Dominic's family – mother, father, siblings, wife, children, etc. This letter was written Tuesday and delivered today. Dossou's uncle, the chief of police in Savalou, just arrived and the family is meeting as I write this.

Last night Dossou visited me and tearfully asked if I'd still be his friend after he goes to work on the farm. I assured him that nothing will change my devotion to him and his family. It's so sad to see him giving up hope for a better future. He's in survival mode. Needless to say, I've done lots of grieving for the family. I want so badly to take away their pain, but I know that only God can be their peace in such a time. Please be in prayer for this matter.

I know God has a plan. I just can't see it yet. Last night I suggested to Dossou that he pick a day for us to fast and pray. He chose Friday – that's the 17th! I then told him that not only will the two of us be praying and fasting, but seven others in the US will be with us.

THE POWER OF GOD

3/18/00 Letter…
On Thursday night, I saw a ten-year-old boy, the one who just started voodoo masquerade, swallow a razor blade. It's a double edged razor blade like the type we use to remove paint from glass. I thought it was a trick of some sort until someone explained that it was real. It's voodoo, of course. Before being able to eat razor blades, they do a ceremony where they make 2-3 small incisions on the back of the left hand. They rub the blood with some voodoo concoction and rub the wound. Afterward, they can eat razors without damage. Dossou said he used to do it before accepting Christ. He showed me the small scars on his left hand.

3/27/00 Letter…
Dossou and I were invited to a masquerade voodoo ceremony. We sat quite far away on the terrace of the tailor. I was seated next to one of the chiefs of that sect. Without any warning, the most powerful voodoo came over and began spinning. There were two stick boys instead of the usual one, but they could not stop him. He hit me, and not lightly!

Anyone else would have "died". I felt nothing. The spirit had absolutely no power over me. However, the voodoo definitely realized what had happened because he instantly stopped. His stick boys, Dossou, and a couple of others saw what happened, but no one said anything, including me. Later I asked Dossou if he knew why I didn't "die". He said it must be because I'm white. I said, "No, it's because I have the Spirit of God in me and the devil can't take me out."

Also, the masquerader lost much of his power and became dazed. He returned to the ceremony area and continued to dance. However, very soon thereafter, he and another voodoo came out of their costumes. One of them came straight at me with a sword raised. It took three men with sticks to hold him back. The chief seated next to me quickly ordered me not to move. Afterward, we quickly returned home.

When they remove their outer costume, it symbolizes that the voodoo are angry. People take off running. Villagers believe that Satan himself inhabits the voodoo at this point and fear seizes everyone.

The voodoo chief later met with Dossou and me. He initially requested money to pay the voodoo for "my" offense. I flatly refused.

He then just begged me to keep quiet and not disclose how I had affected the voodoo, making him lose his power.

I think the masquerade voodoo finally realize that I don't fear them. Whereas most people run from them when they walk around the village on ceremony days, I don't run. If they approach me, I stand my ground. For example, I had taken a young child to my house for some candy. As we were returning to her family compound, a voodoo approached me. I put the child behind me to shield her and spoke openly to the voodoo.

He kept coming at me, stepping closer and closer, but I refused to back up. He realized I wasn't moving and backed away. Come to think of it, I think it was the same voodoo that hit me last night!!! I later found out that it was the same voodoo.

Needless to say, I think the war is on. I'm realizing that it will be a tough battle. Satan has chosen his strategy to hit as close to the heart as possible. It's personal.

AN EERIE VISIT

Dossou has decided not to pursue another trade. This week he'll be moving to the Allagbé farm to begin farming full time so he can take care of his mother and siblings. At first, he was really sad, but he's now resigned to the fact and is encouraged to do well in farming. He's even going to let me plant a garden on the farm since I have no land here and the house isn't completed yet.

When Dossou moves to the farm on Wednesday, he's giving me his room at his father's compound where he now lives. Even his mom agreed to it. I always go to their compound for some privacy and to get away from people calling on me all day long. Even when I'm in my house, people shout for me even if they don't see me.

At the Allagbé compound, there's a door to the enclosed compound so I can relax, visit and help them prepare food. They don't see me as "white"; they see me as part of their family. Anyway, Dossou has given me his room so I have a private retreat. That is a beautiful gift. When he told me that he and his mom both decided to give me the room, I was near tears.

In yesterday's bible study, we discussed religion versus a relationship with Jesus. I asked how many people could describe their relationship with Jesus. Dossou's answer nearly made me shout. He explained how he loved masquerade voodoo before he accepted Christ. There were nights that he would even sleep in the ceremony area the night before a ceremony. After accepting Christ, he initially missed the voodoo. However, now that desire is gone and he only wants Jesus. You could see the excitement in him and others also commented how mellow and mature Dossou has become. This was good for him to hear.

I have a part-time bible study member named Fedias. He switches between here and the Celestial Church, a probable cult. Two weeks ago, his father-in-law was brought to Aklampa from the Ivory Coast where he'd been living. About one year ago, two people placed a curse on him. He has gotten progressively sicker so they brought him home to die. They took him directly to the Celestial Church for healing. He has been there for two weeks and is getting worse daily.

I knew nothing of this until Fedias came and asked me to go pray for the man. Dossou warned me that the man was at the Celestial Church. Thank

151

God for the warning. As Fedias and I walked to the church, I asked what sickness it was. He plainly responded, "Sorcery, Satan."

When I arrived on the church grounds, I was ordered to remove my shoes. The grounds are like a commune. People are living in lean-to huts on the open grounds. The place is very orderly. All women had their head covered and many people had on white gowns and "chef-like" hats which is their "proper attire". Everyone is bare-foot.

We walked past the main church building to an area set up for their outdoor Friday worship service. It's an area surrounded by a two-foot high cement wall. At the front is an "altar" with statues and flowers. It resembled a shrine.

The spiritual atmosphere was eerie. No wonder Dossou nearly begged me not to go. It is clearly a cult, even though they somehow claim to know Jesus. I thought of Jonestown. At one point, the pastor came out and saw me. Clearly, he knew who I was. How many white people live in the area? Yet, he stood staring at me for a bit, turned around and walked away. He didn't even say hello.

Now, let me explain my prayer with the man. Of course, I prayed before going. I took my bible and sat on the ground next to the man. He was lying outside. I read some scriptures pertaining to Jesus healing demon-possessed people. Then I felt led to read Psalm 91 aloud to cover and protect myself.

Fedias and I sang "Alleluia" for a while and then I prayed. There was not much reaction from the man. When he later sat up and looked at me, I could see the demonic presence in his eyes. The eyes didn't even look human. They were light blue gray and glossed over. He's being treated with herbs since doctors say that no medicine can help him.

He was coherent enough to speak to me a bit. He knows English, but cannot hear well. He claims to know God and to be a Christian. My question in my spirit was, "Which God?" I instructed him to fight this spiritually. I told him that Satan hates the name of Jesus and his best weapon is to continually call on Jesus' name. He kept saying he'll call on God, but I couldn't get him to say Jesus. I told the man and Fedias that calling on God in Aklampa is deceiving because Satan has nearly everyone convinced that he is God. After all, Satan is "the god of this world" as stated in the Word. As of today, the man is still alive, but not well.

The day after I prayed for the man, the pastor ordered that he be removed from the church grounds. Until I arrived, they hadn't let anyone but family members, who were also Celestial members, see the man. I somehow believe Fedias didn't ask permission to let me in, but no one had the nerve to stop me once I arrived.

A BLOODY ORDEAL

3/28/00 Letter...

Today was a great day. Jonas, my chauffer took Dossou and I to Sowiangi, a village 17 kilometers further into the bush. The village is about 25 years old and comprised of mostly Aklampa people. I guess it's technically a very large farm. Tuesday is market day and I wanted to see this village. It was lots of fun and I knew tons of people.

I also visited the school and met the headmaster. Where the Aklampa schools have an office for the headmaster and concrete structural classrooms, this school is a two-room clay structure. The headmaster sat on a bench under a tree in the school yard. They currently have ninety-four students. For secondary school, students must travel to Aklampa.

We also visited another farm/village about ten kilometers further into the bush. Amazingly, I knew a few people there too.

On our way home, our car came upon an accident so we stopped. A motorcycle and bicycle had collided. The motorcycle driver was badly wounded. He had a deep gash in his forehead and blood was everywhere. There was a pool of blood on the ground. The man's entire face, arms, t-shirt, etc. were soaked with blood. I grabbed my tissues and a bottle of water and went to work. I did say a quick prayer of protection. The man wore an AIDS prevention t-shirt. Of course, I had no gloves, but everyone was just standing there and not helping.

I washed his face and applied tissues, but the blood kept pouring through the tissues and down his face. At one point, I had blood all over my hand. I strongly felt led to pray and asked his permission to pray. So, there I was, standing among ten to fifteen bush people who've probably never seen a white person, having one hand on the man's forehead and one hand raised to Jesus and prayed.

An observation on the issue of blood in Aklampa. When someone in voodoo is hurt and bleeding, especially from the head, it is not "lawful" to touch them. Therefore, my ministering to him was a double shock to bystanders. Not only was I white, but I was breaking their voodoo "law".

By the time I finished praying a short prayer, the blood had completely stopped! Please understand that the tissue I had used right before the one I applied before beginning prayer was soaked with blood within seconds.

The tissue I put on before praying was nearly clean! It didn't even soak through one layer! I don't know how many people noticed, but the man noticed, and so did Dossou. It was a good lesson for Dossou to see God's power.

Now God is up to something because I later found out that the man is, of all people, the son of the king of Aklampa!

Yesterday, the accident victim was at my house before 8 am to thank me. He had a bandage on his head so I couldn't see the wound. However, he returned again this morning with no bandage and almost no wound. It was amazing, the power of God!

A huge gash and now not even a scab over the wound. Only a slight bump. I know that man realized the healing was miraculous. I told him it was Jesus.

SOMETHING'S UP

4/6/00 Letter...
I'm going through a difficult time. It's definitely a spiritual attack. I have
a feeling someone is performing voodoo curses over me. There's a
heaviness that I feel. I'm confused about many things. No matter what I
do, I cannot truly enter into worship. I've therefore resorted to reading
Psalms, sometimes aloud. It's very difficult to explain. I've gone from
being a praise team member at Village Baptist Church to not being able to
enter into the presence of God. It's strange.

My biggest "attack" is regarding money. Another 70,000 cfa has been
stolen. (A month earlier I had had 11,000 cfa stolen which caused many
arguments and had villagers wanting me to turn to voodoo to root out the
thief. I refused. God knew who was stealing His money so I let him deal
with the culprit.)

I had my money hidden where no one could possibly have found it, and no
one had access to it. This is a serious problem. I was nearly sick over this
matter, but decided that this can't be fought in the physical realm.
Therefore, I've begun praying for God to hide my money from any
demonic thief. This is wild!

4/7/00 Letter...
I'm really having a tough week. I feel depressed, and that's very unlike
me. I don't want to return home. I'm just very irritable. Everything and
everyone bothers me. It takes every bit of strength to be nice to people.
Therefore, I stay close to home, or go sit in Dossou's family compound.

I guess I feel very alone. I know God is with me, but even He feels distant
right now. I'm reading my bible and praying more, but I feel worse each
day.

Dossou returned from the farm this evening and also noticed and
commented that there's something going on with me. He knows something
is wrong and was told that there are some voodoo sects that are angry at
me.

I also knew something was up because elders have come by this week to
see what I know about voodoo. It originated with Cyrille. We need to
handle this as Christians and not feed into their politics and gossip. I said
I'd like all involved parties (at least eight people) to sit down together and
openly discuss any problems so no one can lie. I refuse to handle this in

voodoo "he said, she said" fashion. Besides, I'd like to know what they think I know that is secretive. Something is definitely amiss.

NOT DEAD YET

4/16/00 Journal Entry...
Last week I saw a fifteen year old boy on his deathbed. I was originally told that he was dead, but that his eyes wouldn't close. They actually considered him already dead and had given up all hope of him living.

I was told that his sickness was the result of a witch's curse. They had taken him to the Celestial Church. That 'church' couldn't treat him. They took him to a hospital in Wessé where doctors tried but were unable to treat him. Therefore, he was sent home to die.

They figured he would die that very day. The coffin was prepared and waiting for him. He lay on the floor with his eyes wide open and slightly rolled back. You'd think he was dead except for his twitching arms. I sat with the mother and asked if I could pray. I told her I was praying to Jesus. I put a hand on the boy's hot arm and prayed. I then told the mom to get water in the boy if possible so he doesn't dehydrate from the fever.

Well, two days after praying for him, he was not only alive, but was up and eating. Oh, the power of God! Also, what a powerful testimony to the village.

5/8/00 Letter...
I noticed a need in Aklampa as it relates to the hospital we are building. Many medicines are available either here or in Glazoué. However, people don't have the money to pay for medicine.

For example, a good friend has malaria. The "doctor" in Aklampa prescribed multiple medicines for him. He needs to find someone to travel to Glazoué to purchase the medicine. The cost is 7,500 cfa. I didn't have the money to give him, or I would have paid because he's a good friend, faithful in bible study, and always helping me. He has spent two days trying to gather the money, but couldn't. I couldn't stand to see him so sick and going around trying to find money. Exerting this energy is only making him sicker. I finally gave him 2,000 cfa last night to cover the cost of the quinine. The other prescriptions were for vitamins so I gave him some of my multi-vitamins.

I've had a headache for four days. I'm eating Tylenol like candy and it doesn't help. The pain is in my eyes and neck so I think its tension. I also have a strange rash on my hands and forearms. People say it is from the heat. I hope they are right. What worries me is that I had a little bit of this rash a few months ago and it left scars. I'm using anti-bacterial soap, so I don't think it's the water. Also, it's nowhere else on my body. It itches! I'm thinking its from the stress. The other night, I applied powder before going to bed to stop any possible sweat. That didn't work. Also, last night was cool, but I have more welts this morning and I did not use the powder last night. Also, I'm not using any new detergents, soaps, beauty products, etc.

GRACE

5/9/00 Letter…
I was given a cat because my friend knows I love cats. I named her Grace.
Aklampa was shocked to see the cat playing with a ball and jump into my
lap for attention. At first, I didn't want a cat because I was originally told
that only witches usually have one. I later learned from a number of
people that lots of people own cats that have nothing to do with witchcraft
or voodoo. They're pets just like dogs. Well, now I have a baby kitten
who loves attention, and chewing on my toes.

As I'm writing to you now, my cat just learned how to open a door. She
jumps up on the handle and hangs on until the door unlatches. She jumps
down and pushes the door open. Her goal is to get to me so she can sit on
my lap, her favorite activity. During bible study today, she sat on my chair
and slept. I sat on the edge of the chair. She loves being around people.
No other cat in Aklampa loves humans, much less would sit on a lap.
People come by my house just to watch this cat.

I taught the cat to play with a small ball. This was especially
surprising to the villagers. I soon gained a nickname that stuck. The
literal translation of my nickname is "The cat plays ball."

5/12/00 Letter…
I've had three good days. God is speaking again. It's so wonderful. It has
been so long since I've been able to break through during worship. The
other night in prayer I felt like a hand was on my head and God said he
wants my mind. I must take captive every thought that is not from Him. I
would not be proud to reveal my thoughts of the past few weeks. Not
pretty at all.

I also have such peace, even though I have only 3,000 cfa (approximately
$6) to my name and money hasn't been delivered yet and it's Friday. I
had sent a note to Cotonou two weeks ago stating that I'd be out of money
by now, and if there wasn't money to send, to call my mom. I've heard
nothing, but am not surprised. It's apparent that someone is angry with
me and this may be an attempt at revenge.

Here's the funny part. I'm not worried. I'm almost excited to see how
God will provide for me considering there is absolutely no one in the
village from whom to borrow money and 3,000 cfa isn't even enough
money to travel to Savalou and call home. A one minute call is 2,400 cfa.
I have water and food to last me another week or so. However, I'll not be

eating meat for a while, but that's fine too. This is part of the cost of following Christ and I don't mind. I admit that I have one small concern – I'll run out of fuel by Sunday and that means no refrigeration for food or water. God will work that out too.

5/13/00 Letter…
It's Saturday morning at 7:20. It's been an interesting night and morning. Last night I was praying. I had just begun to pray in the spirit when a voodoo procession went by the house, singing, dancing and playing instruments. All of a sudden, I was praying in a new language which was much fiercer. I believe the Holy Spirit was praying against the demonic forces passing. I could feel the battle.

Around 6:30 this morning, I was lying in bed talking to God and contemplating his peace and goodness. Again, a voodoo procession walked by and I felt led to pray against the forces of evil. A few minutes later, I faintly heard the procession again and assumed they were on another road. However, I believe God told me to get up and go to the window and pray over each person in the group.

I figured if it's God's will, the procession would walk by my house. Of course, they did. I stood at my open window, hands raised and prayed that the darkness would be destroyed and the light of Christ would enter their lives. Some saw me, but I didn't care. Unbelievably, within five minutes, another voodoo procession passed and I did the same thing. As I wrote this, another procession was nearby but didn't pass. The battle is on. Let's be praying.

5/15/00 Letter…
I found out the reason for all the voodoo processions. Turns out a young man and woman were joking around and she accidentally hit him on the head. He's a voodoo member and apparently you can't hit a voodoo member on the head, even if accidental. No matter what the cause, the voodoo must take revenge.

This situation is sad because the two are good friends. The voodoo will meet to determine the amount of money, goats and chickens the woman must pay. Also, the voodoo march around singing against her, cursing her.

I asked what happens if one voodoo member hits another voodoo member. Then all the sects come out and it's a huge problem. Even the husband of a voodoo member cannot hit his wife on the head without voodoo involvement.

Isn't it obvious that voodoo is NOT God? Still they are blind.

It's Monday. No money has arrived. Amazingly, God is still providing as I knew he would. Fina, my house help, gave me 20,000 cfa to purchase fuel. Dossou's offered me 7,000 cfa if I need it. I told him to wait a while. Is God good, or what?!

5/22/00 Letter...
I've been helping different people in the village with their work. I help Dossou's mom and another Akognon woman prepare leaves that hold a cooked cornstarch gelatin. Also, I tie bags for salt and soap for three different women. I've shelled peanuts to prepare them for planting. I've ironed clothes, helped a tailor hand stitch hems, etc. Today, I broke corn kernels off dried corn cobs to prepare for planting. This one gave me a small blister on my thumb, but I don't mind. I have to fight to help people because I'm white and they think I shouldn't work. I'm here to work, and I love it all.

PAPA ALLAGBÉ

You'll never guess who came to bible study yesterday? Papa Allagbé. That's Dossou's father. He's one of the highest, if not THE highest, voodoo chief in Aklampa. He's publicly known as a killer and witch. He's admitted that when Dossou first left voodoo, he was upset with me. However, he now sees that I'm not like most church people. He noticed that I don't condemn people in voodoo, I separate the people from the voodoo and just condemn voodoo. Therefore, he felt welcome to come to bible study.

Papa Allagbé actually participated and at one point said that the people of Aklampa have been blinded by Satan and voodoo, but people are starting to realize voodoo is from Satan and are leaving voodoo to follow God.

Now, what do you make of a comment like that coming from a voodoo chief? An amazing thing is that I prayed about people being blind and asking God to remove the blindness. That was my opening prayer in English with no interpretation. Papa Allagbé doesn't speak any English. If it were any other voodoo chief, I'd be sure it was deception, but I've spent much time with his family and consider them my closest family in Aklampa.

During my first year in Aklampa, Papa Allagbé's family was the family with which I was closest. They treated me like a daughter. I knew Papa Allagbé was initially very upset when Dossou accepted Christ. Dossou had been worried for his own safety from his father.

I had a private meeting with this patriarch. I knelt before him and begged him to allow his son to leave voodoo. He informed me that, "We tried you", meaning they somehow tested me to see what power I had. Based on his status, I'm sure he and some others put voodoo curses on me to try to harm me. He noted that he realized my power and I could have Dossou. He didn't seem to realize that I wasn't the person who "had" Dossou. Jesus did.

RAIN

5/23/00 Journal Entry…
I traveled to Dassa on Saturday to call home. I am out of money, but someone from the village borrowed me enough money to make one phone call home. Fina also found a free ride for me to Dassa so I could call. There are no phones in the village or in Glazoué. A group from the village traveled to Dassa for a graduation ceremony and let me ride along. I am very grateful.

On Saturday as we were traveling to Dassa, Laman made the comment that rain will fall in four days (they count the current day as a day, making it Tuesday). I said possibly. He said they have a meeting, and rain will fall. I didn't know what he meant until today.

I was told earlier today that they are doing a special voodoo ceremony to make the rain fall. It should have begun raining over a month ago. The crops are in danger of dying.

Everybody had complete faith that rain would come. No one doubted the outcome. I was "instructed" to attend this public ceremony. I was later admonished by Dossou and Fina because I should not have attended this dangerous ceremony.

I had been ordered to attend by a high government official who was visiting his home village of Aklampa that day. I also later learned that his motive for sending me was to have me killed. He had given directions that I was to be deceptively taken into the main voodoo structure to have me murdered. However, my escort refused to obey the order. Instead my escort obeyed his mother and made sure I was protected, not taken near the temple, and brought safely home.

Before the ceremony even began, rain fell for about ten minutes. I was informed that rain always falls on the day of the ceremony. It's "African spiritual power."

Let me try to describe the ceremony. There were the usual drummers and dancers. However, the dancers were in voodoo attire with red paint on their feet, beaded necklaces, etc. The male dancers wore extra-short African wrap skirts, a piece of fabric tied around their chest, and a necklace. This was nothing like the masquerade voodoo. This was serious stuff.

The dance was very different and had a definite pattern. It wasn't "jovial" like most other public ceremonies – they were very serious and deeply into their "worship". The demonic presence was obvious. You could tell people were possessed by the sounds they made, like animals screaming, and strange dance outbursts. One man near me in the crowd became possessed. He began screaming, ripped off his shirt and ran into the circle. He then began doing cartwheels and summersaults on the ground. It was very animalistic. People tried to protect him so he wouldn't hurt himself. At one point, three different men were doing this.

The strangest sight was a woman who lives behind me. At one point, she clearly became possessed. She was talking to someone, but I don't know if it was a real person or not. Her face contorted and completely changed. Her mouth moved to one side of her face and then the other. There's no natural way a face could have done that. Then her left hand went up in a claw and she looked as if she were about to attack. All of a sudden she became fearful and ran and hid a small distance away. When she came back a few seconds later, the demon seemed to have released her, but she was quite dazed.

Also, there were lots of small confrontations where one demon would try to attack another. It never ended in an actual fight because people always pulled them apart. It was very strange.

Many people wanted me to take photos. Some people argued that I shouldn't, while others wanted me to take photos to record for their history. This is a quite powerful voodoo and it's supposed to bring trouble to people who try to take photos. However, I was assured that I was safe to take photos because I was invited.

Amazingly, when I arrived in Affinzungo for the ceremony, there were only a few light clouds in a mostly blue sky. All of a sudden the sky turned black and the wind picked up. People began running to leave. Toto, Antuno's daughter, told me to leave with her. Good idea. Less than thirty seconds after I arrived home, the rain began pouring – an unbelievably serious rainstorm. One minute there were blue skies with a few light clouds. The next, the sky was totally overcast and raining.

Here is my question: I know God controls the weather. I know voodoo is of Satan. Why would God allow the rain in response to this ceremony? To me, it makes these people further believe that voodoo is of God.

In studying this issue, I believe that God is a merciful God and had mercy on the people. They needed the rain to survive. Also, Satan is

called the god of this world. He has power to bring rain. Satan still has to bow to God's divine will, but I believe God allowed the rain because God was merciful to the people.

Dossou returned from the farm a few days later and was upset with me. He heard that I had attended the rain ceremony and was not pleased with me. He said he'd stayed at the farm Tuesday just so he wouldn't have to go. He said I should not have seen Satan working like that and I could have been hurt. However, I had no idea what I was going to see and everyone told me to go. Actually, I was 'ordered' to attend. Dossou pointed out that "everyone" is not Christian. Good point.

MEDICAL ADVICE

5/24/00 Letter…
I'd like to start something in Aklampa like our church is doing in Nigeria.
I have only one patient now but would like to establish five to ten patients.
A month of hypertension medicine can be supplied for 1,000 cfa. I don't
know how good the medicine is, so I'll have to do further research and
work with a "doctor" in Aklampa.

It's difficult for me to help in the schools, but it seems as if everyone comes
to me for medical advice. I'm no doctor so I just give common sense
advice. For example, I've seen babies with a fever and the mothers have
them swaddled in cloth. I tell them to remove the clothes and get water
into their systems.

Also, last week a woman came to me worried because her one year old boy
won't eat regular food. He just wants breast milk. I asked her if she was
producing enough milk. She said yes. I told her not to worry because her
baby is very healthy (even a bit chubby) and she should make sure she is
eating healthy because her nutrition is passed onto the baby. It's the only
thing I could recommend.

5/24/00 Letter…
A man just arrived with money for me. He was the same man who brought
cement for the hospital on Saturday. There was a letter dated 5/18, last
Friday, which means the money was in Cotonou before their last trip to the
village. They knew I was out of funds. Why didn't he send the money last
Saturday with the cement? Why wait five extra days? I'm guessing it took
mom calling Emmanuel, who then called Cotonou to determine why the
money had not been forwarded to me yet. Oh well, I'm safe and God
provided so abundantly for me that I'm just thankfully praising Him.

Here's an example of His goodness. Yesterday as I was lying down, I felt
that I should go through a box of journals/papers. I haven't gone through
that box in four months. I didn't want to go through it, but I felt a strange
urging, as if I would come across a note or message to encourage me. I
didn't find a note, but I found 10,000 cfa! I know God put it there for me.
Is He great, or what?!

ONE OF THEIR OWN

5/25/00 Letter…
I had a delightful African experience on Friday. I decided that I wanted a waist chain like all the women in Aklampa wear. Although some have fetishes which are voodoo, most are just traditional fashion.

On Thursday, I bought the beads and asked a friend to find someone to make it. My next door neighbor who gives me breakfast each day saw the beads and got so excited. She and another lady decided to come over and make the chain for me. They sat on my deck and made strands of beads, thirteen strands total and woven together at the ends for a string tie. It took over four hours.

I was so touched that I nearly cried. The women are absolutely thrilled and refused to take money so I bought them firewood to show my appreciation. The chain is made with very tiny glass beads. It's less than one inch in diameter, even with all the strands. It's worn under the clothes so no one sees it, but I've had lots of women feel my waist and squeal with delight.

6/4/00 Letter…
Bible study this morning was truly a blessing. I had a record 21 people. We had to borrow benches and a few children sat on the floor. God is amazing. It's also encouraging that people are retaining some of what I teach them.

I've also learned two simple praise songs in Fongbe. One song is about 2 Corinthians 5:17. At one point, everyone was clapping to a song and Fina even stood up and danced for Jesus. I was so happy that I nearly cried. I LOVE JESUS!!!

A DESTRUCTIVE PLOT

DECEPTION BEGINS

During my first trip to Africa in 1998, I had met a gentleman who became a close friend. During my stay in Benin, this friendship developed into a relationship. I had been led to believe this relationship would result in marriage. However, this relationship ended painfully with a phone call from America informing me that, when approached and asked directly regarding his motives with me, the gentleman denied any relationship or discussions regarding marriage even though his brother had been involved in the marital discussions.

I was assumed to be lying about the relationship. Although the truth was later revealed through the testimony of family members and copies of his "love letters", the damage had been done. I was now considered a liar.

One of the enemy's most successful tactics was to discredit me. Somehow, some members of the village and those associated with the village took great interest in my personal life. They couldn't believe that I was 30 years old and content to be single. There were numerous questions as to when I would marry, who I would marry, when I would bear children, and on and on. It was exhausting. Speculation often arose regarding possible relationships.

There was a small group of people, comprised mainly of people who were originally from the village but now lived in the city, who wrote letters to my pastor making false accusations about sexual affairs. Because my pastor and I had been so very close and he knew my character, I believed he would see right through these incredulous lies.

I was wrong.

5/30/00 Letter…
What a past 24 hours. As directed, Godwin came here to meet with me. I was prepared through lots of prayer and things went very well. I have been deceived about a few things. Needless to say, this relationship is over. Amazingly, I have peace and am not worried. I am a little sad today, but the Lord is my strength. I'm not in Africa for a relationship with people, but for God.

Godwin also informed me of a few things that shocked me. Now I know why Emmanuel was worried for me. I learned that the MAFA association in Benin has actually been discussing my private life in their meetings, thanks to Henry. A comment was made that I am having an intimate relationship with the "village rat", referring to Dossou. I also learned that letters and phone calls have taken place regarding this "situation". I'm shocked. No, actually, I'm not. What can you expect in spiritual warfare?

I'm about to be very defensive, so please forgive me for the following. I never hid Dossou's past from anyone. Yes, he was real bad, and he'll be the first to admit that. My understanding of the bible is that when we repent and turn our lives over to Christ, He washes all of our sins away and forgets and forgives the past. (2 Cor 5:17). Unfortunately, man doesn't seem to be able to do the same. What makes me angry is that I've spent months on my knees praying and helping him to leave voodoo. As past letters can attest, this was no picnic. I fought hard! I praise God often for the transforming power of the blood.

I recommend that the next time some unsaved person reports on Dossou, or me for that matter, ask them if it's based on actions since Dossou left voodoo. I'm upset that this garbage is still happening and even more upset that it's affected my relationship with my pastor.

We really need to pray for discernment about Henry. He definitely has two personalities. For example, I learned that in addition to instructing the young man to take me into the voodoo temple at the rain ceremony with the intent to harm me, he and Bernard also walked into bible study, totally disrupted it, and even teased a voodoo member for attending. The voodoo member got embarrassed and left shortly thereafter. I had been witnessing to him for over two months. The enemy is at work in Aklampa!

Freda, please forgive me for my attitude today. I guess this stems from the pain of the division between my pastor and me. Based on his letter, he seriously doubts my call. Therefore, I've got some decisions to make. I've put the ball in his hands. If he wants to stop supporting my "African vacation", I'll have to make some decisions about my future. All I can do at this point is stay on my knees and keep fighting this war. I see this so clearly as spiritual, even if it is manifesting in the physical by destroying my relationship with my pastor/teacher/friend/mentor/brother. The enemy is serious in his attack.

I believe with all my heart that I came here in God's will and timing. I'm exactly where God wants me.

Emmanuel heard so little from me, yet heard an onslaught of gossip and lies from a number of sources in Africa. Our telephone conversations were strained, at best. I truly believe what he said to me was said out of love and concern, but I received it in criticism, and vice versa. The enemy seemed to literally sit between the telephone lines and distort and twist our conversations. I do not remember having any easy conversations with him during my time in Africa.

6/3/00 Letter…
I've done lots of praying since Godwin's visit earlier this week. You cannot even begin to imagine how hurt I was by the letter from home. This letter was filled with false accusations and chastisement. Unfortunately, assumptions were made without ever seeking understanding of my side of things.

It was devastating. Anyway, I've been doing lots of praying and God keeps telling me that this is spiritual, not physical. I truly believe the devil has strategically attacked every angle of my life: my relationship with someone close to me in Africa, my relationship with Emmanuel, and my ministry. He seriously wants to destroy me. It is so evident. Satan is using non-Christians and voodoo worshippers to do it.

Let me explain: I've mentioned my guard. He's very close to Henry. He's also very wicked and has even told me himself how it's no problem for him to go to voodoo to harm someone. I have to pray every day for protection from my own guard. I asked Godwin if I could fire him and use the excuse of saving money, but Godwin said that it's not possible. He fears that my guard would take revenge and attack me at night, and possibly kill me or destroy my property.

My guard and Henry have been feeding the association (MAFA Benin) information that I'm sleeping with the "village rat" and Dossou has moved in with me. In reality, Dossou has moved to the farm with his family. They've also said that I'm doing no ministry in Aklampa. I'm not even going to justify that comment!

I hear that letters and phone calls have been made to different people in America. This is outrageous. I almost have to laugh. What makes me not laugh is that people in America seem to believe all of this. It is shocking that those so close to me would believe such foolishness. I thought they knew me better than that. From the letter from America, I gather that they seriously doubt my call and my walk with Christ. Why can't they see that this is a war!

TERRORIZING A VILLAGE

6/4/00 Letter…
A new voodoo sect began last night. It's so powerful and dangerous that they notified people over a loud speaker (think of the TV show M.A.S.H.). They warned everyone to be indoors early and not leave your house for any reason, especially women. If women are seen, the voodoo cut off the breast of the woman.

They also have authority to murder. This voodoo sect is known for sacrificing humans, not goats and chickens. The members began publicly marching around the village yesterday afternoon. I only saw them from a distance. They were chanting in Yoruba and I didn't recognize any of the men, but they were all young adult men. This sect is known for its evil actions. Great! That's all we need in Aklampa. More evil.

We were in the house and locked in by 8:30 pm. Fina was very afraid because she's seen this sect at work in Lagos and knows that Aklampa's spiritual atmosphere is much more powerful. While she went home to bathe before 8:30, I anointed the house with oil and prayed for our protection. I was not at all afraid because I claim Psalm 91 over my life.

When Fina arrived and locked up the house, she begged me to close and lock my windows, since I always sleep with my windows open for cool air. I refused to "hide" from voodoo and told her that if the demons wanted to get in, windows would not stop them. I had a good night's sleep and wasn't worried at all. Whenever I heard the voodoo, I'd pray in Jesus' name and within seconds they'd be gone. I don't even think they came near the house.

6/8/00 Letter…
Last night was wild. My generator died because we ran out of fuel. There is a fuel shortage in Benin and the prices have gone up. I sent for fuel a few days ago, but still no fuel has arrived. It should be here today. Anyway, I digress…

The new voodoo sect I mentioned earlier will come out for eight nights, not just one night as I had thought. I had heard them briefly a few nights ago, but last night I got first-hand experience. I was told they don't like light and that's why they've stayed away. Other people feared they would knock out my generator because they don't like the light. Anyway, it wasn't ten minutes after my generator died that I heard them coming. It was wild. With all other voodoo, you hear them walking and chanting.

With this group, you hear absolutely nothing, except this strange whirling noise in the air.

I knew God would protect me, but it was still unnerving to know that demons were in my yard! All of a sudden, the whirling stopped. I'd have loved to see into the spiritual realm at that point. I believe a battle was taking place. I laid very still but felt the huge presence of evil. I believe the voodoo came to my open window. I couldn't see them because my back was to the window and I was praying, but I felt them.

Fina also said this morning that she heard them come into our yard and was terrified. She also heard them the other night when they went into the next door neighbor's compound because her window faces that direction. After about two minutes of silence, I heard them again, but they were no longer in my yard.

Here's the strange thing. When the voodoo came into the yard, my cat went crazy. She cried and cried and was afraid. She sleeps in the main salon, but wanted to come to my room very badly. She's never done that. Fina said the cat was frightened the other night as well when the voodoo went to the neighbor's compound.

I wish I could say that I was totally calm, but it was a very eerie feeling. The adrenaline was pumping.

Now here's a funny story. Right after the generator died, a firefly flew into my room. I didn't know Africa had fireflies. To see a bright light fly into your room in this atmosphere is unnerving. I knew it wasn't of God because I felt no peace by that light. Therefore, I nearly began to cast out demons in Jesus' name, until I called to Fina in the adjoining room and asked if Africa has fireflies. I had to laugh at myself. I thought a firefly was a demon! I just thought the timing was too strange and the light was so bright that it lit up the entire room.

6/9/00 Letter...
I've been reading Proverbs and really feel I need to be a faithful manager of my employees. My only difficult one right now is my guard. It's hard to believe that my number one human adversary in this village is the one person I pay to protect me. He does no work and sometimes doesn't even show up for work until 10:00 pm. He's supposed to begin at 3:00 pm.

If I ask him to do something for me, such as calling the electrician to service my generator, he will not do it. It is so frustrating. I pray every day for wisdom on how to handle this. I know I can't let his wickedness intimidate me. Yes, he may try to harm me, but I serve a powerful God. Please pray daily for this situation.

My guard told me why this voodoo god hates women. The god of the sect is a woman who died in some horrible way. She hates women and if she sees a woman, she wants her dead. To date, the voodoo have seen one woman, but they didn't catch her and are not sure who she was.

There are faults in their theology about this voodoo and I can prove it's demonic. 1) How can one woman die and have her one spirit operating in Lagos, Cotonou, Aklampa, etc. at one time. Demons are not omnipresent. 2) It's appointed unto man to die once, and then judgment, not float around causing trouble. They're clearly demons who are out to kill, steal and destroy.

Last night was a weird night. I couldn't sleep because I have a cough and there was a mosquito inside my net. It had already bitten me four times. I turned on my bedroom light in an attempt to find and kill it. Within one minute, I heard the new voodoo sect coming toward my house. I said aloud in Fongbe "The voodoo are coming". I flew out of bed and shut off the light. I knew they had seen the light and were not pleased. They came right to my window and made their whirling noise.

All of a sudden, my window was lit with a bluish light. The whirling stopped. I thought at first someone was shining a flashlight, but realized that's impossible, given the situation and type of light. After about one minute, I heard the voodoo whirling, but at a distance. Then, the light vanished. I believe it was an angel protecting me. I wish you could have seen it. Over and over the voodoo came to my house last night, but I had total peace.

Later That Day...
Well, I'm off to bed. The voodoo are out early tonight. I have learned that the whirling sound is made with a wood reed tied to the men's arms and they swing their arms. When finished, they walk very lightly to a new spot and whirl again. They put the fear in people so their "secrets" won't be released. I was informed that since I'm a Christian, they will leave me alone, but I should pray, just in case they do try to attack. I chuckled at this.

However, due to their evil nature – sacrificing humans, especially women - - I recognize that it's still satanic and dangerous. It is especially dangerous for me since I stand against everything they believe. Good night.

6/11/00 Letter...
God is absolutely awesome. I had sixteen people for bible study today.
Not one of them understands English well, but some know a bit so we got
by because I spoke as much Fongbe as possible. Of those sixteen, four
have already accepted Christ. Five more people accepted Christ today,
three young adult men, one grown man and a young adult woman. I was
so excited.

One young man's first question was how to greet the voodoo
masqueraders now that he's following Jesus. He knows he can't avoid
them. I told him that he can no longer bow to them and it's a good time to
be open and tell people that he now follows Jesus and can no longer do the
things he used to do. This boy loved the masqueraders so it will be a
challenge for him.

My guard told me last night that he knows Jesus. He said Jesus is the
person who created him. He further explained that his mother and father
created him and, therefore, they are Jesus. He claims everyone who
knows their parents knows Jesus.

This was too crazy to even respond because he was taunting me and I
refuse to play his games. I told him if he seriously wants to discuss Jesus,
I'd love to sit with him or have him come to bible study. He laughed at
me. I seriously believe he's demon possessed. He's deeply into voodoo.
He is one of the most evil persons I've ever met. Please pray that God will
take revenge and actually save him. That would be the best revenge. I'd
love it. My prayer for him: "God, go get him!"

6/11/00 Letter, 8:30pm...
My guard just informed me that the chief of the new voodoo sect ordered
that we turn out all the lights in the house at night. We do, except for the
hall light and the terrace outside, but Fina has begun shutting off the hall
light. She's absolutely terrified and hasn't slept since they've begun.

I learned today that the new voodoo sect is coming out for another week.
This is crazy. They've terrorized this village. They had even wanted to
come out yesterday afternoon and force everyone into hiding. That was
impossible, and crazy, because it was market day and everyone is out and
outsiders come to the village to sell their goods. Where would they hide?

Anyway, back to my terrace light. My guard refused their request. This is
the first smart thing he's done. He believes that if we turn off the light,
they'll try to get in and harm me or steal something. I didn't think they

176

were doing things like that, but I'm wrong. Even if they did try to get in, I know God would protect me or work all things for His good.

6/12/00 Letter...
I am seriously living in Satan's camp. The new voodoo sect didn't come out last night because another voodoo sect was out. A young man hit his mother in a fight. The mother is a voodoo member. Therefore, the voodoo are out marching around the village.

I was just in my room when I heard strange shrieking/screaming in a high pitch. It was drawing a crowd. I looked out the window to see the commotion. A group of mostly women, about fifteen women and four men, were in voodoo attire and definitely on a mission. They were marching and chanting. A few of the women were clearly possessed and making shrieking noises. They carried wands and weapons. The handles were wood, but the blades were metal. Some are all metal and painted red.

I felt such a painful burden. It was so evil and sad.

Remember the woman I told you about from the rain ceremony whose face distorted when she became possessed. She sells food next door to my house. As this procession passed, she greeted the marchers with a voodoo greeting and bowed to them. They placed their hands on her and "blessed" her.

A few hours later... The man who beat his mother is also in voodoo. As a punishment, they took him to the voodoo compound across the street from my house and his own members beat him. I was working on my deck when it began. I could see the men chasing someone and seriously beating him with tree branches.

He had welts all over his body, especially his chest and back because he was forced to remove his shirt. He's been directed to pay 18,000 cfa, three goats, and nine chickens to the voodoo. They'll use it as a sacrifice for the mother.

I feel like I'm living in another era of time, not the 21st century. It's like I'm living in The Discovery Channel. It seems unreal. I have to go now, because my cat is jealous and just sat on this page and is trying to eat my pen...

6/13/00 Letter...

I went to the Sai's father's farm today. It was lots of fun, mostly because I didn't do any work. They wouldn't let me do anything except serve water and take photos. For farms of older men, they choose one day and all the young men in a family go to that farm and work for a day. Sai, Amalyn and I took breakfast to them. It's about a two kilometer walk from my house. I also took my camera.

We sat in the middle of a field under a mango tree for shade. I was surprised, and somewhat disappointed, to see that all of the people who came were workers from Dossou's father's farm. I expected all the local young men in the family to be there, but no one came. This is strange, because Sai's father is chief of his family. Also, all the men, except one, aren't even of the same tribe. They're Fulani, not Fongbe. I recognize them from the Papa Allagbé farm.

I took lots of photos for them. As we prepared to go, I grabbed a shovel and made them teach me how to farm. All twenty men stopped working to watch me. When I caught on, they cheered for me. Sai laughed at me, so I dumped dirt on his foot as he stood beside me. This brought more laughter. They all invited me to the Allagbé farm and said they'd even build me a hut to bathe in privacy, but my toilet would still be in the bush. I just may take them up on the offer and spend a day or two on the farm.

A PERSONAL VISIT

6/15/00 Letter…

I want to relay an incident to you and get your input. I told you about the new voodoo sect in the village. They quit coming out last Saturday. However, on Tuesday I couldn't sleep because they kept making their whirling noise along with a new sound I've not heard before. To make matters worse, I had another mosquito in my net and it kept biting me on the face. It was really annoying. I wanted to turn on the light to find the mosquito, but didn't want to "offend" the voodoo. I laid awake a long time, very frustrated.

In the morning, I asked Fina how she had slept, knowing she is terrified of this voodoo sect. She slept fine. She heard no voodoo. I thought that was impossible because they spent a long time right outside my window. She insisted that the voodoo never came out. I asked my guard if he heard them. He said that no voodoo came out. I also asked Sai and Dossou. Once again, no voodoo. I absolutely know I was wide awake and not dreaming. I had even sat up and taken a drink of water.

Sai and Dossou think that one voodoo was sent here to scare me. They know I don't fear them like the rest of the village. I then remembered that Cryille stopped by to visit on Tuesday. He NEVER comes here any more. He asked Fina and me about the voodoo. I told him that I have nothing to fear as a child of God. I don't know if my telling Cryille this has any relation, but that night the voodoo were at my house.

What doesn't make sense is that both Fina and Bernard slept here yet heard nothing. I believe Dossou and Sai's reasoning, but I think it was demonic and spiritual. Why was I the only one to hear them?

There's a huge gas crisis in Benin. There's no fuel being transported into the country. Yesterday morning, there was no fuel in Glazoué, except for roadside vendors. In Dassa, there was fuel at the station for 350 cfa per liter. By yesterday at 4pm, all stations were out of fuel. The roadside vendors in Glazoué and Dassa were selling fuel for 600 cfa/liter. By the time we arrived in Aklampa, the cost was 800 cfa/liter. I praise God that I have 2.5 – 50 liter kegs of fuel here which will last two weeks. However, we began shutting off the generator at 3:00 am, instead of 6:30 am. Even if I had tons of money, I refuse to pay 800 cfa/liter. That's over $1/liter.

Due to the crisis, I had Jonas, my regular chauffer, and one other chauffer who's on standby when Jonas isn't available, come here asking for fuel –

at cost! If it had been anyone else, I may have refused. However, I gave them one 50-liter keg of fuel this morning. They are planning to travel to Bohicon today to buy fuel in bulk since it's still available there at a reasonable cost. They promised to return the keg of fuel to me tonight. I hope all goes well for them. I guess this is ministry as well. They noted my willingness to help had to be from God because the fuel owners in the village have refused to lower their prices.

EVIL PLANS BUT ANGELS PROTECT

6/15/00 Journal Entry…
Laman came by the house today with an interesting story. Nafi (Henry's sister) told him that Emmanuel will take me home with him when he comes here in August. Is there any coincidence that she's my guard's closest friend and is rumored to be sleeping with him, even though she is already married to another man? I told him to believe nothing he hears.

My guard is acting like my best friend lately. He knows about the rumors and that I know he's spreading lies. I also told him that I'm onto his and Henry's little game. I let him know I realize that he is my #1 enemy and the person most likely to perform voodoo on me. I told him that I'm not afraid of him. Dossou and Sai now think he's afraid of me.

6/15/00 Letter…
Dez and Gab are in Aklampa and brought me two boxes from home. One is a box I sent from mom's house before leaving America last July! It is filled with aspirin, deodorant, etc. I was so happy to see that box. I was sure someone had stolen it. Yesterday I also received a letter from mom dated November 5, 1999. It was incorrectly sent to Shanghai, China.

Oh, I also got a notice that I have a package in Glazoué. I traveled there to retrieve it yesterday and was told that the post man had gone home and to come back tomorrow. I asked him if he realized that I lived in Aklampa. Going to Glazoué again costs time and money. I couldn't sway him. I don't know when I'll go back. I may go with Dez today and take a motorcycle back to Aklampa. I may get a sore bottom, but I'll have fun and save money. I've learned that I love motorcycles!

6/15/00 Journal Entry, Later That Day…
I'm such a bush person. I'm sitting in the motor park in Glazoué waiting for Azondaken to return from Bohicon. He went to buy fuel because there is no fuel in Glazoué or Dassa. I came here to get a package from the post office. I tried to get it yesterday, but the man had gone home. I came here today with Gab & Dez.

As I was sitting in the carpark, a taxi scooter driver asked me what man was with me when I was in Glazoué two weeks ago. I thought he was referring to Sai, but he said the man was tall and either had long hair or some type of head covering. Could it be an angel?

He noted that the man followed me to the post office. However, I took a motorcycle taxi to the post office down the road and could not have possibly had another human with me. The taxi driver also noted that the tall man followed me throughout the market. In the physical realm, I was completely alone during those times. I believe I had an angel following me. I didn't see the angel, but others clearly did.

A WET JOURNEY

6/16/00 Journal Entry…
Yesterday's trip from Glazoué was quite an adventure. As of 5:30 Azondaken hadn't arrived and the heavy rain began. By 6:00, a car was heading to Aklampa. Still no Azondaken so I left with that car and a driver that I had never met or seen before. The journey took 3.5 hours! At one point, it was raining so hard that we could hardly see the road. The windshield wipers didn't work, and in most places, the water completely covered the road.

I felt led to sing praise songs aloud. At first, I was a bit intimidated, but I knew I must obey. Within minutes, the rain stopped.

Our first adventure occurred at a concrete spot on the road – like a tiny bridge over a stream but with no side barriers. It simply drops off. Well, the water was flowing (raging) over the road as we approached the bridge. I knew the car would be carried to the side. I was right!

Our car began floating to the edge of the road – my side. We nearly went over until I said, "Jesus!" We made it across, but had water up to our ankles in the car and the car died on the other side of the bridge.

So there we were, next to a raging stream with a stalled car. Everyone exited the car, and some of us, including me, pushed the car in an attempt to jump start it. Nothing worked. I felt led to pray with the driver. So there I was, with eight people watching me, as I held hands and prayed for the car and driver. I then told him to get in and start the car. It nearly started, then died. He worked a bit more and it started. We were on our way. I'm sure I was quite the sight, pushing a car in my bare feet with water past my ankles.

We started and stopped many times because the car overheated. We added at least 60 liters of water as well as my bottled water and some muddy field water. Before we reached the village of Assanté, Azondaken had caught up with us. We arrived home at 9:30 pm.

There were nine people in my car – four in the front seat and five in the rear. Two men were from a different tribe and they refused to help push the car. It was disgraceful. During one stop at Hogo, they began preaching their Muslim religion. This was after they had seen me pray with the driver and help push the car. They didn't talk too long because another man in the back seat set them straight.

As I prayed throughout the journey, I kept wondering what was happening in the spiritual realm. At one point, the Lord said, "Look who's in the car. They worship satan." I really feel demons played a large part in this journey. At one point, the car wanted to cut out and I began rebuking demons. It began to run better as long as I prayed.

Even through it was a long and dirty journey, I felt total peace and knew God was with us. I also know he wanted me in that car, and not Azondaken's newer car. I was there to minister, pray, give water and food, and keep the mood light. The driver was very thankful for all my help. I hope I did all that God asked.

RUMORS ABOUND

6/21/00 Letter…
Gossip. This village loves it. I think it's a way for people not to focus on their own problems. Henry's sister, Nafi, is unbelievable. She, my guard and Henry are truly up to no good. Here's the latest rumor. Ojo supposedly gave me 2 million cfa to hold for him. I stole the money and gave it to Dossou. Now, Ojo is mad at me and the Akognon's are mad and want to kill Dossou.

Is this crazy, or what? Here's another one. Nafi told a man, who directly approached me, that Emmanuel is coming in August to take me home.

How about another? Henry spoke to the Gendarme of Savalou, who is Dossou's uncle. Henry asked the Gendarme if he knew I was sleeping with a bunch of people in the village.

Henry did not realize that the Gendarme knew me personally. While visiting Savalou a few months earlier, I had been a dinner guest in his home. The gendarme did not disclose our knowledge of each other.

This is wild. It all stems from one little jealous group. I will not react because I'd be stooping to their level. However, I make sure that I live in a manner where people with any sense know that I'm not living in sin. Some other people know these rumors are false and want to write Emmanuel. I've told them not to. I truly believe God will reveal all evil and that a tree is known by its fruit.

However, please pray for everyone's discernment. There's lots of politics going on. I can't wait until Emmanuel's house is completed. I can move away from this garbage, settle in, and live in peace.

TWINS

6/23/00 Letter...
Dossou's older sister Therese has become a good friend. Yesterday morning, she gave birth to twins, one girl and one boy. By 5:00 pm, she was home. I could never give birth in Aklampa. One word kept going through my mind -- germs! Everyone came by to hold, toss and touch the babies. The favorite activity seemed to be sticking their dirty fingers on the babies' mouths. It was hard to keep my mouth shut.

Today I went to visit them and stayed most of the day. I decided to help her. Her mom cooked as I cleaned and swept floors. Later I held the twins while Therese cooked, did some laundry by hand, and boiled water for baths. Yes, she just had two babies 24 hours ago.

I finally forced her to lie down for a bit while the babies slept because they kept her awake all night and she's absolutely exhausted. She fell asleep in less than one minute. People kept coming by to visit. I let them see the babies, but refused to let them wake her. She needs all the rest she can get. She now has four little ones at home to raise. Her husband farms and takes good care of them. He just built another house which is nearly finished.

People keep asking me when I'm having my baby. Therese and I smile because we both know I need a husband first. Most people thought I was engaged, or already married, but they are slowly figuring it out. A few days ago, an older man flat-out asked me if I was married. I said, "No".

FASTING

My view of life as an American is definitely changing. I'm beginning to carry items on my head! Before, Africa seemed so foreign. Now, America seems so foreign. I've asked and asked God how long I'm to be here. He's saying nothing except, "You're no ordinary missionary."

Bible study was interesting today. Actually, a conversation before bible study threw me off. A MAFA Benin member was visiting for a funeral and was staying here. I told him that my bible study lesson today was about fasting. He told me I'm wrong for teaching new Christians about fasting. He said people without the Holy Spirit cannot fast. (He comes from a denomination that believes the Holy Spirit does not indwell all believers.) I told him that I teach and believe that the Holy Spirit is given at the point of conversion. He also argued that they cannot fast because they are not baptized. He said I should have water baptized them long ago. I informed them that I have already written my pastor on this issue and we will handle this.

Also, he said I can't let them fast on Mondays because God began creating the world on Monday and hadn't accomplished too much yet. Wednesdays through Fridays are good. There were a few other wild comments such as not fasting only one day because that's not enough time for God to forgive your sin. Oh brother…

However, I refused to be shaken and the lesson went wonderfully. I taught on fasting because a family member is very sick and I felt that God wants our group to fast and pray for her. She's a little older than me. She miscarried in March but part of the placenta was left inside her. This caused infection. She began bleeding over a week ago and has been in a hospital in Savalou since then. She nearly died.

On Friday, we heard she began bleeding again. We are all very worried for her, especially her younger brother, Dossa, who accepted Christ two weeks ago. Their parents are dead and the woman is basically Dossa's mother.

I felt led to fast and pray tomorrow. We decided to fast from 6:00 am to noon – no water or food. The people are so excited they asked if they can all meet here at 6:00 am to begin the fast as a group with prayer. Also, they all want to return at noon and end the fast together. Even the farmers want to make the special trip back. Is God good, or what?

I've decided to cook lunch for all who fast and come here at noon. It should be lots of fun.

6/26/00 Letter...
Six people showed up at 6:00 am for prayer. However, ten total people fasted and showed up at noon. They were all so excited. Oh, my heart swelled with excitement to watch new Christians see how good it was to fast and how God sustained them. All three of the new converts who accepted Christ two weeks ago went to the farm today and went without food or water. This is a serious denial, especially given the heat. One other member went to the farm last night which is over 12 kilometers away, but returned just to break the fast together.

The woman recovered completely.

They are begging me to do a Wednesday night bible study as well. They want to be like Village Baptist Church in America. I'm not sure how to structure it since my Sundays are already structured like Village's Wednesday night gatherings.

A MURDEROUS ATTEMPT

7/3/00 Journal Entry…

I'm sitting at Dez's house in Cotonou. I'm on my way to a doctor/hospital. I was very, very sick yesterday. I think it began Thursday, but was more noticeable on Saturday evening. I thought it had to do with my stress level, which is on overdrive. I also received a letter from Nigeria which added to my stress.

By Sunday morning, I had a fever, severe diarrhea and my body was extremely sore, especially my back. My back had been bothering me at night for three days. By 10:30, I was crying and nearly delirious. I was gasping for breath. Sai, Dossou and Fina were really worried because every time I moved, I was in so much pain that it took my breath away. They wanted me to go to Cotonou but I would not have survived the long journey. They finally convinced me to go to a clinic in Affinzungo. Azondaken brought his car and drove us. God is amazing! When we got to the clinic, the head doctors for the entire region were in the village. (This is the first time they had been in the village in six months!)

I had three real doctors treat me. I was severely dehydrated from the diarrhea. They gave me an IV drip. Luckily, Fina begged them and they let me go home to do the IV because the facilities in the clinic are not modern, or sterile. I would have had an old cot in a plain cement room with no electricity, etc. The doctor agreed to allowing me to have the IV at my house. Fina brought the IV, which had seven different drugs, in two glass bottles. I actually had a bush IV drip! They hung the bottle from the electrical wiring on my wall and ran the IV line into my arm.

The female doctor was gentle and the IV insertion wasn't too bad. The drip began at 1:00 pm and ended at 9:30 pm. The first one had to drip very slowly due to all the drugs. We were instructed that if it dripped to fast, it would cause a heart attack. She explained this to everyone over and over that it must drip very slowly.

I finally fell asleep. I awoke to the sound of Dossou opening the hallway door, coming to check on me. God's timing is perfect! I woke up in time to see my guard turning up the drip so it was literally pouring into the IV. He quietly left the room as if nothing was wrong. Dossou also witnessed this and we quickly slowed the drip and anxiously waited to see if I reacted in any way. I was fine.

If Dossou hadn't opened the door at that exact time, my guard would have successfully murdered me. My guard stayed in the back room and kept entering my room to check my IV. Needless to say, I didn't sleep again that afternoon.

The only other incident was at dinner. I sat up to eat and was doing fine. All of a sudden, I felt nausea, my heart began racing, my breathing shortened, and I began shaking terribly. After ten minutes, it subsided.

I feel much better now, but the people of Aklampa forced me to come to Cotonou to see a doctor and make sure I am treated. Bernard (the singer) even offered to help me financially to travel. The people of Aklampa are amazing. All my church members came to see me, as well as many, many others. Jonas, my regular chauffer, met us at the hospital on the other side of the village and waited until today to travel to Cotonou to make sure I was fine. He stayed on stand-by all day. Azondaken, the chauffer who transported me, my crew and doctors to and from the village hospital, also stayed on stand-by all day. This is a real sacrifice for chauffeurs since their income is derived solely from driving people out of the village.

The people in the village were so wonderful, especially Fina, Dossou and Sai. Dossou also rented a motorcycle for the day to make sure we had immediate transport for a doctor, if necessary. This ordeal was very tough on him. He had to leave the room a couple of times because he couldn't handle it. He was so scared that I was going to die.

We left for Cotonou at 7:00 am on Monday. Aklampa came out in large numbers to wish me well. So, here I am in Cotonou.

I later learned that most of the village believed I was about to die and thought they would never see me again. They had come to say their final good-byes.

After visiting a doctor and running lab tests, results revealed that I had a bad case of malaria.

7/7/00 Journal Entry...
I'm back in Aklampa. I was so excited to get home. The people I love missed me so much. Antuno said she was really worried and just sat around all the time. So far, I've had more hugs from people in Aklampa than they've probably ever given since hugging is not their custom.

On Monday and Tuesday, some of my church members even fasted and prayed for me. I was so touched.

Everyone is shocked by how much weight I've lost. I feel good, but am weak from the trip. My back is still sore, but the doctor doesn't know the problem.

I continue to struggle with back pain due to sciatica, especially when I get sick. I believe that bout of sickness caused permanent damage to my back in some way. Am I discouraged by this? No way. It is a reminder of God's abundant protection and sufficiency.

SPIRITUAL OPPRESSION

7/9/00 Letter...
Something is definitely amiss in the village. Sai came here this morning and told me that Aklampa believes I'm leaving in August. He said he's been secretly praying that I stay.

Also, a woman who I thought liked me came to greet me today as we were about to begin prayer. (I'm too weak to lead a full bible study, but some wanted to come and pray together for a short time.) What I found odd is that she always greets me from the fence and has never come to the door, especially if she doesn't see me outside.

She greeted me, did a little dance, said something about God, and then handed me 100 cfa. She gave me money! I knew something was not right. I went back into the house and told Fina, Dossou and Sai about the interaction. They became upset. Fina grabbed the money from me and said I'm not to touch it or buy anything with it. It's voodoo. Fina angrily said, "If they can't kill you one way, they'll try other things."

We believe my illness was partially spiritual. For example, in Cotonou, I was feeling quite good and had lots of energy. I now feel pain and weakness. I believe this stems from my guard's group.

7/11/00 Letter...
God is definitely giving me insight into some things. I believe my guard did some voodoo curse on this house while we were gone. Here's why I believe so. Fina admitted yesterday that she was unable to sleep the first two nights after returning to the village. Every time she closed her eyes, she saw voodoo members' faces chasing her and trying to choke her. She told Sai and he brought her his bible. Sunday night she slept with the bible and slept better.

Also, I've been feeling weak since returning here and the medicine has no effect. I couldn't figure that out. I was feeling so much better while in Cotonou.

Also, while I was in Cotonou, one of Therese's twins became very sick and nearly died. People hinted to her that it was voodoo getting back at her for befriending me. When I went to her house yesterday for the first time since returning, I was shocked to see how sick he was. I was afraid he would die in my arms.

I was so impressed by her reaction to me. She handed me the sick child and told me to "work Jesus on him". She's not a Christian. I had feared that she wouldn't want me near the baby, considering all the rumors. Yet, she knows me and put her trust in my God. I sang and prayed for him. Today, he's much better. He's no longer bluish gray, his eyes didn't roll back and he's eating again. As soon as I went to visit her today, she handed me the baby and said, "Work Jesus".

Anyway, back to my guard and the house. Odd people have been coming to greet me and asking after my health – people I don't usually visit and who are deeply into voodoo. I decided to fight back. After Fina left to go bathe last night and my guard went home to eat, I anointed every door and window in this house, covering Fina and I with the blood of Christ and casting out demons and breaking off any curses performed against anyone associated with me. Fina slept great, the twin is much better and I feel great today! Satan got whipped again by Jesus!

I firmly believe I'll be under serious attack until Emmanuel arrives and leaves. Nafi and Bernard have informed everyone that I'm leaving with Emmanuel. I believe they will try anything to make that happen and to save face. They'll feel foolish when I'm still here.

7/14/00 Letter...
Godwin just informed me that Emmanuel said that I'm to stay in Henry's house in Aklampa until after they've left Aklampa. This is shocking. I'm very hurt and feel like they don't want me around. What in the heck is going on? My church family is coming to visit, I haven't seen them in over a year, and they don't even want me to stay with them. I guess they see me as a true Aklampan and don't want me around too much. I know it has nothing to do with space because that house easily sleeps sixteen people and I'm only one person. I can't even believe this.

What's going on at that end, because this it too wild? I had heard all this prior talk about having a house big enough to hold everyone and not being separated, yet now they were separating themselves from me. Here I was so looking forward to preparing the house and spending time with them. Oh, well. Such is life. Anyway, please don't tell Emmanuel. He has enough issues with me and I'm trying not to cause any more.

AN OPEN DOOR - PRAISE IN THE ENEMY'S CAMP

7/23/00 Letter…
*God is unbelievable. Ephesians 3:20 truly came true today. God does
more than we can ask or imagine. Before I tell you about today, let me
give you a bit of background.*

*Lately, I have been going to Therese's house. She is Dossou's sister. Her
house is in an area of the village called Azonwhé. I used to sit under the
big tree near her house and visit with the people. Now that Therese has
had the twins, we usually sit at her house. I've gotten to know quite a few
people and they are excited to have me visit with them.*

*Last Sunday, Therese came to church and went home and told everyone
about church. Now, when I go there, people come to the house and beg me
to sing Jesus songs. I've, therefore, been teaching Christian songs to the
people of Azonwhé, including some voodoo chiefs.*

*On Friday, Sai informed me that Azonwhé is the largest voodoo area of
Aklampa, and I was crazy to be singing "Jesus" songs there. I knew it had
a voodoo house and that masquerade voodoo ceremonies take place by the
tree because of its open space. However, I never realized that it was the
deepest spiritual point of the village. Sai worries that if I sing about Jesus,
the voodoo will try to hurt me (as if Aklampa voodoo hasn't already
tried!).*

*Well, I refused to stop going, despite some jealous comments by my
neighbors. Also, I refused to stop singing, praying and talking about
Jesus. I've also boldly stated that voodoo is satanic and not good. I do
this in a non-offensive manner and make sure they know that I love the
people, but want to destroy their voodoo. Through God's divine way,
these people are open to me and we have a great time. Humor is key.*

*Now to today. I fasted yesterday for today's service. This morning I felt
led to anoint the front room where we meet and pray. I prayed for God to
station angels at the door and block out any and all demons, but to let the
people enter. I somehow anticipated something great today, because the
prayer was different and I felt a real battle brewing.*

*By 8:20 am, Michael had arrived in the village. He's Henry's brother who
went to school with Emmanuel and is truly a Christian. He leads a church
in another area of Benin. However, he's spoken to Emmanuel and would
like to help me start a church here. His prayer was for God to build a true*

church of Jesus Christ in Aklampa, not one that compromises the Word to appease the people.

A total of thirty-six people attended today. Eight people accepted Christ. And, all the Christians wanted to repent of past sin that they had been hanging on to and have a fresh start. What's more – four of the people to accept Christ were from Azonwhé. At least nine people from Azonwhé attended. Is God amazing, or what?! Also, I had at least two very deep voodoo members attend, one being Dossou's father's other wife who I've been inviting.

I had people sitting on chair arms, tables, a fold out bed, benches, etc. The children sat on the floor. I think its time to order benches. Each bench seats about five people and will cost about 4,000 cfa. I'm getting estimates this week.

I have no idea where some of the people came from because a group came that I've never met. Two of these people accepted Christ. God just brought the people.

At the end of the lesson, I had an open question time. One of the men from Azonwhé asked about going to heaven if you are a nice person, but don't go to church. (Sounds a lot like America.) This led to a discussion about a true relationship with Jesus versus religion/church tradition. God truly removed the blinders today. It was so wonderful.

Also, part of my invitation was very specifically about choosing to leave voodoo and fetishes. They had to choose to stop putting faith in fetishes and turn totally to Jesus. People commented that they are willing to do this. YES!!!!

Today, Satan had seven people snatched out of his lying hands. I love it. All power lies within the blood of Jesus!

Of the thirty-six attendees, six were children, four were women and the rest were men. I've invited women and told the men to bring their wives, but mostly men seem to be attending. I wonder if God is preparing a generation of men who will break off the traditions of idolatry that their forefathers worshipped and raise up men who will stand for Jesus.

This makes me think about last week's lesson on Daniel 3. I asked what they would do if the king of Aklampa told them to bow to an idol or be thrown into a fire. I even gave them the option of bowing and thinking they could just repent later. I did this to test the seriousness of their faith.

195

Their response, quoting Dossa, was "I'd tell them to lead me to the fire because I won't bow." I nearly shouted with excitement.

These are real issues they are facing and I'm so happy to hear that they would, and are, refusing to bend in their convictions. I somehow think I'm teaching survival training. For example, they have questions about what to do if their father sends them to buy a chicken that will be used for a voodoo sacrifice, or if someone brings them food that's been part of a voodoo sacrifice, or how to react to voodoo masqueraders who approach them. In this case, they used to remove their shoes and bow to the ground for them. I tell them to keep wearing their shoes and not bow to the devil.

7/23/00 Letter...
Cosmos, a member of the MAFA Benin association, is in the village doing electrical work, or leading that department, in the building of Emmanuel's house. He is visiting from Lagos. He arrived on Wednesday and stayed in this house. He's a Christian. We've become good friends. He was surprised to see how well people in Aklampa react to me. He commented that the others, referring to the MAFA Association, need to come to Aklampa and really see what I'm doing before listening to rumors. He was a great encouragement to me and I thank God for him.

A SEIZING OPPORTUNITY

7/24/00 Letter…
It's been a wild morning. I was just about to take my bath when I heard a commotion in the compound behind my house. I assumed it was an argument because the men living near me seemed to have married hot-headed women and the women are always fighting with each other.

I saw some men running to the scene which was odd. I opened my window to see what was happening. The neighbor's eleven-year-old daughter had fainted and was seizing. They were carrying her to her house located directly behind my house. I knew something was very wrong.

The Holy Spirit strongly urged me to grab my oil and go pray. My flesh didn't want to get involved because this particular family doesn't like me much and has been spreading rumors about me. However, I decided to obey God. I ran out and around my house and went into the house where they had carried her. Amazingly, people got out of the way and ushered me into the room. It was quite a sight. The girl was completely naked and covered in feces, even her face. She was seizing. Her eyes were rolled back and she was literally foaming at the mouth.

I asked her mother, a voodoo member, for permission to pray. She agreed. I anointed the girl with oil, grabbed her and began praying. I don't recall all that I prayed, but at one point, the Holy Spirit revealed that this was demonic. I began casting out demons and breaking off curses in the name of Jesus. Within one minute, she was conscious and her bodily functions were under control. I even got her to look at me and acknowledge me before leaving.

As I left their hut, I was met at the door by her father who speaks English. He is involved in many different voodoo sects, and was constantly bragging that voodoo was so wonderful. I asked him, none to nicely, if he really thinks voodoo is so good, because the kind of voodoo god he serves kills children.

I returned to the girl's home approximately 30 minutes later. She was weak but resting well and spoke to me a bit. She hadn't been sick and this has never happened to her in the past. It is definitely demonic. I wonder what was going through people's minds, especially those who understand a bit of English, as I prayed and rebuked demons. I'm sure it was a testimony to the power of God to overcome demonic forces.

I later learned that this incident was the result of a curse that one person put on the young girl's mother. These people see how horrible voodoo is, yet they follow it faithfully and "cheerfully". They are truly blind.

WISE COUNSEL

For months I was wrongly accused of having an inappropriate relationship with Dossou. I'm not sure how things changed, but believe the enemy began planting thoughts in my head and I didn't notice when my feelings began changing from a simple friendship to something more serious. I was suddenly attracted to him. We became closer and began considering a future together. Although this seems crazy now, for some reason it seemed completely logical at the time.

I began to sense an unhealthy connection to him, almost like an addiction. It was a strange feeling that is difficult to describe. I continually prayed, asking God's direction for this relationship. Following are some devotions and journal entries from May 2000 leading up to a devastating set of events:

5/11/00 Journal Entry…
My devotion was in Matthew 6. I had a wonderful prayer time last night and this morning. Oh, how I love Jesus. At one point, I felt pressure on my head and believe Jesus wants my mind. I love the peace of God. I'm going through some tough things right now, yet I have peace.

I also think it is no coincidence that Dossou has been at the farm for six days. That is God's will.

5/15/00 Devotion…
Interesting devotion in Matthew 9:35 – 10:16. 1) Jesus gave the disciples authority to cast out demons and heal every sickness and disease. He didn't say to heal only some, but every. 2) Beware of wolves who act like sheep. Be wise as a serpent and innocent as a dove. Discernment is the key.

5/22/00 Journal Entry…
I have a wild thought I want to record just to see what the future holds.

I'm reading Matthew 13, the parable of the four soils. Some seed was sown on rocky places. He instantly received it with joy. But he had no root and lasts only a short time and quickly falls away. Sounds like Dossou. He hasn't been to bible study in over a month, and when he attends, he sleeps.

Also, he has a profound effect on my life. His presence has brought jealousy, confusion, and emotionalism. Most importantly, my devotion and prayer time greatly suffers when he is around. Now that he's been at the farm, my prayer life is back on track and I see more clearly. He also tried to destroy my relationship with others who seem to pose a threat to him.

God was clearly warning me that there had been a change. Although God was using Dossou mightily in my ministry initially, Dossou wanted more and greed set in. He wanted me, not Christ living in me. I didn't realize it then, but in a desperate effort to further our relationship, Dossou began to lie to me, and had others lie for him as well, including his friends and family. I did not find out about these lies until August.

A few comments about my relationship with Dossou. Throughout my stay in Africa, the enemy used a variety of different strategies in his attempt to destroy me. One of his early strategies may have been to bring Dossou into my life. Did the enemy plan for Dossou, a high priest in voodoo, to come into my life, destroy my relationships, and bring about my downfall? I'm not sure.

However, what Satan may have originally meant for evil, God worked for the good. Dossou was the first convert to Christianity and, through his friendship, was used by God to teach me many of the inner workings of the village.

Early on, God used this relationship mightily to advance His kingdom. Dossou kept me informed of the tactics of the enemy and those trying to destroy me. He informed me of rumors of voodoo ceremonies against me, protected me from direct attacks, directly saved my life on at least one occasion when my guard attempted to kill me, warned me against eating in certain circumstances that could harm me, and chastised me when I unknowingly walked into dangerous territory. He also, on numerous occasions, took me to visit people who needed prayer and healing. He believed in the power of Jesus to heal and deliver.

Do I believe Dossou accepted Christ? Yes. Do I believe God used him mightily to teach me about the culture of the village? Yes. Do I believe he had left voodoo? Yes. Do I believe the attacks on us were real? Yes.

The following was written after I had spent extensive time seeking God's will regarding my close relationship with Dossou...

7/27/00 Journal Entry ...
God said he would have an answer for me today and he did. It came via
Cosmos. He just arrived from Lagos and sat with me to encourage me on
my mission and then spoke about decisions I need to make. I mentioned
Dossou's name and that started the ball rolling.

He informed me that people have reported to him that Dossou is lying to
me and that Dossou needs to prove the truth to me. Also, as long as the
real truth is unknown, I must keep a distance. He also counseled me that
all of Aklampa has heard what Dossou is up to and it may reflect my
ministry negatively. I can't let anything stand in the way of my work here
for God.

Also, Cosmos sees it as a potential problem when Emmanuel comes
because he won't possibly approve of this close relationship if Dossou is
deceiving me. I know he's right and I agree with him.

7/28/00 Letter...
I've prayed about it and I now want to remain in my current house while
the others are visiting. First, the house won't be painted and I'd rather
move once the house is complete.

Also, I have a small fear that all the villagers coming to see the Americans
will be difficult for me. I think I've become somewhat of a loner. When
Ojo and the others are here, lots of people come to the house, usually
looking for a handout. I find myself retreating to my room to read or
crochet. I think it will be more peaceful and I can live more normally
while they are in the village.

I guess being the center of attraction and having all eyes on me for a year
takes its toll. I now dearly relish privacy, of which I get very little. Even
when I'm in my bedroom, people shout into the window for me and some
even come up to the window to try to look inside if it is open. Yet, I can't
close the windows because I need the light and cool air. The new house is
much more secluded and quiet. I will probably miss all the activity.

7/31/00 Letter...
It has been raining every day since the rain ceremony held in the village a
few nights ago. A few voodoo members have made a point of coming to
me and bragging that voodoo has the power to bring rain. Oh, how blind
they are.

8/3/00 Letter...

Still raining every day! August first was a big holiday -- Benin's independence day. I cooked food and invited some church members to visit. Godwin and Gab arrived. It was good for them to see my ministry in action. In the afternoon, I convinced my regular chauffer to take us to the Adidemé farm for a visit. On August 1st, everyone celebrates at the farms, whereas New Years is celebrated in the village. I went in true African style - ten people traveling in one car. I had a great time.

We visited people's houses, and ate and drank lots. I drank soda, but there was lots and lots of alcohol being consumed as well. We also saw the masqueraders who travel to the farm on this holiday. The celebration is split between three major farms. Sowiangi was the largest, but I wanted to visit the family farm where I knew everyone. Besides, the Allagbé farm is nearby so I was able to see these family members as well.

THE VISIT THAT CHANGED EVERYTHING

A group of people from my church visited Benin in August 2000. Emmanuel had built a mission house in the village which was completed just prior to their arrival. The group spent approximately three weeks in Benin. They spent about three days in Aklampa.

Initially, I was so excited to have them visiting me. I couldn't wait to share my life and ministry with them. Unfortunately, things transpired very differently than I had expected. The enemy had devised quite a plan to destroy me. He nearly succeeded.

8/16/00 Letter…
I've been to Cotonou and am back in Aklampa with the Americans. I'm having a good time, but feel as if I'm juggling two lives. I sleep at Henry's house, go to the other house for breakfast, group devotion, activities and lunch. I then return to this house to rest and then spend time with my friends from Aklampa. Around 5:00 pm, I return to Emmanuel's house until bedtime. I don't want to neglect any group of people. Therefore, I'm exhausted.

On Sunday morning, my bible study was amazing. At first I thought it was going to be disastrous. My core church members spent an entire week preparing and practicing songs to sing for the Americans. They also did some serious outreach. Bible study was to begin at 10:00 am and the Americans said they'd be there. However, at the last minute, they decided 10:00 was too early for them and decided they would not attend. I was crushed and felt so sad for my obviously discouraged members. At 10:20 am, I sent a message to the group that my members had planned a special service in honor of their home church in America. They said they'd come, but to start without them.

You should have seen the sadness on their faces as they began to sing songs. I felt their pain. Also, there were over 80 people packed into the room. I decided to praise Jesus, in spite of my home church family's seemingly disregard for the ministry, and for their brothers and sisters in Christ in the village. I stood and danced, which caused others to do so as well.

You should have seen their faces brighten when the Americans finally arrived around 11:00 am. Pastor Michael interpreted and all went well. Five people accepted Christ and another five rededicated their lives to Christ. We sang songs at the end and everyone danced.

That night at dinner, Emmanuel apologized for being late to service and said I have a very fruitful ministry. He also met with me later and said he'd asked Pastor Michael to move to Glazoué so he can be a regular interpreter and assistant. Now we need to find a location because the house will not contain all the people in this growing ministry. I think the school would work. I know God will provide the space.

MOUNTING THE ATTACK

Dossou and I had grown close and spent more and more time together. I did not realize the depth of the connection until my pastor visited Africa.

When my pastor arrived in Africa, I openly discussed this relationship with him, sharing as much information as I had about Dossou. However, Emmanuel thankfully did his own research and discovered the truth – that he was already married. When I learned the truth, I was shocked. I was directed to sever all ties to Dossou and his family.

Then the enemy went wild. I was accused of having known that Dossou was married, and of lying to my pastor. I was devastated beyond words. It was as if I had been slapped in the face (Dossou's deception), and then cut through the heart (accused of lying to my pastor who was my dearest friend).

My lack of judgment would be costly – very costly. It would cause others to believe all the gossip and lies that had begun months ago. It provided "proof" to those in authority that all of Henry's forthcoming accusations must be true.

While the group was visiting Aklampa that August, the enemy attacked from multiple sides. In addition to the Dossou situation, Henry mounted his attack to bring his "prophecy" (that I would return to America in August) to pass.

When I tried to defend myself and tell the truth, things only got worse. I was strongly reprimanded. The truth contradicted the lies, and I was the one being accused of lying. Amazingly, Christians were believing non-Christian voodoo leaders!

Henry wrote me a letter while the Americans were visiting, copying Emmanuel and others. In it, he praised me for my work and noted that he had not witnessed any negative behavior on my part.

Then, after a number of meetings, he wrote a second letter a day or so later, notifying us that he could not guarantee my safety in his house any longer. The letter was received late in the evening. We were forced to move me out of his house in the middle of the night.

8/18/00 Journal Entry…

Things are so crazy that I'll have to begin with today's developments and go back later to the past few days.

Beginning at 11:30 pm, I officially moved out of Henry's house. It took two car loads and lots of people. We even carried the generator, the cat, and a 50-gallon metal water drum by hand. It is now 1:30 am, and I'm in Emmanuel's house, but I don't know for how long.

Henry came to the house and met with Emmanuel. He made lots and lots of accusations about me and accused me of spreading rumors. This was a day after writing me a letter praising me and noting that he hasn't seen me do anything negative.

Emmanuel is so angry with me that he wants me to return to the states. It is all so crazy at this point. It is so out of control that a special meeting is being called in Cotonou to sit everyone down to find out the truth.

There are so many other things that I'll just list them and detail them later:

1. Bernard (my old guard) has met with many people trying to retain employment in the new house. **Remember, this is the same guard who repeatedly tried to kill me.**
2. I am being accused of lying.

At this point, Emmanuel has lost all confidence in me.

SPIRITUAL WARFARE

As I prayed, I realized a few things, based on scripture:

1. We aren't fighting flesh and blood, but powers and principalities. This is spiritual warfare.
2. Emmanuel himself recently said my ministry is very fruitful, but doesn't seem to believe so now. A tree is known by the fruit it bears. Bad trees cannot bear good fruit.
3. People are leaving voodoo and turning to Christ. I refuse to compromise the Word to allow voodoo. The enemy is mad that I openly speak against voodoo and wants me out.
4. Rumors have been flying for months that Emmanuel is coming to take me home in August. Isn't this a huge clue that the enemy's been scheming for a long time.
5. They falsely accused Jesus as well. He didn't defend himself. If they persecuted him, they'll also persecute me.
6. "You'll be handed over to be questioned. Don't worry what you'll say. The Holy Spirit will give it to you."

My plan of action is to pray, fast, be honest, and let God win this battle. The enemy seriously wants me out of here. There have been threats made on my life. It's become so dangerous that Emmanuel is worried for my safety. However, if I have to die here, it's ok, as long as I'm in God's will.

8/19/00 Journal Entry...
Matthew 5:11-12: "Blessed are you when people insult you, persecute you and falsely say all kinds of evil against you because of me. Rejoice and be glad, because great is your reward in heaven, for in the same way they persecuted the prophets who were before you."

John 15:18-19: "If the world hates you, keep in mind that it hated me first. If you belonged to the world, it would love you as its own. As it is, you do not belong to the world, but I have chosen you out of the world. That is why the world hates you."

Matthew 10:16-22: "I am sending you out like sheep among wolves. Therefore be as shrewd as snakes and as innocent as doves. Be on your guard against men; they will hand you over to the local councils and flog you in their synagogues. On my account you will be brought before governors and kings as witnesses to them and to the Gentiles. But when they arrest you, do not worry about what to say or how to say it. At that time you will be given what to say, for it will not be you speaking, but the

Spirit of your Father speaking through you. Brother will betray brother to death, and a father his child; children will rebel against their parents and have them put to death. All men will hate you because of me, but he who stands firm to the end will be saved."

Thoughts:
- We must base the truth on the Word of God and consider the source of the information.
- I am not afraid for my physical safety.

GRIEVING THE LOSS OF A FRIEND

8/20/00 Journal Entry…
We are back in Cotonou. I totally feel like an outsider with the Americans, especially with all the garbage happening. I feel much more comfortable around Cosmos, Godwin, and the villagers.

My relationship with Emmanuel is cold at best. I feel as if he believes all the rumors and thinks I'm still secretly holding onto a relationship with Dossou and am involved in voodoo, etc. I don't think he sees that this is a spiritual attack. It is wild that he believes the lies said by a man who belongs to all the evil societies in Aklampa, yet doesn't trust a Christian whom he's personally mentored and trained.

Also, we've not even had one conversation about my life in Aklampa. He basically ignores me as much as possible.

I am grieving the loss of my relationship with my pastor, who was also my teacher, mentor, friend, and brother. I feel as if he's completely written me off. I had hoped he would be an encouragement and that we'd spend some time together. However, I believe that he has been spending all his time with Michael and wants him to take over my ministry. Would I fight for that? You bet! I was originally told that Michael would only interpret for me and nothing else. Now it seems that he's been put into a leadership position.

Emmanuel and Michael are secretly going behind my back to see if I am still involved with Dossou. They don't believe my word that the relationship has been severed. Also, I have been informed that they have given my new guard as well as a family elder permission to beat Dossou if he comes near me.

I am shocked that Dossou so blatantly lied to me, and so did his family and friends. This is not good at all. Didn't they think I would find out the truth? It's a relief that I no longer feel responsible for the well-being of his family. What a heavy burden I was carrying.

8/21/00 Journal Entry…
Today's group devotion was touching. One of the Americans led and spoke about being separate from unbelievers. I almost felt like someone had spoken to the leader and the devotion was done because of me. At first I refused to comment, but felt led to admit to the group that the Aklampa spiritual atmosphere does affect me and I have to be very careful.

209

As Emmanuel closed in prayer, I silently wept. I believe he prayed the prayer for him and me. **I believe he was also grieving the loss of our close relationship as well.**

GROUNDRULES

8/24/00 Journal Entry…
As it stands, there is a formal meeting set with Godwin and a few others to "set me straight". I'm apparently breaking cultural rules that I don't know about. I agreed that I need someone to show me the ropes. I came here with little knowledge of this culture.

Also, I've been informed that my generosity is not good because it's putting a burden on my home church. However, most of the stories are lies – such as me putting a family up in a hotel. I want to meet and get everything out and clear. I don't want these issues again.

Without my input, Michael has been hired to assist me. I'm not comfortable with him, but I'll pray about it. I can see him taking a controlling hand. I need to get very clear direction on his duties so there is no confusion. I believe he will have problems with my non-traditional ways. I don't know his views on women being called into ministry.

I found out later that he is against women in ministry and did everything possible to change my non-traditional methods.

There are a number of African church traditions that I tried to keep out of my church, such as forcing women to wear head coverings, men and women sitting on separate sides of the church, and forcing people to dress up for church. I was living in a poverty-stricken village. I was not concerned about dress. I just wanted the people to come and learn about Jesus. I was concerned with their spiritual life, not their physical appearance.

Once Michael joined the ministry, these traditions were quickly implemented. If a choir member arrived for practice improperly dressed, they were sent home to change. The girls were sent home to get proper head coverings. I had limited power to stop these changes since I had been ordered to allow his influence.

8/25/00 Journal Entry…
Yesterday was a tough day, spiritually. I feel like people are trying to break me. It took lots of energy to hold my head up and keep my mouth shut. There was a MAFA meeting that Henry was invited to, but he never arrived. He's been fired from the hospital building oversight committee. The truth of his character is being revealed.

Godwin spoke to me a bit yesterday and told me not to worry at all about our upcoming meeting. He's said that there is no problem. He also said that he and Gab will employ spies throughout Aklampa to keep an eye on Bernard so he doesn't harm me. I knew he was my biggest threat in the village. I must remember to tell my employees to watch out for him and not let him near the house.

Bernard is up to no good right now. I have been informed/warned that if I return to the village, it will cost me my life.

I spoke to my mom and told her some of the hurtful rumors that have been spread. She was great and responded, "What do you expect. The voodoo want you out and will do anything to see that happen."

8/28/00 Journal Entry…
So much has happened. Where do I begin? On Saturday, we had our meeting. Godwin, Michael, Emmanuel, the church secretary, and I were in attendance. It was an official Village Baptist Church meeting regarding the present situation in Aklampa.

The meeting began with all the issues over the past year being laid on the table. I was also informed of some of the rumors, originating from Henry:
1. That the entire village is complaining about my close connection to Dossou.
2. That I am committing sexual immorality with multiple men and the village is calling me a prostitute. **Although this was not true, and the village adored me, this comment devastated me. This comment was the most hurtful and would ring in my mind for years, even affecting my marriage.**
3. That I've been initiated into a cult and I sit among them.
4. That I know every voodoo leader and that I'm out at night with them and don't return until morning.

I was informed that 1) Henry is behind some of this mess. 2) All the people in the village are liars. They smile to your face but stab you in the back. I am not to trust anyone.

Although they admitted that the rumors are lies, I was strongly reprimanded nonetheless.

As an outcome, the following rules and guidelines now apply:
1) I cannot have a close relationship with anybody from Aklampa without the express approval of my pastor or his brother Godwin.

2) I must distance myself from Dossou's family. I am not to have any interactions with him whatsoever. **Before this, I spent the majority of my time with his family and had grown so close to them. My lifestyle would completely change.**

3) I cannot eat outside food any longer for fear of poisoning and voodoo. I must now eat at home and alone. Fina will prepare all my food in the house. **I had been accustomed to eating village food on a regular basis. I so enjoyed eating with the villagers and it saved considerable money.**

4) I am not to show any partiality to church members. My first priority is to be a missionary, not a friend. I am to treat the faithful and the non-faithful the same. I am to minister to everyone equally.

5) I am not perfect. No one is. However, if I am corrected and refuse to change, I will be dismissed. I must be open to correction.

6) I am not to forget who I am – a missionary in a 100% voodoo village.

7) I am no longer to use my own money for ministry. If there is a need, VBC will look at it and determine if it is worthy of funding. **Before now, I would use my personal money that had been sent by VBC to purchase teaching materials, benches, medicines, etc. This was all to stop.**

8) I am not to assume that I know the village better than people who were born there.

9) I am to practice humility and not be too forward. I am not to involve myself in conversations with others because I apparently say things that are not appropriate.

I asked for examples on the last two items, because I was unaware that I had offended people from Africa. I don't remember any being given. However, being raised in an American culture, I'm sure my forwardness and boldness could have been negatively perceived in a male-dominated culture. I know that women are viewed very differently in Africa. Maybe some men were unaccustomed to me offering my opinion and being confident of my beliefs.

I know that I was very forward while living in the village. I had to be. I was living in the enemy's camp trying to convert people to Christianity. I was confident of my calling and bold in my proclamations. However, I do not believe I was acting out of pride. It was impossible to walk in pride when living under such spiritually adverse and physically difficult conditions.

It was a tough and humbling meeting. I know God wants me here. And, I know my close ties to Dossou cost me dearly. The discipline isn't fun, but that's where poor choices and deception lead.

The Americans left on Sunday evening. I was happy to see them leave. Not a tear was shed.

Although I was already wounded, I felt as if I were kicked and kicked and stabbed over and over and over again. It took over six years to recover from the events of these few weeks. I don't think anybody understood the devastation.

Within a few short weeks, I had lost Dossou, someone who was very dear to me and such a great part of my life in the village. I also lost my pastor. In addition to being a pastor and mentor, he was like a brother and best friend. Oh, the pain. I can't even begin to tell you of the sorrow…

I'M STILL HERE......

8/28/00 Letter...
I'm off to the village this morning, but want to get this in the mail to you. I forgot to give it to Emmanuel.

I'll start another letter in Aklampa to recap all that's transpired while the Americans were here. To sum it up, it was nothing like I expected. I thought I'd have a wonderful time, but it was very tough because the enemy had truly been busy. There are many hurtful rumors going around, some about my relationship with Dossou. Turns out he lied about something that affects my ministry. That hurt so much. I had actually believed him, his family and friends. What a fool I was. Oh, how it damaged my reputation. Why can't people just be honest?

Anyway, it's a long story and I pray it's over. This has severely damaged my relationship with Emmanuel and that's the most painful. It will take lots of work for him to trust me again. Please pray for us. How can I be effective if my pastor is not behind me? I need to be more accountable to him so he's not in the dark regarding my ministries and activities.

One more prayer request. Pray my ex-guard out of my life. It's come to my attention that he's capable of doing anything to get rid of me. He wants me out! It's so bad that Godwin informed me that they have found secret spies to make sure he doesn't harm me.

8/30/00 Journal Entry...
I had a long conversation with a friend in the village. He assured me that the village is not saying bad things about me. They are happy that I have learned the truth about Dossou and they are upset with Dossou for hurting my reputation. If Dossou comes near me, the village has orders to beat him and send him to jail. Everyone is keeping a close eye on things. Godwin believes Dossou may even try to hurt me. However, most of the village adores me and would kill anyone who harms me.

I was also informed that the village has noted how different I am, in that I no longer go out.

Fina warned me to be very careful with people. Even a handshake can affect me through voodoo. I'm thinking its time to hire a new regular chauffeur because Dossou is working for my prior one.

The Oro voodoo came out last night. They spent most of their time around my house. Usually they pass by and go into the village. Their outing definitely had lots to do with me. No problem! I prayed and felt peace. I have no intention of running from them.

8/30/00 Letter…
No one ever said being a Christian would be easy -- or boring. Life has been very difficult since returning to the village.

I felt really strange returning. I knew I faced much – including a new home, new guard, new rules, rumors, and death threats. I've really had enlightenment on a few things. Had I known some of this earlier, I'd have saved myself much pain.

Regarding my old guard, he's keeping a pretty low profile. I've not even seen him. However, he's still spreading lies and rumors and I have been told that he's vowed to kill me if I step foot back in the village. Well, I'm back and his ego's bruised.

My new guard, Napoleon, is wonderful. He's very protective. He, Fina, Sai, and others around me make sure I'm never alone in the house and when I go out, they make sure they know exactly where I'm going. I stay in public so no one can harm me without witnesses. I also carry a walkie-talkie.

Regarding my cat, she was doing great until she went missing last Thursday evening. I have been informed that Bernard killed it and ate it as a warning and revenge. I miss my cat so much, but refuse to let people see that it affects me. I don't want a new cat, especially if people are going to kill it for revenge. I just try not to think about how she used to run out to greet me when I came home, or take a nap curled up beside me. I was really attached to her. She even used to sit under my chair at bible study. People joked that she was a Christian cat.

Regarding Dossou, oh boy. I've learned lots more about him since returning. He's lied about so many things in recent months and people kept quiet because he'd get things (like clothes and food) from me and give it to them. He convinced his family and friends to lie for him.

As it stands, he knows he cannot come near me. If he does, the villagers have directions to beat him and have him taken to jail in Glazoué. His family cannot come to my house due to their involvement in the lies.

Have I seen Dossou? Yes. Every time I go into town, he's there. It's like he knows exactly where I'm going. For example, my new guard's wife had a baby yesterday morning. As I was returning from visiting her, I passed Dossou on the road. I didn't even see him coming down the road because I had been talking to my guard and greeting a few people. Dossou said, "Welcome". I simply greeted him and kept on walking.

Also, today I took my bicycle to the buvette (a bar/restaurant that also sells limited supplies) to buy batteries. I went there directly from my house. As I pulled up, there was Dossou talking to a friend alongside the road. I ignored him and went about my business.

At the same place on the road, I greeted and thanked the man who serviced my bicycle. While doing this, Jonas, my regular chauffer, pulled up to chat with me. Dossou had been doing an apprenticeship with him. As Jonas and I visited, Dossou walked near and greeted me. I responded and then pulled Jonas to a distance to visit. I told Jonas that I received notice of a package in Glazoué and need to go, but cannot go with Jonas on a day that Dossou is with him. He let me know that would not be a problem.

After greeting a few other people, I returned home. Jonas was there to inform Fina and me that he's letting Dossou go and will not train him any longer. The entire village is in an uproar over what Dossou has done to me and Jonas wants no part of the problem.

You may think it cold how I treated Dossou. However, I had no choice. I had been deceived and hurt badly by him and his family. Furthermore, these were the conditions of my staying in the village as a missionary, which was much more important. I was committed to ministering to the village and agreed to any conditions placed on me, as long as they didn't contradict the Word of God.

So, how do I feel about all of this? First of all, I'm human. I was so sad that our relationship was severed. I truly cared for him and his family. Now, I'm angry that he lied to me. I'm also angry at myself for not seeing the warning signs and believing only what I wanted to believe. It's also been humbling to walk back into a village where people are talking about you. It's hard to keep a smile on your face when everyone asks how you are and look like they want details.

Through this entire ordeal, I praise God. He has truly been my strength. I'm holding onto Him, knowing that when this is all over, I'll have come through a little higher than before. However, a storm is never fun when you're in the midst of it.

I love the new house! It's so peaceful and my entire daily schedule is better. I took one of the dining room tables and made an office. I'm sitting here now looking out onto the road and watching people pass and return from farm. There are not many other houses near here so there's no drama. I finally feel like I am in a home. Fina prepares hot water at night and I sit in the main salon on the sofa and read and drink a cup of tea before retiring. The little things really do matter.

I thank God every day for his blessings.

USURPING AUTHORITY

8/31/00 Letter…
I woke up in a good mood, but now am not. Michael, the man hired as my interpreter, paid me a visit. He entered the house unannounced and that disturbed me. Fina, Bayou and Napoleon were not here. I told him that it is not proper to just enter the house without warning.

He then proceeded to tell me that we was told that he should move into this house when he's in Aklampa. I told him that I feel quite uncomfortable about that since no one has said anything to me. He then told me how my bible study will now be a formal church service and told me the order of worship. I vetoed that idea as well. We are moving to a more formal service which is needed because of the number of people, but I don't want a "traditional" church. I want the Spirit of God to be able to move and the people to be able to ask questions and learn.

Freda, please pray that I have some discernment regarding this man. I know he's going to be a good interpreter, but something in my spirit is so uneasy. I pray it's not me being defensive. He's a Christian and really wants to change this village for the better. However, I feel as if he has his own motives and is trying to manipulate people into getting his way.

Please don't share this information because those in authority over me seem to trust Michael 100% and I don't want any issues. Maybe I'm just too testy. Michael's one of my new "rules" so I need to carefully handle this situation. I want peace in my house and a successful ministry in Aklampa.

9/4/00 Letter…
I went through a few seriously tough days, but by Saturday evening, I was better. I'm having a real difficult time getting over the severing of my relationship with Dossou. I wish I could just say it was no big deal, but I seriously cared for him and he was such a big part of my life. We were great friends. I was also very close to his family. I'm going through a grieving process because it's as if they have died. I'm not allowed to go to their house to visit and they are not allowed here.

His sister, Therese, and the twins came to visit on Saturday afternoon. I met her on the terrace of my house. I couldn't help crying. She also cried. I had to inform her that she cannot come to my house and I cannot visit her. It was tough! Anyway, she quickly left. However, Uncle Vincent saw her arrive and became angry at me, even though I told him that I told her to leave. It was crazy.

I saw Dossou's younger brother recently, and was informed that the brother is very mad at Dossou for lying and causing this mess. Anyway, I hope the pain soon goes away. It's no fun having your family ripped away and having no human support nearby.

Needless to say, I was a mess on Saturday. I spent most of the day crying and had decided that I'd stay here until next July and then leave. I knew it wasn't God's will, but I wanted out.

OLD SCHOOL, NEW SANCTUARY

By this time, my ministry had grown and we no longer had enough seating space to meet in a house. Thankfully, the village allowed us to use one of the old school buildings as a place of worship and teaching.

On Saturday night, I was praying and felt led to go anoint the school building that we're using as a church.

I asked Sai to join me. It was about 8:30 pm. We anointed the building and prayed. I clearly felt the Holy Spirit's presence. We then walked a circle around the one room building and claimed the ground for Jesus Christ, not for voodoo. (The new voodoo, Oro, routinely meet there at night.) By the time we left, I felt renewed and my spirit was lighter.

School building where we held church services.

I returned home and as I began to pray, I heard the Oro voodoo in the bushes outside my window. I began laughing. I knew they were in for a shock when they went to the school. Well, God definitely won a battle that night. For the first time ever, they didn't go to the school. Also, they only went to one area – my guard's family compound. They were protesting the lights at my house.

I sent a message to them through my guard that if they have a problem with my lights, they need to come see me. Of course, they won't. What's even more victorious is that nearly every person in my guard's family compound attended my church today – at least twelve people.

221

We had our first church service in the school room. We had eighty-four attendees. We had a choir of six girls and seven boys. I have an usher/attendance person. My guard did child control. It all just fell into place. We were seriously short of borrowed benches, but the headmaster of the school is meeting with some people this week to ask if we can borrow benches from the school until we build our own.

I taught on Proverbs 3:5-6. It was a relaxed atmosphere where I routinely ask if people have questions throughout the lesson. One woman said she's an idol worshipper and wanted to know why she can't come to church and still worship idols. I explained how idolatry is of Satan and you cannot follow Satan and God at the same time. She said she didn't want to give up idol worship, and if my church says she has to give it up, she's ready to get up and leave the service. I told her that I'm only teaching what the bible says. I asked her to stay until the end of the lesson and if she believes I'm teaching falsely, we'll help find her a "church" to fit her desires. She agreed to stay.

I went on to explain the passage and drew an illustration that life is a path. As long as we don't know Jesus, we cannot be following God's path. I drew a path on the chalkboard with many forks and asked people if their life is similar in that the path of their life twists and problems come and they don't know where to go. I then gave an invitation – one to accept Jesus and ask him to take over in their life and another for current Christians to acknowledge they need Jesus to guide them in all their ways. Nearly every adult responded. The woman who nearly left earlier stood to accept Christ!!!

Well, as you know, my church is ruffling a few feathers. I know I have "spies" who attend and then report to the voodoo what's happening. One of the "spies" is Laman. He attended yesterday. I could tell he wasn't exactly happy with the responses. He said he had a comment at the end. He said that I shouldn't tell people they have to leave idol worship. They should be allowed to practice both and slowly leave idol worship. He also encouraged the woman and another man not to leave idol worship.

I boldly stated to him, in front of everyone, that this church refuses to compromise the Word of God. Jesus was the last sacrifice. I refuse to tell my members they can still participate in idol worship and still follow Christ. I said the devil and God are enemies. I notified him that I will not let anyone intimidate me into allowing my members to practice voodoo.

He wasn't too pleased with my response. I'm sure he's reported me by now. Even Michael commented after church that my response was great and he's heard that the voodoo know something is changing and they're afraid. HAH!!!

God is truly teaching me how to look to him for strength and He always comes through. I'd had such a humbling week, but look how God blessed on Sunday.

BANTÉ – A WAR CRY

9/5/00 Letter…
Yesterday was a crazy day in Aklampa. At around 9:30 am, I bicycled into town to purchase eggs. I knew something was drastically wrong because everyone was outside, women were upset, and the men were carrying guns. One of the nurses in the village stopped me to inform me of the situation.

There's a village called Banté which is about 40 kilometers from Aklampa. Last week there was a motorcycle accident and a man from Banté and a woman from Aklampa died. Someone stated yesterday that the people of Banté blame Aklampa for the death and want revenge. They claimed that people of Banté were on their way to Sowiangi to kill people. Sowiangi is a village 17 kilometers north that originally began as an Aklampa farm. We heard that Banté had declared war on Aklampa.

You wouldn't believe the chaos that broke forth. Men retrieved their guns and took off for Sowiangi, some by foot. People from all the farms dropped everything and came into Aklampa. They literally dropped everything and ran. People even left food on their fires. I saw women run from Aklampa to the farm to bring their families home.

People were declaring that Aklampa will obliterate Banté. One old man even stopped me and asked me to buy bullets for them. I refused, but said I'd go home and pray. These people mean business in war. For example, my neighbor didn't return from farm immediately. We asked him why not. He said he had four bullets with him and was sure to kill at least one person before they killed him. Amazing.

Well, it all turned out to be a rumor! No one from Banté came to Sowiangi. The rumor was actually started by an Aklampa man. I couldn't help but laugh at the stories of people forgetting their shoes or bikes and just taking off running to the village to safety. Or the man who spent 10,000 cfa on bullets and didn't use a one. He's quite angry.

It was wild to watch the people prepare for war. It was just like an old western film, with an African twist.

A GROWING CHURCH

9/9/00 Letter…
Life is never dull. Turns out I'm upsetting some people because I'm teaching that to follow Jesus, people must give up idol worship. They want me to compromise and say they can practice both and maybe gradually leave idol worship. No Way! People's lives are at stake. We'll see what happens tomorrow in church. By the way, praise God. The headmaster has agreed to give us all the benches we need until we get permission and funds from America to build our own. I wrote Emmanuel on this so I'm sure it will work out fine.

This afternoon begins my first "New Beginner's Class" for new Christians. It will be three weeks long and meet each Saturday after choir rehearsal. Week one will explain their decision to accept Christ. I want to make sure people understand and are serious about their decision. Week two will explain prayer, bible devotion, and putting faith in Jesus to be their new guide.

Week three will specifically deal with leaving the past, specifically voodoo practices. I'm still praying about the exact outline, but this will be a biggie. So much has been ingrained into them since birth. It's important for them to claim freedom in Christ from all past bonds. I intend to expose some of the lies of the enemy – such as "once initiated into a sect, there is no way to leave, even if it involved blood".

I also plan to teach them how important it is to get rid of all idols, fetishes, and music associated with voodoo. Sai said he has heard of other churches having members throw the stuff into the river. I feel led to burn them so they are totally destroyed – no selling them or giving them to someone else. I'm thinking this "ceremony" could be a fourth week of graduation. I'm still praying about this because I don't want to take it lightly. I know I'll be attacked from the enemy on this one, so I have to make sure I am under God's direction and cover.

Guess who came to visit? Cyrille. Remember him and all the problems I've had with him in the past. He came by to greet me and asked for my permission to come to church again. He says he'd like to leave voodoo, but sees no way out because his father refuses to let him out. His father is the Oro chief as well as chief of a few other sects. I told him that if he's serious about coming to Jesus, he can truly get out. I need to be VERY discerning on this issue because I don't believe he really wants out of voodoo. His visit had other motives.

225

Here's an ironic incident. As Cyrille was visiting, my front terrace light burned out. Cyrille was the tallest person present so he changed the bulb. He's a member of Oro and the Oro are upset about my lights. Yet, one of their own members wound up changing the bulb. God sure has a sense of humor.

8:10 pm...
Pastor Michael never arrived to teach the class. Therefore, we had to postpone the New Beginners Class until next week. I had ten people present, but no one who spoke English well enough to translate. I'm thinking about going through the three lessons with Michael and Sai so Sai knows them well enough to aid me if Michael isn't here for the classes. These classes are important and I hate to postpone them. I felt bad because one attendee had traveled from the farm just for the class.

I had a bit of fun adventure today. Jonas, the chauffer, stopped here on his way to Glazoué. He dropped off his wife to visit with Fina. I told Jonas I wanted to drive. He handed over the keys. He hasn't seen that I can drive, but he's heard that I am able. We took off and he said I should go to Glazoué with them. I said I couldn't because they're not returning until morning. I have class and church and I hadn't prepared. About three miles out, I stopped the car to turn around. Jonas refused to go back and said I should walk back. I laughed at him. He hailed down a motorcycle and some strange man brought me home. Jonas knew him and assured me my safety.

As I returned, the men laughed, but the women cheered that this woman can drive. I've only seen one other woman drive in Aklampa. You don't even see many women on bikes or motorcycles, except as passengers.

9/13/00 Letter...
Sixty-one people attended church on Sunday. It was a tough service because Michael again did not show up to interpret. Fina had to interpret and she doesn't understand things well. At one point, I had to have Sai interpret by speaking "Fronglais" (that's my own language of combining French, English and Fongbe). I've still not heard from Michael who's been hired to interpret each week. I hope all is well.

I've decided I like my new neighborhood. I have only a few neighbors and they are quiet and friendly. The people staying with Uncle Vincent are very nice and humble. Their children are well-behaved. The father is a school teacher.

Every afternoon I teach Sai English. It's amazing how quickly he's learning. He's learning to speak and read English. I usually have a few others who join in the learning.

9/17/00 Letter...
Seventy-nine people at church today. Thank God that Michael arrived to interpret. Sai, Ayena and I fasted today for all the sickness in our church. We also had a healing prayer time during service. The three of us met before church to pray and read scripture. After praise and worship, we had our sick members come forward. We anointed them with oil after reading scripture. I prayed for the first two people and then Ayena took the lead for three people. Sai then led for three and I took the last. There was no confusion and it flowed so smoothly. The people were all standing in a bunch, some sitting, but God led us to the same person as a group.

Oh, how wonderful to have people to minister with me. There was no pettiness or jealousy, just eager ministry. It's wonderful to see these two young Christians being bold in their walk. If a church member is sick, the gather other faithful members and go pray for that person – sometimes twice per day. Also, by Friday or Saturday, they're asking what scripture I'll be teaching so they can study the passage.

AN UNWELCOME VISIT

Yesterday morning I went to the school/church to sweep it out as I do every Saturday morning. As I was working, Dossou appeared at the window/open wall. He greeted me. I initially greeted him and then ignored him. He didn't leave so I thanked him for lying to me and causing me so much trouble. He didn't have much to say. He was there less than two minutes when a child came to help me. Dossou sneaked away, thinking nobody saw him.

Not only did someone see him, they walked to Uncle Vincent's farm to "report" me. I was summoned to Vincent's house late yesterday and questioned. Vincent was angry at me and asked why I am still talking to that boy. I explained my conversation with him and swore that I initiated nothing. I had even reported the incident to Fina earlier in the day.

This mess is crazy. I'm tired of no one trusting me. Never in my life have I been in a situation where I was being "watched" and distrusted. No matter how I try, Vincent, Michael, - everyone - thinks I'm up to no good. I've totally changed my movement and lifestyle in that I never go into town alone. If I do, I carry a walkie-talkie and I report exactly where I'm going and when I will return.

Before, I'd routinely go out alone for a walk or visit, or to work with villagers and minister to them. Not anymore. Most days, I don't even go out because I can't think of a "necessary" place to go that would be allowed. Yes, I feel like a prisoner at times. They say it's for my protection, but that's not their real motive. Last time I checked, God was doing a good job of protecting me.

So, how am I emotionally regarding Dossou? That's tough too. I don't want him back as a friend. He lied about an important issue. Yet, I wish I could say that I feel nothing. I have really tough days. He was such a large part of my life in Aklampa. I had someone to eat with, laugh with, and just visit with. I miss that interaction so much.

I also grieve that this friendship was so costly to so many people: his family, my ministry, and especially my relationship with Emmanuel. What a costly error in judgment.

Freda, remember the close of our last telephone conversation. You said that you truly believe that I'm called here and you trust me. You have no idea how your encouragement has helped me. Over the past two to three

228

weeks, it's been that remark that has given me the courage to stay here and pray through this storm. God uses you mightily. Thank you soooo much.

9/19/00 Letter...
You won't believe this. I know God is truly at work in Aklampa. The prefect (chief magistrate) of Glazoué arrived in Aklampa yesterday and outlawed Oro and the masquerade voodoo! Can you believe it!? I've specifically been praying against them and have even been burdened to pray for some of their specific members. This ruling takes away the main voodoo sects for young adult men. God is so awesome!

Also, three of their members greeted me this morning. They came asking for their mother who was injured over two weeks ago and has a very sore knee. They've tried everything else. I read James 5:13-16, anointed her with oil and prayed. You bet I prayed for their salvation and release from voodoo as well. I know they understood some of it because they speak a little English.

Turns out all of Aklampa has heard what Henry and Bernard tried to do to me in August. At lunch in Glazoué, a chauffer commented that he knew they want me either out of the village or dead. The conversation began when he asked why I no longer eat food out in Aklampa. I responded that it was because 1) it often makes me sick and 2) people fear poisoning. He responded, "Henry and Bernard". I hadn't made any reference to them at all and had no idea he would know anything about it. I have to laugh because it is so evident that they totally failed and have been shamed. God got victory again!

I also found it interesting that, just a few months later, Bernard, who continually attempted to harm one of God's chosen, had his entire cashew crop burst into flames, ruining his income source for years to come. I never retaliated, but chose to trust God.

"It is mine to avenge; I will repay. In due time their foot will slip; their day of disaster is near and their doom rushes upon them."
Deuteronomy 32:35

BATHING WITH COWS

9/19/00 Letter…
OK, now it's time to laugh. Let me tell you about my journey to and from
Glazoué. I had a package at the post office that I needed to retrieve from
Glazoué. I now travel via motorcycle because it is much quicker, cheaper
and more fun. We travelled via the road through Ashanti, which is a
different route than the one in front of my house.

The road was horrible! The rains had made the muddy roads impassable.
At some points, I had to walk because even the motorcycle couldn't find
dry passage. It was quite the adventure. We thought the road would only
be bad the first six kilometers and then be much better and passable.
However, we were stopped by another motorcycle coming from Glazoué
and were told that there was another stretch that was worse. I thought,
"No way". I was wrong.

For a two kilometer stretch, the road was a virtual mud hole. At one point,
I dismounted the motorcycle to walk half a kilometer. I needed traction so
I took off my thongs and walked barefoot through the mud to the very edge
of the road at the edge of the bush. I still had mud squishing through my
toes, but I had some traction. Along the trek, there was a truck stuck in the
mud. The men would go and get branches and lay them on the road for
traction and then push the truck a few meters and start all over again.
However, they had a chuckle seeing a white woman walking barefoot
through the mud.

Once we made it through the mud, we drove to the nearest stream along
the road. We climbed down its bank and washed our legs, feet, arms,
shoes, etc. in the muddy stream. Thank God I wore a nylon sweat suit over
my shorts outfit. Once I arrived in Glazoué, I took off the sweat suit and
was relatively clean.

Anyway, as we 'bathed' in the stream, a man led his herd of cattle across
the stream. He smiled and waved. It's not every day that he sees a white
woman bathing in the stream where he was herding cattle!

Needless to say, we took another route home. This was another adventure.
Not ten minutes into the ride, the spark plug caused problems and the
motorcycle died. We worked on it, but there was a wiring problem.
Another cycle came along and my chauffer asked him to give me a ride to
the next village's mechanic and drop me off to wait while he pushed the
cycle.

*So, here I was on a stranger's motorcycle riding to the nearest village.
Then, I sat at a motorcycle mechanic's hut until my driver arrived. I was
safe and had no problems.*

*After repairing the bike, we were off. Within two or three kilometers, the
cycle began acting up again. I thought he'd stop in Wedémé at a
mechanic, but we kept going. Right past Wedémé, we had to stop again
due to a problem with the wiring leading to the accelerator handle bar.
He undid the wire and manipulated it manually with one hand, pulling on
the cord for gas while steering the bike with the other hand.*

*There were two problems with this scenario: 1) It takes lots of strength to
hold the cord, and 2) You need two hands to maneuver through the many
muddy spots. It was a tough trip for my driver, but we arrived home
safely. He's an amazing driver and always puts my safety first. He's not
even a formal chauffer. I'd never let anyone else carry me on a motorcycle
to Glazoué with these roads. Most drivers are too careless.*

*Anyway, I kept thinking that this adventure is one that should have been on
video because it was absolutely wild. A definite journal entry!*

MORE DEATH

9/21/00 Letter…
It's been a sad morning. Right after we held morning prayer at my home,
a car sped past. People began crying. The mother of some of my church
members died. She's young and has four children under the age of fifteen.
I'm quite close to two of her children. She took 'medicine' to abort a
pregnancy and it killed her.

Right now, I'm waiting for Fina to bathe and we're going to visit the
family. The woman is Sai's sister-in-law. She's also the aunt of my
motorcycle chauffer. Jonas, my regular chauffer, just stopped here. All he
could do was cry. It is difficult to see grown men cry. I think this is going
to be a very tough day.

9/24/00 Letter…
The funeral ceremony was difficult. Although the baby had aborted, the
placenta had not passed. The doctor's had already warned her against the
procedure because she was over four months pregnant. She took the
medicine on Wednesday to try to lose the placenta. When complications
arose, her brothers rushed her to Savalou to a hospital. She died there.
Her husband didn't know that she was pregnant nor that she had aborted
the baby. He found out she had died when they returned to the village
Thursday morning.

I spent Thursday and Friday with the families. I am exhausted. I tried not
to cry, but how can you not cry when a fifteen-year-old boy cries out for
his mom. He was so broken. He just sat with me and sobbed and sobbed.
Also, to see people openly sobbing is difficult when they're the people
closest to you.

The burial was Friday morning. We took photos of the family with the
body. It's sad that the only photo these children will have of their mother
is her dead body with a piece of white tape over her mouth. After they put
her in the casket, the family asked me for prayer. They had to ask the king
for his permission (for this break in African tradition) because she's a
relative of his. He agreed. We gathered our church members and I
prayed with the husband and children. To my knowledge, the woman was
not saved. The husband had accepted Christ the Sunday that the
Americans were visiting Aklampa.

After nailing the casket shut (imagine hearing the hammering of a casket
being nailed shut – not a joy), they placed it in the back of a small truck

and drove to the cemetery. At least 400 people followed, most on foot. I travelled in Jonas' car so I didn't have to make the long trek on foot. Jonas cried the entire journey. At the cemetery, people reflected and read poems. They then lowered the casket into the ground and poured the dirt. We drove back to the family compound where we sat for some time until the king announced that the ceremony was over and we could leave.

On a lighter note, yesterday was my one year anniversary of being in Aklampa. I invited eight friends over for Coke and bingo. They loved playing bingo. It was a riot. They were here for only about ninety minutes, but it was nice. They were almost all Christians and they initiated to open the evening with prayer. How touching.

What a year! Overall, it was great, except for the last month. Life for me is certainly different from a year ago.

By the way, this house has too many bugs. There is netting on the windows, but it doesn't stop the smaller bugs. There are these tiny beetles that are everywhere at night. I think there's so many bugs because we're next to the bush. For example, as I ate dinner, three of these things dropped into my plate! If I die in this village, it will be of insanity over these bugs! Oh well, a new diet plan – no dinner.

PAIN AND BITTERNESS

10/5/00 Journal Entry...
I'm reading Job. Job went through a tough time, yet never blamed God. Even all his friends turned on him and accused him of sinning. I can really relate to him.

I am hurt beyond words by people who were so close to me, and now have falsely accused me. I had expected their visit to be uplifting and encouraging. All my expectations were shattered. Although I was completely open and honest, and shared everything I knew, it proved to blow up in my face.

I feel so much bitterness. I expected encouragement and support. However, I was given discouragement and accusations. Some people don't believe I'm called to be here. I feel as if I'm being met with unforgiveness. How quickly people forgot my integrity, character and service.

I am now expected to live by man-made rules, which hinders God's will. An example is that I'm to separate myself from "those" people, referring to people in the village. I'm not to have any confidences and close friends with anyone in the village. Do others in ministry live by that standard? Is that even possible?

Before, I was so happy spending time freely getting to know people. Yes, my close ties do Dossou damaged me. However, what about all the other people? I was free to visit with people and minister to them. Now, I am a prisoner. Whereas I believe the bible teaches we are all equal, I have been directed that we are not equal and I am to separate myself from "them".

Lord, I have so much pain. I need serious healing. I would also like you to help me forgive and forget. I know Satan would love to destroy this relationship with my friend in America. I don't want that to happen. Please help me.

Also, I am a bit overwhelmed at how unhappy I've been. I want to go out, but don't want to give anyone reason to doubt my walk with you.

Have my close ties to Dossou killed my ministry in Aklampa? Is the punishment for my being gullible and making a poor judgment call that I should go home a failure?

God, why are you so quiet? Have you turned away from me? Please don't do that. Gina

10/10/00 Letter...
You asked if I believe Dossou gave up voodoo and accepted Christ. I don't know how to answer that. I really do believe he did. However, he's not been to church since I returned to Aklampa. People (and Dossou as well) have said that he's afraid because everyone is threatening to beat him if he comes near me. However, they've told him there's no problem for him to come to church. Please pray for his walk with Christ. I asked Sai secretly if he thinks Dossou left voodoo, and he believes he really did.

I really miss Dossou. I lost someone to whom I could tell anything and with whom I could pray. Oh, how I wish we had remained friends. I know he's lied about so many things in an effort to get closer to me. It backfired and this has been painful for everyone involved.

I have an interesting neighbor. My neighbor attends my church, but his wife is in voodoo. There are days when she's going to some ceremony and becomes possessed. She squawks like an animal. Everyone gets out of her way because they realize it's a voodoo demon. Part of me wants to lay hands on her. The woman is a trip.

She has a daughter from a prior marriage who is also up to no good. As an example, I was sick on Monday. Fina had gone to the market. I heard the front door open and close, but no announcement. I knew it wasn't Fina so I walked out to see the girl standing in the salon. Now, no one is supposed to enter the house without permission. She asked how I was feeling and touched my head and arm. I felt something was amiss. I told her that Fina wasn't here so she had to leave. As I shut the door and walked to my room, I saw her watching me through the window. I walked straight to my room, grabbed my oil, anointed myself and bound any curse that may have been brought.

When Fina returned, I reported the incident and even reported what the girl was wearing. Fina went to talk to her and she denied even coming here. We then knew for sure that she was up to no good.

NEW BEGINNER'S CLASS

I wanted to tell you about my New Beginner's Class on Saturday. It's for new Christians, but I'm asking all church members to take it. It's only three sessions. The first two sessions deal with understanding their decision to accept Christ, prayer and bible devotion. The third session deals specifically with leaving voodoo. I knew this was going to be sticky because that's the last thing the devil wants me to boldly teach. I teach about the power of Jesus' blood over any past voodoo initiations. I dispelled some of Satan's lies such as being committed to a sect for life with no way out, as well as the lie that ancestors coming back to inhabit live bodies.

I expected five students to show up who had completed the first two classes. All five attended, and so did at least twenty others. They weren't invited as such. Many of them stayed after choir rehearsal. Most were youth. My first thought was, "Oh, boy, my secret tactic will be no secret." Then I realized how important the message is to the youth. At one point, I asked for a show of hands for how many people had been initiated into a voodoo sect before accepting Christ. Nearly every hand went up – even for some boys as young as ten years old. I almost started crying. Satan grabs them as babies.

I very plainly spoke about relinquishing any supernatural power they hold, asking Jesus remove any demons that influence them. I also said they must get rid of all voodoo fetishes, idols, music, etc. because it gives the enemy legal ground to be present. I also said they can't slowly leave voodoo. Either they follow Jesus or follow voodoo, but not both.

One of the young men had grown close to John, one of the young American boys who visited in August. Since John's witness to this young man, he has been totally faithful to every meeting, class, service, and choir practice.

It was a great class and we sat for a long time answering questions. Even after the rain began to fall, people refused to leave. By the time we left, I had to walk through water nearly up to my calves to get home. Was it worth it? YES!

10/22/00 Journal Entry…
It has been a spiritually interesting twenty-four hours. We decided to do a prayer walk last night. There were five of us. We set the time for 10 pm.

However, at around 8:00 pm, we heard Oro voodoo preparing to come out – yes, they have been allowed back.

Sai quickly went to Michael's house to notify him and said we wanted to pray at 9:00 pm, and pray that they don't come out. Everyone gathered at my house and we decided the prayer focus which included claiming the road in front of my house which is at the entrance to the village. The prayer walk was powerful. I feel like it was the beginning of walls crumbling. It was interesting to watch people's reactions to our prayer. People readily recognized what was happening.

Interestingly, we came across the leader of the Oro voodoo. He greeted me, but I didn't respond because I was in deep prayer.

In victory, Oro did not come out last night!

This morning as we gathered for daily prayer in front of my house, two men came over to join us after we began to pray. One man I didn't know, but the other was an Oro leader! God works in mysterious ways.

SICKNESS AND DEPRESSION

11/1/00 Journal Entry…
It's been a rough few days. What's new! On Monday, I became very sick with a 102 degree fever, diarrhea and vomiting. Kiki took me to the nurse in Affinzungo who gave me two painful injections, and put me on malaria medication. It was a tough day, but within hours of the injection, I began to feel better.

However, in light of how sick I was, we decided that I should travel to Cotonou on Tuesday morning. I slept most of the way. I'm tired and my head aches, but I feel a bit better. I know some of this is stress-related.

I spoke to my pastor this morning. We had a long visit. I broke down and shared with him how I feel as if I've failed him and God. He denies it. I told him how important he is to me and how I've let him down. He doesn't see things that way at all. He said that he even preached about me yesterday. He said many Christians never lead another person to Christ, and to look at how much I've done.

I even shared how I felt like giving up, but couldn't sit under him as a failure. He reminded me that God never fails. I countered that I've failed God. Emmanuel denies that.

He's worried about my mental health. So am I. He says that if I need to come home, he'll come get me next week! That's commitment.

He also shared that he never wants anything to come between us. I told him how much I value and love him and Freda.

So, what do I want? I want peace, but don't know how to get it back. I want to please God and Emmanuel. I want somebody that I can lean on and trust in this village. I want to turn Aklampa upside down for Christ. I want an effective and fruitful ministry. I want to succeed in God's eyes and my pastor's eyes.

During this time, I slipped into a deep depression. I spent days on end laying on my bed and just letting the tears flow out of my eyes until I ran out of tears. I wept and wept. I felt completely hopeless. I remember times that I would pray for God to take his hand off of me and let me die. Yes, it was that deep. I just wanted to end life. I never considered suicide, but realized that if God let me go, it wouldn't take

long for the enemy to take me out. These were the darkest days of my life.

11/2/00 Journal Entry…
I spoke with Freda this morning. She believes I was being affected by a spirit of oppression and depression. She prayed for me. She also shared that God knows I'm not perfect and knew the mistakes I would make, but He still called me. I never thought of that.

She reminded me to look at David – a man after God's own heart, yet he had committed adultery and murder. Still God loved him and used him mightily.

I have to stop condemning myself and get back on track. She told me to look at what God's done in the village through me and realize that God still wants me here.

MINISTRY AND MANGO TREES

11/5/00 Journal Entry...
Today was amazing. We started our church at Mangavisa (a farm located about 7 kilometers from the village).

Let me describe the setting. We sat outside on a bench while many sat on the ground or stood. We sat under the shade of two mango trees. Even though the temperature was nearly 100 degrees and very hot, it was cool in the shade due to a light breeze. The people came as they were: no bath, children with no clothing, topless women, etc. It was wonderful. About fifty people, mostly young men and children, attended.

I taught a simple message of Jesus. They asked good questions regarding sin as it relates to Adam and Eve and what rules need to be followed to accept Christ. I explained John 3:16 and 14:6. During the invitation to accept Christ, six people initially said they wanted to accept Christ. I asked them to come forward for prayer. They came forward and dropped to their knees without even being told to do so. Many others followed. A total of twenty-three people knelt to accept Christ into their life.

I prayed and had them repeat a prayer to make sure they understood their decision. It was so beautiful and I was so honored to be present for such an experience. I never dreamed that I'd be sitting in the bush teaching the bible under a mango tree. Wow!

We also visited a farm about two kilometers further down the road. They also want us to start a church there. We're going there next Sunday and then they'll join us at Mangavisa thereafter. Many of them are from a different tribe and speak a different language.

A DECEPTIVE VISIT

11/11/00 Letter...
What a day! It actually began yesterday evening. I was sitting on my deck listening to music when Dossou and another chauffeur's apprentice drove by and honked. Dossou motioned that he'll return. I haven't seen him in over a month. I went in the house. Soon I heard a horn honk and thought it was the chauffer delivering my fuel. It was an apprentice. He initially mentioned my fuel so I thought they were there to deliver fuel. The apprentice got out of the truck to talk to me.

He then said he didn't have any fuel. I told him to tell his boss to bring my fuel today. Before the apprentice could speak to me about his reason for visiting, Vincent walked up. The apprentice refused to speak, got back in the vehicle and took off. Vincent confirmed my suspicion that Dossou was in the vehicle.

While I was away at the farm today, a different apprentice came to my house to visit me. Fina said I was gone until noon. He said he had a letter for me and left quickly, yet Fina saw no letter. Fina told me to be careful today because something was strange about the visit.

After returning home and bathing, I felt STRONGLY led to anoint myself with oil and claim Psalm 91 over my life. I needed it. Not an hour later, I had a visitor -- Dossou's brother from Savalou. I was alone so I asked Rosalind, Vincent's daughter, to join us, both as an interpreter and witness. His brother asked what happened between Dossou and me. I told him. He tried to defend Dossou and his family by claiming that Aklampa lied to Emmanuel and me about Dossou. I clearly explained that Dossou brought the brunt of the problem by lying about his past. I said Emmanuel would not have cared about what Aklampa said about him. Emmanuel wanted truth and Dossou lied.

His brother literally begged me to forgive Dossou and not forget him. He said over and over how much Dossou cares and wants to be my friend again. I said I no longer wish to reconcile the relationship. I forgive him, but there would be no rekindling of any friendship.

It was a wild visit. At one point, Rosalind stepped out of the room and the brother asked me to sneak to Affinzungo to meet Dossou at his grandmother's house. I refused. I made it very clear that no one is forcing me not to see him. If Dossou wants to see me, he should come to church and meet with Michael and me.

241

Now, here's the wildest thing. At one point, Dossou's brother asked me if I was sleeping at night. There's no way anyone could know that I wasn't sleeping well. Only Fina, Sai and one other person know, and none of them would have said anything. I clearly believe that my sleeplessness and confusion were caused by a curse of some type. Also, why did God tell me to anoint myself? He knew what was going to happen.

Well, I reported everything to Fina and Vincent. Fina is upset and Vincent's planning to go to the Allagbé compound and inform them that the family is to stay away from me if they want to avoid jail time.

This is too wild. Now onto other news.

I've spent the last four mornings working on the farm. It is peanut harvest time. I'm helping Sai. We walk the two kilometers to his farm, straight through the bush. I sit on the ground and pull the peanuts from the plants. I stay until noon. It gets too hot and I'm not about to get sunburned. I'm already really tan.

11/11/00 Journal Entry...
I discussed this Dossou situation with Michael. He opened up and shared some things about Emmanuel's August visit. Emmanuel was convinced that the Allagbe's had done some ritual on me because I clearly wasn't thinking normally nor seeing things correctly. At this point, I'd agree.

I also told Fina about Dossou's visit. She is livid! She's ready to have him arrested and sent to Glazoué.

I'm going to be open with everyone about everything so there will remain peace in my house. I do not want politics or division.

This whole mess makes me realize how important prayer cover is.

11/12/00 Letter...
My problem continues...

Dossou's now claiming he never stopped here, while at least three people saw him, and that his brother never came here with the intent of discussing Dossou. Someone's threatened him and he's angry and threatening to come to my house, claiming he doesn't care if he is shot and killed. I decided this is enough! I told Michael this morning that we need to meet with Dossou instead of listening to third-party information, threats and lies. *I want this issue resolved and don't think it will be over until people hear directly from me. Dossou needs to clearly understand the situation.*

After our church services today, Michael and I went to Dossou's house. He wasn't home. We left a message that we want to meet with him on Thursday when Michael returns to Aklampa. We told him to not listen to rumors, but to be calm until Thursday.

Satan is having a ball and I intend to deal with this matter openly and honestly so God will get the victory.

To top things off, the apprentice with the letter returned. There was a real letter, but he also wanted to talk about Dossou. He begged me not to sever ties with Dossou. He also told me that Dossou needs money. Aha! That's why all this is coming up. I told him there will be no money. However, then I said that if Dossou really wants to see me, he will be at Thursday's meeting.

We had a great afternoon service at the farm. We travelled to a small farm about one mile past Mangavisa. The plan is to have these two farms join us as one church at Mangavisa, but we promised to go to the other farm today. They wanted to hear what we believe to see if it is in-line with their beliefs. Amazingly, nearly the entire farm is Christian. They're tied to the Assembly of God church but must travel many miles to attend church services in a different village. This farm doesn't speak Fongbe. It's an entirely different tribe and language. Therefore, they have to travel long distances to go to church. However, they are interested in joining us.

I taught in English, Michael translated into Fongbe, and a tribe member who speaks Fongbe translated into their language. It was an unforgettable experience. At the end, they asked me to sing a song in my native tongue. They then sang a song for me in their language. I loved it. I wish I had had a video camera to capture the dance and song. It was very touching.

The plan is that we will meet each week at Mangavisa. If they join us on any Sunday, we will interpret into the two languages. They even had their pastor from the church present. I didn't know who he was until the end of the service, but was getting lots of "Amen's" from him. For a minute they got stuck on denominations, but I stopped that trick of the enemy. We're not sheep stealing or asking anyone to be Baptist. We're here to teach the bible to God's people and build the Kingdom, not a denomination.

By the way, over eighty people were present today. It was strange to see this group of Christians in the bush surrounded by all non-Christian farms. These people had bibles and know their Word. Amazing!

Needless to say, I'm exhausted. Four days farming and a full Sunday. I think I'm not going to farm tomorrow. Fatigue!

MUFFIN MIX

There were times during my stay when finances and food supplies were very tight. Sometimes, money had been sent, but there was a delay in the delivery of the money to Aklampa. To make matters worse, the exchange rate decreased while prices for fuel and water were greatly increasing. Therefore, my money didn't go nearly as far as it had the previous year, and my church had limited resources.

Fortunately, my mother sent care packages which included food. She sent Vienna sausages, potato chips, candy (a favorite of the villagers), as well as muffin mixes. There were no ovens in the village so I had no way of baking muffins. However, on more than one occasion when the food supply was scarcely low, I mixed the muffin mix with water and ate it as a meal. Not the most nutritious, but I survived.

The care package food also came in handy near the end of my stay when my house help turned against me. For reasons I am still unaware of, her attitude suddenly changed. I began to notice multiple (new) voodoo markings on her body.

One day she handed me a bowl of soup, prepared with spaghetti noodles, water and chicken broth. I looked into my bowl to see hundreds of ants in the soup. When I noted this, she had no reply and walked away, assuming I should go ahead and eat it. Another day for muffin mix.

There were also other times when I sat down to eat and distinctly heard the Holy Spirit tell me not to eat what was placed in front of me. I knew the food had been tampered.

I don't know how many times I ate food that had been poisoned or tampered. I prayed over each meal and ate, unless the Holy Spirit directed me to abstain.

There were other times that she simply refused to cook for me.

Sometimes during this difficult time, I sent a close friend to secretly buy me food in the village. I knew I had been ordered not to eat village food, for fear of poisoning. However, I was in a tough situation. I needed to eat. This incensed Fina even more.

Before August, I had often purchased and ate food prepared in the village. Locally prepared food never bothered my digestive system, except for one instance that I purchased some rice with a red sauce from a woman in the village. I didn't know that the sauce had been prepared with the equivalent of bleach. Villagers can handle this chemical, I didn't do so well. Other than that instance, I had loved these foods immensely.

A MOTHER'S WORRIED PRAYER

11/17/00 Letter...
I've decided not to go to Cotonou for Thanksgiving. There's no money. I messaged Ojo to call Emmanuel and have him call mom and tell her that all is well and I'll try to call over Christmas, if I can leave Aklampa.

Regarding the Dossou saga, Michael and I went to meet with him. He did not show up. However, he came to the house this morning. I told him that Michael would be back on Saturday and to go meet with him. I cannot meet with Dossou alone. I must say that Dossou looked rough. Even Fina said he looks sad. Overall, I praise God because when I saw him, I felt nothing, except healing. Thank you Jesus.

Dossou finally met with Michael and me on Saturday evening. He profusely apologized for lying and we discussed the issues. He wants to be friends again and be able to visit me. I said that is not possible because it would negatively affect the ministry. However, I agreed to do what I could to restore him in the village. People are treating him very harshly and literally threatening to kill him. I will be civil with him when we cross paths in public so people realize the issue is settled.

We also spoke much about his salvation and the need to attend church. He came back to church yesterday. We were standing outside when he arrived. You should have seen the stares and gasps. I walked over and greeted him and so did Michael. Michael's going to try to disciple him. God's timing is perfect because I couldn't have handled this last month. Healing is wonderful. Also, ironically, I was teaching on Matthew 18:15-20 – forgiving a brother who repents. Coincidence? I think not.

A few days later...
I've made a new friend, Gilles. He lives next door and was the mason on Emmanuel's house. He's now building a new school in another part of the village. He's been in the Celestial Church for 16 years. He was very helpful to me last month when I was going through such a tough time. Since he didn't grow up in the village, he doesn't think like a local villager. Therefore, he was very helpful in putting some things into perspective. He quoted lots of scripture which helped.

During my time of such deep depression, my mom was sensing that something was very wrong and could do nothing but pray since there was no way to contact me. She prayed that God would send someone into my life to comfort me.

Gilles started to visit me each day. He sensed my deep sadness and would stop by to encourage me and began quoting scripture. We soon grew close and became interested in each other.

Per the "rules" that had been laid out in August, I contacted my pastor's brother to discuss this interest and received his approval to pursue a relationship with this man. In retrospect, given my mental state at the time, I had no business getting into a relationship.

However, God has an interesting way of working things out. After receiving approval to have a relationship, we began a relationship. My pastor approved of our marriage, but for our safety, requested it be kept secret from the village, until after my return to America. Everyone agreed this was best. Various families in the village believed I should belong to their family, and to have married a member of an unrelated family could be potentially dangerous for members of Gilles' family.

RENEWED HUNGER

12/1/00 Letter to Emmanuel and Freda...
God has really been dealing with me for the past two weeks. It began with a renewed hunger for His Word. Everything seems new, even scriptures I've read over and over. New truths are unfolding. For example, I'm reading Acts for the third time since August. God used Peter mightily and even miraculously freed him from prison. This wasn't new to me, but in meditating, I realized that this is the same Peter who denied Jesus three times! Still, after the denials, God used Peter. Is that mercy, or what? I've been a Christian for six years and am truly beginning to understand mercy. It is so unwarranted.

As you know, these have been some really rough months. They were definitely the worst months of my life. I was seriously spiritually oppressed. At times, I truly wanted to not go on. I felt hopeless.

November has been a month of supernatural healing. I truly needed Emmanuel's insight and prayers. Satan had convinced me that Emmanuel was fed up with me and our relationship was destroyed. Where did that leave my ministry? It was horrible. I praise God that Emmanuel exposed the devil's lies. People underestimate the importance of a pastor's support. God used him to expose these lies, and begin a healing process.

Freda, you were invaluable. You correctly recognized that I was under spiritual attack, especially by a spirit of depression. When we prayed on the telephone, I immediately felt a spiritual burden lift. I was my old self again. I could laugh again. Thank you so much.

I've just begun re-reading a book that has been a blessing. I want more of God! I hunger for his divine presence. I realize my focus here has been wrong. I got caught up in worrying about getting people in the church. I can get a hundred people in a church, but if the presence of God is not there, they won't last.

In the pressure to establish a "real" church, I've developed a program driven church, not Holy Spirit driven. Every week, it's the same format. I go and ask the Holy Spirit to teach and guide us, but do I really let Him do it? I want more! I want real worship!

I've been frustrated because the choir is not serious, especially the women. Every week they come forward to accept Christ! I'm starting to think I should not do a weekly invitation because it's a joke. Many people come forward, but the same people do it every week. It drives me crazy. Please pray for me in this area. I need wisdom.

Anyway, regarding worship, I've been frustrated that the choir isn't worshipping. They're just singing. It's a big difference. Well, yesterday, God said to me, "How can you expect them to usher in my presence. They haven't ever experienced my manifest presence. But you have."

I felt foolish. Of course, how can I expect people who've never really worshipped God to understand that God's glory can fill the house? That's my job. I believe once they really experience God's presence, lives will be changed. I've been focusing on teaching the Word, which is good, but not allowing the Word to come to life. I have to stop worrying about results, do my job and let God bring the growth and results.

This morning in worship, I believe God showed me that He wants me to teach Sai one or two worship songs and have us do a time of worship on Sunday. Nothing fancy, just real worship. I'll let you know what comes of that.

So, that's where I am spiritually. I feel things are about to change. I need to be open and let God use me and get the job done.

I have no idea how long I'm to be in Aklampa. Do I know what I'm supposed to do after that? No, but I have lots of ideas of what I'd like. I just don't know God's plan yet. I feel like I'll be returning to California and serving under Emmanuel. I don't know that I ever want to be formally ordained. If I am, it'll be because God wants it, not man. I also have no desire to do old-fashioned preaching. Do I think I'll still be speaking? Yes, but it'll be different than before. I guess Africa has ruined my "traditional churchianity" ways. I just want to faithfully serve God and watch him transform people's lives.

You know, God could have sent anyone here just to start a church or two. I know God has a bigger plan than that. It's not about a church; it's about God really being present. He wants to touch these people. He doesn't want dead letters preached; He wants to be alive in the people. People don't need a church, traditions or stuffy doctrine. They need the Father, Son and Holy Spirit.

Lives won't be changed until God touches them. Too many of us "church folk" have become Pharisees – worried about doctrine, but don't want the doctrine to become life. We talk much about all God did in the bible. Well, He's still the same. I want to talk to people about what He's also

*doing now. We can't live in the past. Why don't we see God doing the
same things? Because we've boxed him into our programs and schedules.
We think He can only move in one specific way because that's how He
"properly" did it before. Oh, God! Help us!*

*I have no idea where that just came from. I felt led to write and I opened
to this letter. I've got to go pray. Later.*

12/5/00 Letter...
*Lots of middle- aged men have been dying lately. Two weeks ago, a 50-
year-old man died, and Sunday a 35-year-old man died. From what?
Voodoo curses. Neither had been sickly. The 35-year-old had a backache
for two days and dropped dead. Both men had curses put on them because
of women.*

*The rumor/story of the 50-year-old is that he was a highly educated and
powerful man. While living in Cotonou some time ago, he slept with a
woman and she bore him a child. However, she was already married to
another man. The husband refused to divorce her, so she was forced to
stay with the husband. The 50-year-old man married another woman and
they have children. Recently, the man had renewed interest in the first
woman. The husband warned the man that he had put some "medicine"
on her and if the man tried to get her, he would die. Well, he tried, and he
died. These people do not play around. They take deadly revenge. It's
sad.*

12/6/00 Letter...
*Freda, you're missing something amazing about Africa. African sunrises
and sunsets. They are the most amazing and beautiful sight. I am
awestruck nearly every day. You'd think I'd get used to it, but they are too
beautiful. I love them because God created them. They've become a gift
to me every day. For example, this morning at 6:48 am the sky was a
bright pink. Two minutes later, it was blue. However, the few high clouds
still reflected the pink. The roosters were crowing and the birds were
chirping. This is the morning melody that I wake up to each day.*

*The evenings are equally as beautiful, but not as peaceful because people
are present. I sit on the front steps and watch the sky change colors as the
sun sets. Since this house is at the edge of the village, I get to watch the
sun set over the trees and brush. The other night, the sun was a dark
orange. What a beautiful sight as the sun set through the trees. Many
times, I sit on the steps and sing praise and worship songs to God as he
delivers his evening spectacle.*

12/12/00 Letter...

I've had a backache for eleven days, along with stomach nausea and cramping. I've already gone to the "doctor" here and he's given me two injections for the fatigue and back pain. He also saw a urine sample and noted abnormal color. However, he suggests that I get a thorough checkup with tests in Cotonou. In the meantime, I've begun taking antibiotics today. I'm thinking I have a bladder or kidney infection, but there's no pain during urination.

I'm giving you all the details for you to discuss with Rose, not to gross you out. However, this will gross you out. The doctor recommended that I begin drinking my first morning's urine! Yeah, right! He claims even American doctors recommend drinking the first urine of the day to kill many bad germs. Well, it would instantly kill me, or at least clean out my stomach because I'd vomit. YUCK!!!!!

Anyway, I'm feeling a bit better today and am not in extreme pain. I'm still cramping, but I hope the antibiotics kill it soon.

An amazing thing happened last night. I have been feeling like I will write a book in the future. I asked God to reveal if this was his will. To that end, I received a package last night from my aunt. Enclosed was a short note along with a book. The author autographed and wrote a short note for me and enclosed $10. The author wrote that she's read articles about my mission.

She and her husband lived in my home town in North Dakota for some years and he was our school superintendent. Also, the title is taken from Isaiah 41:30 and has a photo of mountains and an eagle. Remember how many times "mountains" and "eagles" came up in my readings, prayers, etc. before coming to Africa? God definitely has a plan!

FIGHTING TRADITION – SAVING LIVES

I've been getting lots of pressure from Michael to begin traditionalizing the church. He keeps asking when I'll begin regular pulpit preaching. He claims people will become more serious once we install traditional programs and methods. I keep telling him that I have no leading to launch into that type of service. We have added a bible study at 9:00 am before our worship service at 10:00 am. We originally started it on Thursdays, but no one came, as farm work got in the way of attending.

Michael also wants to do pulpit evangelism and mount a stage in Aklampa and play evangelistic videos. I don't feel led to do that either. However, if he feels strongly led, he should go ahead. I told him that I don't always have to be with them when they go out and talk to people. However, I told Michael that we have no money for such a venture and I'm waiting for a response from America regarding money for bible tracts, benches, and medicine. I feel that renting video equipment and speaker systems would not be cost-effective at this time.

However, I don't know God's exact program. I don't want to do anything without His leadership. I'd just be wasting my time if God isn't in it. I want so badly to be a faithful servant and not stand in God's way by doing things my own way.

While I was teaching during our recent service, Michael again disagreed with me about how people should dress for church. He openly disagreed with me in front of the congregation, but interpreted for me anyways. Specifically, he believes women must wear hats/coverings for church. I noted 1 Corinthians 11 and explained the passage.

I've been stressing that dress attire is not important. I am stressing a relationship with Jesus Christ. Once people truly have a relationship with Jesus, they'll dress respectably and that doesn't mean forcing a certain dress code. Michael has sent at least one woman home from choir rehearsal for not having her head covered, and Sai home for not wearing an under t-shirt. This is Aklampa. I sent Sai back to rehearsal dressed as he was.

I've also learned this week that he's spending over an hour preaching at choir rehearsal. He's been directed to teach worship songs, not preach. I just found all of this out this week. When he arrives on Saturday, I will talk to him.

One other funny note about the hat issue. Michael said we must take the bible literally. I said if that were true, Paul's letter to the Corinthians noted that women should keep quiet in the church. Michael responded that we would discuss that later and left. Although I'm sounding negative against Michael, we're getting along quite well.

He did have issues regarding women in church leadership and did not believe women could be called into the ministry. Therefore, he never really did acknowledge my authority as a leader of the church I founded. He appeased me to my face, but continued to teach his own beliefs. I had little power to change this because he was one of the "conditions" of my remaining in the village.

I thank my pastor for his love for the Word and rightly dividing the Word of God and demanding that we do the same.

6:30pm...
I just learned that I have a package at the post office in Glazoué. I hope it's the package sent by the church in September.

Due to my health, I'll be going via car, not motorcycle. I'm going with a driver who makes two trips to Glazoué on Wednesdays. I'll go with the early crew so I'm home early and don't have to sit around for a long time in Glazoué.

A VILLAGE IN UPROAR

12/22/00 Journal Entry…
Dossou has learned that I am involved in a new relationship. He is vowing
to kill anyone who gets close to me. Dossou had heard that I was traveling
to Cotonou for Christmas and is now in Cotonou because of me. I haven't
seen him. However, people fear for their lives.

Voodoo in Aklampa is no joke. It kills many people due to revenge.
Therefore, the threat is real. For example, I was also informed that Fina's
sickness a few months ago was due to Dossou attempting to harm her
through voodoo because he believes she severed our relationship.
However, since she didn't die, people realized that God is protecting her.

I also believe my sickness is from voodoo. Once I arrived in Cotonou, I
felt wonderful.

12/27/00 Journal Entry…
I was informed by my new chauffer that Dossou approached him with
money requesting to be his apprentice. The chauffer realized Dossou's
reason was related to me and refused the offer. He also claims that Dossou
has resorted to all sorts of voodoo to try to attack me.

12/28/00 Journal Entry…
Our trip back to Aklampa was uneventful, but there was lots of activity
once we arrived home. The entire village is in an uproar over me. They
have learned that I've grown close Gilles. I've learned that Dossou is
enraged and has vowed openly to kill him. People have traveled from as
far as Parakou which is in the north of the country to meet with the family
to determine what to do in this dangerous situation. People are
considering moving to Cotonou to avoid the wrath.

I have also learned that two families who formerly voiced their ownership
of me have made threats as well. Interestingly, everyone now loves
Dossou and wants us to reconcile our friendship, hoping a more serious
relationship will evolve.

Fina was approached twice today on this issue. Her mother has had
visitors accusing Fina of destroying my friendship with Dossou. Also, as
she was walking to her family's compound, she passed two women. One
woman did not know her, so the other described her as the "woman who
won't allow Dossou to be close to Gina, but likes someone else and has
plotted for him to marry Gina."

Five months ago the village hated Dossou when he was close to me and did everything to break our friendship. They were then even angrier that he lied to me. Now, they love him and want us to reconcile, and even pursue a relationship. This is too bizarre.

TABLES TURN – A VILLAGE MINISTERS TO ME

1/3/01 Letter…
Happy New Year! I hope you had a great new year's celebration at church.

Sai had decided that Village Baptist Church in Aklampa needs to bring in the New Year in the same fashion as our church in America. For a few weeks, he's been planning a New Year's Eve praise and prayer service. I gave him the ok and let him control it. (I've learned to give people room to lead and not control everything.)

On Sunday after church, Michael told Sai that there would be no evening service because I had vetoed it and that Michael was returning to Glazoué since he had a family program that evening. Of course, Sai knew something was not right and asked me if I had said we couldn't hold a New Year's Eve service. I knew nothing and re-told him that he had my blessing.

Although Michael teaches the choir songs, he didn't need to be present. They should go ahead. I would be present as leadership so there was no problem. The service was held in the compound beside my house so we had light.

The group did great. One of our supporters, who sends his two wives and children to church but doesn't attend because he's a singer who travels most of the time, donated his sound system for the night and joined us in our worship. Therefore, we had a microphone and speaker (think M.A.S.H.) for Aklampa to hear. We began at 11:00 pm and danced to praise songs until 1:00 am.

God works in amazing ways. When I had spoken to Emmanuel, he noted that he was sending me money and I would get it before Saturday. I chose not to wait in Cotonou for it because I wanted to get home. By Sunday, there was still no money and I was completely out of fuel, with only enough to last me part of that night, and only 2,000 cfa ($3) on hand.

My friend Kiki had gone to Dez in Cotonou to check on my money. Dez had heard nothing. Kiki returned that night during our service. He told me the news that there was no money. I became very sad, near tears. It was nearly impossible to even clap my hands. I was at a loss.

At 11:55 pm, we stopped singing so we could pray in the New Year. I had expected Sai or someone else to pray. Sai handed the microphone to me. At first I refused because I'd be praying in English and the people wouldn't understand. Sai insisted. So there I was, completely broken, forced to pray for all of Aklampa to hear.

I'm learning much about brokenness and it is no fun, but necessary. I prayed over Aklampa, claiming the blood of Jesus over every life. I also demanded that the works of Satan and voodoo be rendered powerless. The enemy wasn't happy about that. I wonder what the English-speaking people present thought of that prayer?

After praying, I realized that God has always provided for me and I need to praise him in spite of my physical circumstances. I sang, clapped, and even danced. I had a great time. We had over 75 people attend, mostly non-church members.

After closing in prayer and while we were cleaning up, Kiki approached me and told me he'd come here in the morning and take my fuel kegs and fill two of them for me. That's 36,000 cfa! I nearly cried. What a humbling experience to have someone in the village help me. He is such a valuable friend.

What's more, he arrived New Year's morning, fulfilled his promise and also gave me an extra 30,000 cfa to help me until money arrived. I was overwhelmed.

Also, Fina and Sai fed me all day and gave me holiday greeting cards. I have food but it was a holiday and they took care of me. I spent the entire day near tears. I told God, if this is how brokenness and humility look, it's going to be very difficult for me. Talk about a blow to my pride and independence.

However, we survived. Money still hasn't arrived, but I know it will come in God's time. I think it was God's will for the money not to arrive on my timing. He's teaching me to trust in Him, not physical things. Also, I think it was no coincidence that Kiki offered the fuel _after_ I decided to praise God in spite of my circumstances.

I believe this year will be difficult. I think it'll be a year of God taking away any pride. He wants to make me nothing so I can do something for Him. I wish I could say I'm looking forward to it, but I'm not.

I don't see this as a joyful year, but as a year of transition. I believe I'm laying a foundation here and someone else will build on it. I no longer find joy in living here. It's hard to explain because I love Benin.

I guess it's tough for me because every time I go out in public, I know my life is on the line. I'm not afraid. It's just exhausting being on such alert. I now realize how many people try to touch me and try to take things from me. I realize many of their motives are voodoo. I know there are people who are angry with my teaching that voodoo is satanic. They smile in my face and then do incantations behind my back. Now I know why missionaries usually travel in pairs. You need a partner and Christian companion.

Church services on Sunday morning were sweet. For the first time, the choir seemed to understand real praise onto God. People began dancing. Afterward, we had a time of prayer. I felt led to open prayer with everyone lifting their voices to God. I told them to pray, shout, sing – whatever God led them to do to lift up His name. It was going great and the presence of the Holy Spirit began to fill the building. One woman began to sing softly. I think someone else was humming. We settled into a peaceful mellow waiting upon God. It was beautiful.

All of a sudden, Michael killed the moment and began his traditional prayer that I've told him repeatedly not to do. I was so grieved. He's got this thing about going off and doing his own thing if he feels we haven't done enough praying or preaching. I need to talk to him again because I was so grieved on Sunday, I nearly cried right there. Please pray for wisdom on how to handle this issue correctly.

1/5/01 Letter...
A friend and I did some math last night that I think you will find interesting. A census was taken here a few years ago and there were 23,000 people in Aklampa and surrounding farms. We estimate the number to be about 25,000 now. We then determined the number of truly committed Christians, not just churchgoers. All total, there are less than 25 committed Christians in Aklampa. That's one in 1,000 people. How sad.

There were a few "Christian" churches in the village, but most, if not all, did not boldly stand solely for Jesus. They are syncretistic and mix voodoo or African Traditional Religion with Christianity. One "church" practices more voodoo than biblical principles, holding sacrifices in their church edifice.

Another is nearly empty. There was some disagreement and nearly everyone left. All the young men from that church have joined the masquerade voodoo.

A third claims to stand against voodoo, but their members have some strange "voodoo-like" rituals. Furthermore, one women informed me that she went to that church for prayer for her son and was given a list of "gifts" she needed to buy before prayer or a prophetic word would be offered.

Two people have died in the past two days. Remember the man who sent me a box of poisoned water shortly after I arrived in Aklampa? He's a witchdoctor from Savalou, a town about 40 kilometers from Aklampa. Well, his wife died. I guess he's not such a good doctor, huh? Sorry for the sarcasm, but I'm not too fond of the man. I hope she knew Jesus.

Also, a 20-year-old woman died yesterday. She's married with a child. The story is that her own mother put a voodoo curse on the daughter to kill her.

There are so many people dying lately. They're not sick. They just drop dead. Voodoo is horrible, and it all stems from jealousy and revenge. There's no such thing as forgiveness here. If they get angry, they put a curse to kill you or make you sick. And yet they won't turn to a God who brings peace. Blinded!

1/5/01 Journal Entry…
My devotion today was I Corinthians 9:15-end. Runners run with purpose. Have I lost my purpose and focus? I was doing so well until August when my focus was forcibly changed and I lost steam. Maybe I'm on the wrong course, or have grown weary. I feel my ministry here is closing. I've laid the foundation and pray God will provide a replacement to build on it.

I think one of the things that changed, but shouldn't have, was my freedom to associate with people. For example, I used to visit public gathering areas where I was a great witness to voodoo leaders and members. I was completely open about my beliefs regarding voodoo. I associated with people where they were and used it as a witness. For example, I remember Sai saying that I should not sing about Jesus at Azonwhé, yet I did and people kept asking for more, and even began attending church service.

I've now lost all that contact and witness. My methods didn't sit well with other Christians, but these methods worked and people were coming to church and accepting Christ. Was it any different than going to witness to a prostitute who is on duty, or a drunk while he's on the streets?

I've even joined some men at the buvette (local bar/restaurant). All of them came regularly to my church and all but two are currently active in ministry. Before August, I had lots of Azonwhé people attending church. Now, none.

A MORNING VISIT

1/7/01 Letter…
Oro is back. That's the night-time voodoo that no one, especially women, can see. I'm just fed up with this voodoo. They sat outside my house in the bush next door, and made their whirling noises for at least an hour. I think they sat outside my house to prove a point. I came close to telling them to get lost. I have no fear about challenging them. I know the power of God. However, I need to do it in God's timing.

Last week there was a big bush fire, started on purpose to avoid accidental fires. The fire became out of control and went wild, threatening to burn Oro's bush campsite. The young men ran to fend off the fire. I told one of them that I hope it burns. I said it would be sweet and I'd shout Alleluia. OK, I wasn't exactly humble. I'm guessing he later told the other members – hence their decision to pay me a visit last night.

1/10/01 Letter…
Speaking of Oro, they attacked Michael on Sunday morning. He woke up around 4:00 am to pray. He prays loudly and people in surrounding houses can hear him. He said he was praying when he heard someone try to open the door. He stopped praying to ask who was there. At first no one answered, but kept trying to open the door. Finally, they said, "Today is today. We'll get you today."

Michael told them to come and get him. They tried, but couldn't open the door and tried the windows as well. He said they disturbed him for two hours, threatening him. He had a stick and held onto it for self-defense. This week he is coming to the village carrying a big knife for protection.

This is very serious. I know God protected him because the door should have given way with one good push. It's not sturdy at all. We don't know why they attacked him. He's only here on Saturday nights and leaves on Sunday to return to his home in Glazoué. Michael said he witnessed to the Oro chief and the chief now ignores him and won't speak to him. Something is definitely amiss.

I hear the Oro has now been given authority to come out every Saturday night. It'll be interesting to see what happens this week. We're planning to do a prayer walk on Saturday night.

Also I wonder if any of this ties to me. We'll find out soon enough. I began shutting off my generator at midnight to save fuel and money. Fuel alone takes over half of the money sent to me. Usually Oro stays off my property and doesn't pass the house due to the lights. This Saturday it will be dark so I'm expecting a 'close and personal' visit. One thing I know; I'll be pulling the generator inside the house after we shut if off on Saturday. Most of these boys use their Oro night to steal, as well as drink and do drugs. They're not exactly reasonable, especially once possessed by demons.

WORN OUT

Freda, every day I think more and more about going home. I'm mentally worn out and need a break. I feel like this village is trying to crush me.

Also, I feel like God is showing me more and more that I've completed my task and now it is someone else's turn to build on that foundation. However, I have no idea what God wants me to do in America. I'm praying for a time of rest and recuperation. Going home seems more intimidating than coming here. I'll go back with no home, no car and no job. I start all over.

As I write you now, all the voodoo sects are out due to some fight in the village. They've been out since last night. I can hear the demons screaming through the possessed members. I hate it. It's hard to listen to demons screaming through people. I'm nearly nauseous. Thank God this house is some distance from most ceremonies.

1/16/00 Letter...
Two voodoo sects came out again on Saturday due to the trouble I mentioned earlier. When there was the fight, the voodoo member retreated to the bush, when she should have gone to a doctor. The voodoo sects marched past my house on their way to find their member in the bush and rescue her. They were in their voodoo attire with weapons. They also had pieces of bush branches strapped to their head and limbs. You couldn't ignore their demonic screeches, grunts, chants.

Please, please be in prayer for me. I don't want to go into details, but I'm going through a rough time. I need strength and wisdom from God. I'm worrying a lot about the future and other things. It's too hard to describe in a letter. I've decided to try to go to Cotonou in early February to call you and Emmanuel to talk about some things.

I beg you not to forget to pray for me. Gina

This was the last letter written home.

OUT OF AFRICA

PLANS CHANGE

During a trip to Cotonou, I learned that I was pregnant with Gilles' child. Thinking back now, I was in no mental or spiritual state to have gotten into a new relationship. Living in deep depression and loneliness, I turned to Gilles for comfort. Although I had the approval needed for this relationship, our relationship led to an intimate relationship. This resulted in instant pregnancy.

I told no one. I was so ashamed that I had sinned with my future husband. I initially hid my pregnancy from everyone but one non-Christian girlfriend from college who told me to come home and move to her town. She had an apartment available for me where I could reside. No condemnation. Just love.

The doctors strongly chastised Gilles for getting me pregnant – like I had nothing to do with this sin! Both doctors that I visited strongly urged me to get an abortion. Due to the pressure and shame, the thought actually passed through my mind for a few minutes. However, by the time I returned to the hotel, I had made my decision that I would not abort this child. I have always been against abortion and this was a test for me. Would I stand up for what I believe, regardless of the outcome?

The only reason that I actually considered an abortion was because I did not want to disappoint my pastor. His approval meant so much to me and I already felt as if I had failed him. How could I do this to him now? Surely, it would reopen wounds from a few months ago.

I knew my family would handle this turn of events relatively well, even though they would be worried about my well-being. My mom was always behind me, even when she didn't always agree with my decisions. My dad would be disappointed, but I believed he would forgive me. I knew my three siblings would support me, even though I had made a mistake.

My church family was another story altogether. I had no idea how the church would handle this. I had let them down. I felt so very alone, so very afraid, so very shameful.

How could I face my pastor? He had already heard and believed so many horrible things about me which were false. Now, this would make all the lies seem true. For a few minutes, abortion seemed like the easy way out. However, I knew that although I could hide my sin of sexual immorality by committing another sin of abortion, how could I live with myself? There was no way I was going to sink any deeper into the pit I had fallen.

I decided to keep the child. Great decision. Besides my salvation, my daughter has been the greatest blessing of my life. Only once I had a child did I discover just how much capacity for love God has given us. Amazing.

There are still nights that I kneel beside my daughter's peacefully sleeping body and tearfully thank the Lord for a most wonderful blessing and gift. I also thank Him for giving me a sane mind to make the right decision in the middle of such despair.

Now, I sit here and wonder what transpired in the heavenly realms during this time. Henry tried his best to get me removed from the village, or killed, but was defeated. Others also attempted to get me out of the village before more people were saved. Some even suspected my pregnancy and schemed to try to get people close to me to poison my food to abort the baby and/or kill me.

The enemy thought he had won. I know differently. But I'm getting ahead of myself, aren't I?...

DIFFERENT REACTIONS

I traveled to Cotonou in late January to discuss my pregnancy with Emmanuel. It was a very difficult conversation. We discussed the repercussions of my moral failure – I was to return to America and step down any ministry for two years. I was also advised to marry Gilles. I grieved that he never asked me how I was doing – emotionally, spiritually, or physically. This devastated me.

I mentioned that I did not know where I would stay, and he said that he would discuss this with his wife. When I spoke to Freda, her first question was to ask after my health, emotional well-being, and spiritual state. She was very disappointed with my sin, as she should have been, but was willing to still stand beside me and help me through this most difficult time.

My mom responded as I expected – if not better. She never condemned me, but just told me to come home. She even called Emmanuel and offered to pay for the ticket if the church could not afford it. Now, I'm sure she got off the phone and worried, but she proved to be a source of strength and hope while on the phone with me.

So, I returned to the village to secretly prepare to leave. We did this secretly for my own safety. I was directed not to let anybody know of my plans (even my church family in Aklampa). The only people who were aware of my plans were Fina, Sai and Gilles, but others began to suspect my departure.

YOU KNOW TOO MUCH

2/16/01 Journal Entry…
A local singer came to visit this morning. He's up to no good. I should have known something was amiss because he came to church last Sunday for the first time since August. He came to tell me that he had a dream about me. He'd heard that I'm leaving and dreamed that I had an accident and died. He begged me to change my program. The only change to my plans is that I will leave earlier than anyone thinks.

People are trying to determine what day and time I am leaving, what chauffer is driving me, and what time my flight is leaving. No one would need this information unless they are up to no good.

He also informed me that someone was out to kill me and I wouldn't make it out of the village alive. He said he "heard" about this plot but would not give specific details.

I knew this was a warning with veiled threats.

2/17/01 Journal Entry…
It's true. The village is truly out to kill me. Last night, someone secretly informed me that he knows it's voodoo that has me acting strangely. They correctly recognized it as spiritual oppression. **I was grieving both my sin and leaving the village. I was absolutely spent. I couldn't eat or sleep and felt tormented.**

Someone visited late last night and forced me to close my lower windows. Someone was waiting outside to try to blow voodoo powder through the window over my bed to kill me.

What's more, last night Fina almost died. If she had been at the house, she would have died because she'd have been in her room alone and unable to call for help. She had gone to visit her mother. She began to have severe stomach pains and stopped breathing. They raced her to Affinzungo where she received two injections. She is better today. Everyone agrees that it is voodoo and because of me.

I struggled with Fina's near-death experience for over two years after my return to America. It made no sense that the enemy would attempt to harm her when she was attacking me during these final days of my stay in the village. I had also noticed some strange

markings on her body that I believe were marks of voodoo involvement.

After returning home and while praying one evening nearly two years later, the Lord suddenly revealed to me that it was not the devil attacking her, but was His vengeance for her attacking and trying to harm me.

DIVINE PROTECTION

2/24/01 Journal Entry…

Fina turned crazy on Saturday. She acted wickedly with demands to be "paid off". As we prepared to leave for Cotonou early Sunday morning, I was so upset with everyone due to all the drama surrounding my departure that I couldn't wait to leave. We prayed. I got in the car and we left. No hugs goodbye. Not a tear shed.

The drive out of Aklampa was horrible until we reached Glazoué. We left at 5:00 am and went via the Savalou road, not our normal route.

I had been informed that there was an ambush waiting for me along the other road. They know I always take the shorter route. They may have also been waiting on the other road also, but if so, God hid us from their sight.

I've never felt such evil spiritual oppression in my life as I did during the first leg of my journey. I could feel the satanic attack attempting to kill me. It was horrible and the tension in the car was unbelievable. Even my escort warned the driver to drive very carefully. By the time we reached Glazoué, I was sweating profusely, shaking and nearly had to ask the driver to stop so I could vomit. It was that oppressive.

However, God had his hand on me. At one point, I felt as if we were being carried along by angels. Once we arrived in Glazoué, I felt much better.

I later learned that God had led Freda and Janice, another woman from my church who was on my intercessory prayer team, to urgently intercede for me at the exact time I was traveling out of the village. They had no idea of the timing, but God used them to save my life that day.

After a few days in Cotonou, I returned to America and stayed with my pastor and his family. I was greeted at the airport by Freda and Janice. They greeted me with hugs and bathed me in prayer before even leaving the airport. By their later accounts, I was clearly not well. I was a shadow of my former self and unable to mentally comprehend much. Janice had a word of encouragement for me, but I was unable to receive it. All I could receive at that point was her sweater to warm my body that had been shivering for the past 20 hours.

How did it feel to be out of Africa? I was shocked that everything seemed so modern. I had more difficulty adjusting to life back in America than I had adjusting to bush life in Africa.

After a battery of medical tests, doctors determined that both baby and I were healthy. Throughout my pregnancy, I had nightmares and fears of God punishing my sin by causing deformities in my unborn child. However, that was the enemy speaking, not God. I serve a forgiving and merciful God. Not only did I have a rather easy pregnancy, I was blessed to birth a beautiful daughter who brings more joy to my life with each passing day.

STANDING BEFORE THE BODY

We decided to keep my return to America a secret until the next Wednesday evening after my arrival. My pastor requested that I stand before the body of Christ that evening and briefly share my story as well as reasons for returning home.

Because I had committed sexual immorality, something I had always been so openly against, this was such a difficult time. I really believed the body of Christ would not forgive me for this grave sin so I had decided to move back to the Midwest to be with family and had begun the logistics of the move.

I wasn't excited about standing before the body of Christ to hold myself accountable to them. This was my pastor's idea, not mine. I actually dreaded the idea, but did it to obey my pastor.

That Wednesday as people arrived for our corporate bible study, people were absolutely shocked to see me. Many people didn't even recognize me because I had lost so much weight and looked unhealthy. One of the most memorable moments of the evening was having one of our members call her son, who I had formerly taught in Sunday School, requesting that he hurry to the church for a surprise. When he walked in the door, he ran up to give me a huge hug. Only God knows how I needed that hug. That greeting gave me the strength I needed for the rest of the evening.

Pastor stood to give a brief introduction and then sat on the front pew next to his wife while I went up to the podium to speak. I briefly shared with the congregation about some of my wonderful experiences. I then shared that I had fallen into sexual immorality and became pregnant. Therefore, I was home to seek their mercy, and if they wanted me to leave the congregation, I would completely understand.

I found out later that my pastor sat in the pew with tears rolling down his cheeks, grieving for me and with me.

Amazingly, the body of Christ forgave me and welcomed me home. Thus began my healing. Due to the reception and forgiveness of my church family, I decided against the move to the Midwest.

In retrospect, my pastor forcing me to go before the body of Christ was a very wise decision. It brought the matter out in the open, thus diffusing most of the gossip. Of course, there are always those who wish more harm than good and gossiped behind my back. However, their words had little power. Furthermore, My Father heard what was spoken with their tongues.

I've let my Almighty Father handle things, and He surely has dealt with them.

There were, and continue to be, people who the enemy uses to try to destroy me. They have done everything within their power to destroy and discredit me, even to the point of manipulating someone else into traveling to Africa to "outdo" me.

I instantly recognized the motives behind this wicked plan. The outcome of that manipulation was division between churches and pain to our leadership. The originator of this wicked plan has feigned innocence, but God sees and weighs the motives of the hearts and always exposes wickedness.

This same "spirit" has attacked my marriage and threatened my child. Furthermore, they have tried to destroy my relationship with my pastor and destroy the ministries God has placed in my care. For years, I was intimidated. However, I finally realized that allowing intimidation is giving up your power to that demon. I now refuse to bow to this spirit of intimidation.

"For God hath not given us a spirit of fear; but of power, and of love, and of a sound mind." 2 Timothy 1:7 (KJV)

GONE BUT NOT FORGOTTEN

I wish I could say that the voodoo quit their attacks on me after my return to America. That, however, was not the case.

During my stay in Africa, I had never seen a voodoo doll. I had heard of them as a brunt of jokes in America, but never encountered them.

One afternoon, about a year and a half after returning to America, I was cleaning one of my suitcases that had some memoirs I had brought back from Africa, such as clothing and fabric. I noticed a tan money-pouch in the suitcase that I had never seen before. All of my waist packs and money pouches had been black.

I opened the pouch and found a very tiny voodoo doll, no taller than an inch, safety-pinned to the inside seam of the pouch. It was intrinsically crafted. Although very little and seemingly made of a match stick and fabric, it had a face, body, arms, hair, clothing and belt. Since I knew that I had never seen the pouch, nor a doll such as this before, I was somewhat alarmed.

Gilles had requested that I take photos of the doll for him to review upon his upcoming arrival. I took four photos of the doll lying on my kitchen counter. When I developed the photographs, all four of the photos turned out to be blank photos. There was not even a hint of the doll in any photo. Furthermore, every photo on either side of these photos developed perfectly. I had heard stories in Africa that if the voodoo do not want to have their picture taken and you try, the camera would break. I had also heard that some voodoo things are impossible to be captured by camera. I guess these weren't just stories.

I informed my pastor and his wife what I had found, as well as my husband who was still in Africa. My pastor, having grown up in Africa, became very concerned and sought counsel from Africa on how to handle this issue. He repeatedly questioned me as to whether I had any connection with the doll or if I knew why the doll existed. The reason was that we were directed to burn the doll. Whoever had commissioned the doll would suffer harm if we burned the doll. He was afraid it had somehow been commissioned to represent my daughter or me.

Having absolutely no knowledge of how the doll or the pouch came into my possession, we selected a time for my pastor and his wife to come to my house to burn the doll. My pastor was going to burn the doll and the pouch in my backyard.

After prayer, he soaked the doll and pouch with lighter fluid and lit them. Instantly, my daughter awoke from her nap and began to cry. Freda rushed into the house to comfort her. This little doll, seemingly made of paper and cloth and no larger than an inch tall and a few millimeters thick, took nearly an entire large container of lighter fluid and over 45 minutes to burn! The pouch burned much more quickly than the doll.

To this day, we still have no idea who commissioned the doll or its purpose. However, God knew. I can only imagine the spiritual realm over my home and in Aklampa that day. However, my daughter, pastor, Freda and I were completely protected.

ATTACKING THE INNOCENT

Four months after my daughter's birth, she began having episodes of apparent night terrors that are nearly indescribable. Although they seemed similar to night terrors, they were very different.

Usually an hour after falling asleep for the evening, she would begin screaming in the most eerie, bloodcurdling scream. I ran into her room and lifted her out of her crib to comfort her. She was still asleep and I could not wake her. Sometimes, her eyes would open, but the pupils were rolled back and she was unresponsive. Sometimes the screaming lasted only a minute, other times much longer. The episodes became more and more frequent. During the longer attacks, I would call my pastor and his wife, and they would provide prayer and comfort.

As a parent, I was shaken. I realized that these episodes were spiritually tied to Africa. The group of people who had decided that I would never get out of the village alive had been shamed. Also, there were some who were jealous of my marriage to Gilles. Moreover, they have a belief that any child conceived in the village is the property of the village. They wanted her dead.

I had confirmation that these episodes were spiritually tied to Aklampa. One evening, after my husband joined me in America, we called the village to speak to his family. Since the telephone had just recently arrived in the village, his family did not yet have their own private telephone. We called a central number and sent a message that we would call again in a few minutes. No later than two minutes after the first call, our daughter had an attack – the worst ever.

We continually prayed in Jesus' name to break off this curse and soon the episodes stopped, never to return again. There is great power in the name of Jesus.

I learned that we were actually "lucky" because our daughter actually cried during these attacks. In Africa, the child often simply dies without making a sound.

Psalm 91: "He who dwells in the shelter of the Most High will rest in the shadow of the Almighty. I will say of the Lord, "He is my refuge and my fortress, my God in whom I trust." Surely he will save you from the fowler's snare and from the deadly pestilence. He will cover you with his feathers, and under his wings you will find refuge; his faithfulness will be your shield and rampart. You will not fear the terror of night, nor the arrow that flies by day, nor the pestilence that stalks in the darkness, nor the plague that destroys at midday. A thousand may fall at your side, ten thousand at your right hand, but it will not come near you. You will only observe with your eyes and see the punishment of the wicked. If you make the Most High your dwelling – even the LORD, who is my refuge – then no harm will befall you, no disaster will come near your tent. For he will command his angels concerning you to guard you in all your ways; they will lift you up in their hands, so that you will not strike your foot against a stone. You will tread upon the great lion and the serpent. "Because he loves me," says the Lord, "I will rescue him; I will protect him, for he acknowledges my name. He will call upon me, and I will answer him; I will be with him in trouble, I will deliver him and honor him. With long life I will satisfy him and show him my salvation."

LESSONS LEARNED

A friend with the gift of prophecy once noted, great people make great mistakes. This was said before I even travelled to Africa and became pregnant out of wedlock.

I realized I was not the only person who had made some great mistakes. I joined the club of Moses, David, Peter, and other biblical greats. Although we may think our mistakes are unredeemable, God forgives His people.

God has done so much to redeem me:

Humility: I had been a prideful advocate of sexual purity. I was knocked off my pedestal. I learned, intimately, never to rest on my own righteousness. Oh, how quick the mighty stumble.

When pride came, then came disgrace, but with humility comes wisdom.

Discernment: God has given me better insight into the spiritual realm. He has trained my spiritual eyes and ears to watch and attack the enemy as it approaches.

Dear friends, do not believe every spirit, but test the spirits to see whether they are from God.

Power: I had firsthand experience of the power of God – to heal, to protect, to provide, to restore life, and to deliver.

John 13:3a Jesus knew that the Father had put all things under his power.

Restoration: The Lord once revealed my life to me in a vision of a simple illustration. My walk through this life is like a timeline. As I live a life of repentance, He erases my past – all my past – and only sees me and my future. God has not only restored me, but he has restored broken relationships to an even better state than before.

The Lord is my shepherd, I shall not be in want...He restored my soul.

Protection: In my darkest hour, God never let me go. In my weakest hour, He never let me go. When I begged Him to release me, He never let me go.

Even though I walked through the valley of the shadow of death, I feared no evil, for you were with me, your rod and your staff, they comforted me.

Faith: Faith in God has nothing to do with our circumstance, but everything to do with the will and promises of God.

So I fixed my eyes, not on what was seen, but on what was unseen. For what was seen was temporary, but what is unseen is eternal.

Failure Redeemed: God turned failure into victory. An eye-opening comment was once said to me. I was asked if I was the only person to ever sin within a two-year span. I was reminded that we all have sinned and fallen short of the glory of God. However, God still has a plan to redeem His children.

And we know that in all things God works for the good of those who love him, who have been called according to his purpose.

A Living Testimony: You're reading it.

HEALING

Just a few years ago, God gave me confirmation of His healing. As background, please understand that I was emotional and would cry over the smallest thing. After returning from Africa, I cried very seldom, even during worship. It was as if part of me had died.

I was attending a prayer conference in 2006. In one of the small breakout sessions, a woman began giving a testimony. It mirrored the past few years of my life. As the woman spoke and I sat in the rear of the room, I began to weep and weep. Now, her testimony wasn't especially sad or emotional, but I couldn't believe how it mirrored my life. I knew God was speaking to me. I wept so severely that I had to leave the room to try to compose myself.

Later that evening during a worship session of the conference, I had a vision. The Holy Spirit revealed to me that when I returned from Africa, I was like a lamb that had been savaged by wolves, nearly dead. I saw this savaged, limp lamb being held in the hand of the Father.

Over the years, as soon as a wound would start to heal, the enemy would come and rip off the scab, causing infection to set in and leaving deep scars. I realized that I was still that savaged lamb. God began healing me that evening and I saw the final outcome in that vision - a lamb whose wounds had been completely healed by the finger of the Almighty Healer. The Father then set the restored lamb down and it began running in a beautiful meadow.

During this time, the Holy Spirit also showed me that I was guilty for not sharing my pain with my pastor. I had shut myself off from most everyone and carried all the pain and suffering without revealing the extent of my trauma. How could my pastor and others close to me help me if I did not tell them what actually happened to me? It was nearly a year later before I had the opportunity to apologize to my pastor for not informing him of my real condution during this painful time of recovery, which took years.

I know that one of my weaknesses is letting go of pain and guilt. Being a perfectionist, letting go takes much effort on my part. I also recognized that the guilt had much to do with the enemy whispering lies to keep me from walking in the fullness of God's love, acceptance, and calling.

The enemy continually tried to keep the relationship between my pastor and me broken. The enemy knew that, when this relationship was restored, he was in serious trouble.

Some in the body continue to sow lies to cause division so that their secrets remain unexposed. They have failed, and will continue to fail. I will continue to fight for the Kingdom of God and His truth. I will stand on the wall as a faithful watchman and sound the alarm. Furthermore, I know deep in my heart that God is always victorious, and those who rise up against God have their days numbered.

One of the greatest fears of some people in Africa is that "I know too much". They don't want the enemy's tactics revealed. I have never feared voodoo because I have complete assurance in whom I serve. After all, that was one of the reasons a small contingent of voodoo members decided I would not get out of Aklampa alive – I knew too much. Oh, how victorious is my Savior, my Strong Tower, my Deliverer!

I waited upon the Lord, knowing that He alone could really bring healing. I waited upon the Lord. In the midst of pain and sorrow, I had peace. He promised to expose all the deeds of darkness. Faithful as always, He has exposed motives and wickedness.

It took six years, but I can now joyfully and victoriously say that God has healed me, restored me, and refreshed me. Broken relationships have been mended and are healthier than ever. I learned not to fear man, but to fear God and only concern myself with what My Father thinks. I trusted the Word of God and stood on his promises. He did not fail!

I am that healed lamb who has arisen from the ashes and is joyfully and powerfully running through that meadow!

I am so blessed to have a wonderful pastor who is not just a pastor. He remains a brother, friend, mentor, and godfather to my daughter. I am honored to be his armor bearer. Even in the midst of the storm after my return to America, I knew my calling to support my pastor. Because my focus was on God and not my situation, I refused to waver. I will stand behind him and support him as long as God has me here.

A NEW CHAPTER

So began a new chapter in my life. I'm free of the guilt and wounds of the past. I've stepped back into my calling and service for the Lord. I've learned that, through the strength of God, we can go through the valley and climb the mountains placed before us. Oh, when we reach the mountain top, what a beautiful sight! We are able to look back and really sing, "How Great is Our God".

I've learned to abandon my fears, shut out the condemning voices, and put my hope in the Lord who renews my strength. I've learned to soar on wings like eagles.

Isaiah 40:31: "but those who hope in the Lord will renew their strength. They will soar on wings like eagles; they will run and not grow weary, they will walk and not be faint."

It's been ten years since my move to Africa. So much has changed. Would I do it again? For a long time I couldn't answer that question. But, my desire is to please God in everything I do and think. I've learned why God doesn't always give us all the details when He calls us to GO. If we knew what we were getting into, how many of us would still be faithful and go?

Was the pain worth it? You tell me. It cost me nearly everything, including my physical life, reputation, and relationships with those closest to me. I suffered loneliness, sickness, fear and deep depression.

However, God used these years of brokenness to bring humility, deliver me from the fear of man, and build my character and faith. I've learned to fix my eyes properly on the author and finisher of my faith. Yes, I'm a very different person. But I can finally say that it was all worth it. God has done much to conform me to His image.

Romans 8:28 "And we know that in all things God works for the good of those who love him, who have been called according to this purpose."

Furthermore, there is an active church that follows Jesus Christ in a village where voodoo was the sole authority. Jesus has snatched some from the enemy's grasp of death.

Finally, I was given more than I could have ever expected – the most amazing daughter.

ABOUT THE AUTHOR

Gina Doumaté, born Gina Weigel, was raised in rural North Dakota with loving parents and three feisty siblings. After graduating from college, she moved to Northern California. Shortly thereafter, she accepted Jesus Christ as her Lord and Savior, and has been on fire for him ever since. In 1998, after a short mission trip to Benin, West Africa, she felt the Lord's calling to move to Africa as a missionary for two years.

Both before and upon her return from Africa, she has served as an active member and leader at Village Baptist Church in Marin City, California. She is honored to serve under the leadership of Dr. Emmanuel O. Akognon, whose greatest desire is to teach the unadulterated Word of God, and to have each member be an active participant in the Ministry of Jesus Christ.

In addition to serving at Village Baptist Church, Gina is an advisory board member of Better Africa Foundation, a non-profit organization focusing on addressing issues such as health care, the environment, human rights, and sports opportunities to the people of West Africa. To find out more about Better Africa Foundation, visit www.betterafrica.org.

Gina can be contacted at ginadoumate@yahoo.com.